GOLD ON ICE

Sandra Schmirler

Jan Betker

Joan McCusker

Marcia Gudereit

GOLD ON ICE

The Story of the Sandra Schmirler Curling Team

by Guy Scholz

with Sandra Schmirler, Jan Betker,
Joan McCusker and Marcia Gudereit

COTEAU BOOKS

Edited by Geoffrey Ursell and Nora Russell.

Cover image by Designer Photographics.
Cover and Book Design by Duncan Campbell

Printed and bound in Canada.

Canadian Cataloguing in Publication Data

Guy Scholz, 1958–

Gold on ice

ISBN 1-55050-151-8

I. Curling—Canada—Biography.
2. Winter Olympic Games (18th : 1998 : Nagano-shi, Japan).
I. Schmirler, Sandra   II. Title.

GV845.5.C3S34 1999   796.964'092'271   C99-920140-9

10 9 8 7 6 5 4 3 2 1

401-2206 Dewdney Ave.
Regina, Saskatchewan
Canada   S4R 1H3

AVAILABLE IN THE US FROM
General Distribution Services
85 River Rock Drive, Suite 202
Buffalo, New York, USA   14207

The publisher gratefully acknowledges the financial assistance of the Saskatchewan Arts Board, the Canada Council for the Arts, the Government of Canada through the Book Publishing Industry Development Program (BPIDP), and the City of Regina Arts Commission, for its publishing program.

Gold on Ice is published with the aid of the Cultural Industries Development Fund, Saskatchewan Department of Municipal Affairs, Culture and Housing.

  Canada

To my parents, Herb and Arni Scholz, who taught me the fine line between playing for fun and playing for keeps. — Guy Scholz

To our families, who encourage us to laugh and to cry, to work harder and to believe in ourselves and the power of team. — Team Schmirler

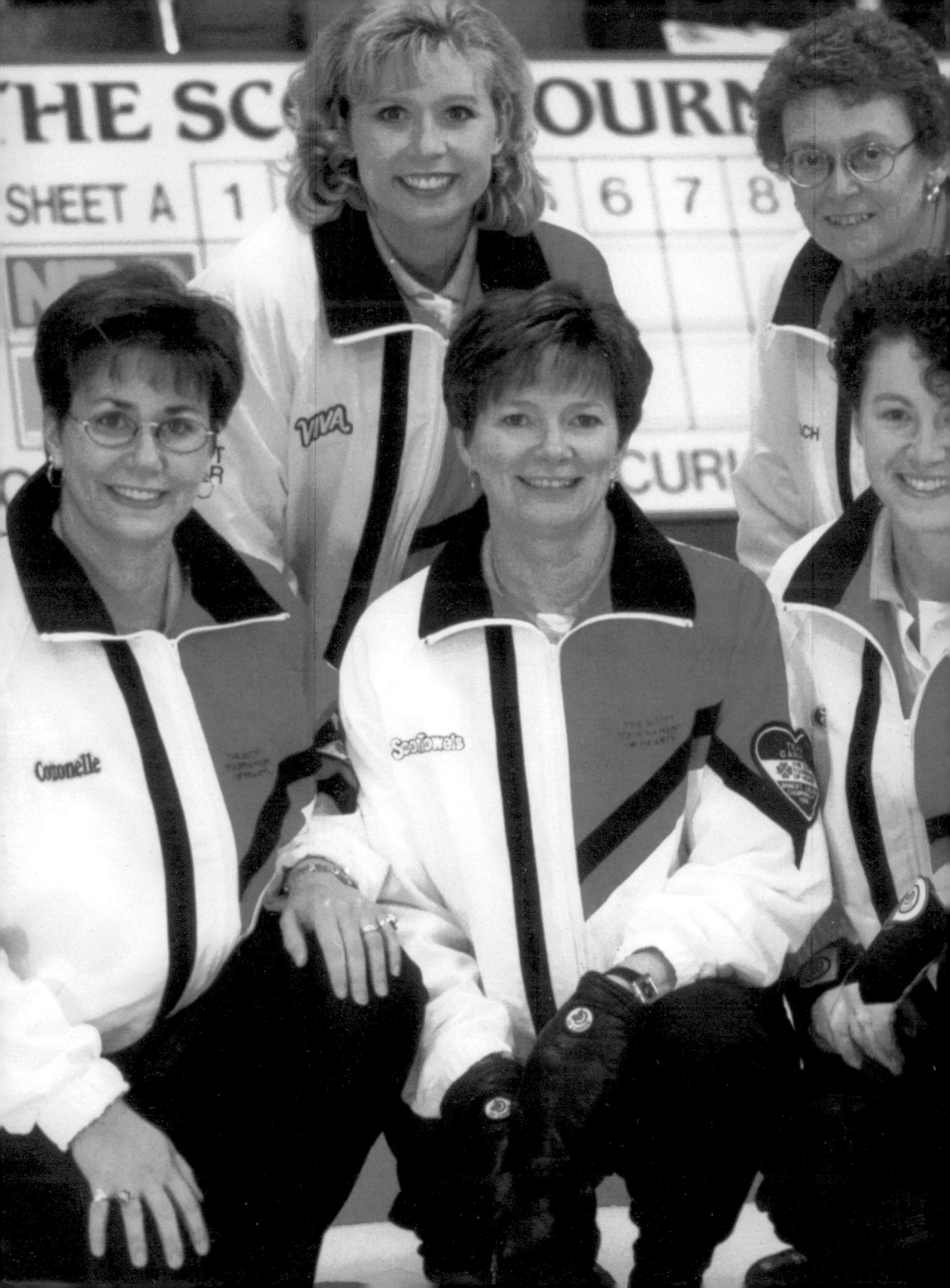
SHEET A
1
6 7 8
VIVA
Cotonelle
ScotTowels

INTRODUCTION

The exhilaration of winning your first Canadian championship is a memory that all champions cherish. The elation of the Schmirler team at the Scott Tournament of Hearts victory banquet in 1993 proved that this team was no exception. There they were, "four little girls from Saskatchewan," as they like to refer to themselves, beaming and bubbling in the glow of a dream come true. All of their hard work had paid off, and they were cherishing every moment of their hard-fought victory over the Maureen Bonar team from Manitoba. They really had no idea of the challenges that were ahead of them at the world championships in Geneva later that year. But it was obvious they were eager to get on with it, ready to embrace that new experience with all their talents and energy.

My experience as team leader for our national teams has given me a great opportunity to work with and observe many talented Canadian women's teams as they have prepared for and performed in world championship play. Canada's talent in curling has been showcased time and again in this increasingly challenging and competitive sport. Each of our national teams has demonstrated the outstanding individual and team qualities that are necessary for success in international competition.

The Schmirler team has been Team Canada 1993, 1994 and 1997, as well as our nation's representative in curling's debut as a medal sport at the Olympic Games in Nagano in 1998. Through working with them, I have had the most wonderful opportunity to see first-hand the evolution of a true dynasty in women's curling. Not since the combination of Saskatchewan curling greats Joyce McKee and Vera Pezer in the early 1970s has there been a team that has dominated a decade like the Schmirler quartet has in the 1990s. These women have been an inspirational model of what being a successful team is all about. Their individual talents and team chemistry have made them the envy of their peers and the darlings of both their home province of Saskatchewan and the country that they have so proudly and ably represented.

There are many qualities that have contributed to these women's present stature in our sport. The Schmirler team has maintained the necessary hunger and desire as they have moved ahead on their journey toward excellence, but have also – very importantly – held onto their enjoyment of each other and of each new experience. Through the ups and downs they have shown courage and welcomed new challenges. They have brought this positive attitude to each championship they have competed in and have reaped the rewards accordingly. They have become a stronger, more formidably-bonded unit with each experience they have faced, whether that experience was positive or negative, whether in their personal or their sporting lives.

Their first game in the world championships in Geneva was a good example of this. They were scheduled to play Dordi Nordby of Norway, a two-time world champion. If that wasn't intimidating enough, they were to play the four-rock free guard zone rule, something with which they had no competitive experience. The competition began with the parading of the competitors. Though quaking on the inside, these women walked out onto the ice surface displaying nothing but confidence and enthusiasm for the challenge ahead. Their expressions, body language, everything in their demeanour said, "Bring it on. We're ready!" They announced their presence on the world stage with a sound drubbing of the Norwegian champions, the game lasting only eight ends.

Along the way these women have learned to deal with the challenges and distractions that accompany those new experiences. Whether these are time changes, cultural differences, the logistical glitches of a championship event, or their own emotions, these women take them in their stride and focus on the job that has to be done on the ice. They pride themselves on letting go of events that are beyond their control. Emotions are discussed openly, and team members together develop strategies to deal effectively with them. This support system is very strong, and has a powerful unifying effect on the team. The team also evaluates each experience to gain from the lessons learned in each. This fuels their preparation for the next event.

Sandra, Jan, Joan, and Marcia consistently bring humour to every new competitive situation. They love to laugh. Whether laughing over a recollection of a team experience or playing a prank on a team member or a member of the support team, they, as they say, "slay themselves." They laugh at and with one another, and no one is exempt from their razzing. One of the prerequisites of belonging to the Schmirler support team is a good-natured tolerance for the pranks they pull. You might find your bed short-sheeted, or snuggle in for a good night's sleep only to find a rubber rat as your bedmate, or find seductive letters from Xena the Warrior Princess in your wallet next to your wife's picture, or have personal items of clothing taken from your hotel room and replaced with interesting alternatives. Fairly innocent, to be sure, but nevertheless it leaves one nervous about when, where and against whom the next prank will be directed.

Their latest was at the expense of the Mike Harris team during the Nagano Olympics. Foolishly, the men asked the women to take their wash out of the dryer while they played their game. The women politely agreed – and then tied every sock and piece of underwear into a string of knots that spanned the length of

Team Canada coach and mentor Lindsay Sparkes, also a championship curler, gave them a blueprint to reach the top.

ii

Custom-made shirts are a "western theme" hit at the 1993 Scott in Brandon.

the hotel hallway. As Joan later asked, "How could they be so stupid?"

Although proudly independent and self-governed, the Schmirler quartet has actively sought assistance from a variety of resource people along their journey toward excellence. They know what they want, and through discussion with coaches, family members, friends, other competitive curlers, and athletes from different sports, they have learned how to get there. They chose Atina Ford as their fifth player and her mother, Anita Ford, as their coach in national and international events, recognizing in these two women the talent and wisdom necessary to fuel their drive to the top. Atina and Anita brought an effective blend of enthusiasm and calm to the unit, and committed completely to the support of the individual team members and the success of the team. The Schmirler quartet consistently uses the little "pearls of wisdom" that resource people offer to energize and refocus themselves when the going gets tough.

An important factor in the Schmirler team's success is that all of their dreams are based in reality. They know they have the skills to win every event in which they participate. They know, too, that their opposition is also very capable, and that they have to prove they deserve the win every time they step onto the ice surface. They expect other teams to play well against them, and they are prepared for the challenges that strong opposition brings.

Throughout their three world-championship crowns and the Olympic gold medal in Nagano, they maintained a sense of wonder about and an appreciation for their success. After all, they're just "four little girls from Saskatchewan." It is this humility and

respect that has drawn me so closely to this team. Along with respecting their opposition, they also have fierce respect for each other and for the game itself. Although team members have very similar interests and experiences in life, they are very different personalities. On this team, members are honoured for their individuality and differences are seen as adding strength and diversity to the team unit, and each member is trusted to carry out her role and responsibilities. This element of trust also lends itself to open and frank discussions, and potentially destructive issues are dealt with quickly.

At the press conference following their gold-medal performance in Nagano, the team was asked about any bonus money they would receive from the Canadian Olympic Association for the win. (This is common practice in many other competing countries, but not in Canada.) Tellingly, their response was to discuss why they participate in the sport of curling. They spoke of the friendships they have within the team, and of the love they have for the game itself. They spoke of competing because they love to be challenged both on the ice and by various demands inherent in competitive curling. They also spoke appreciatively of the support they get from friends and family. Financial awards, though appreciated, are not the motivating factor. It is this attitude, I believe, that has helped them rise to the level of excellence they now enjoy, and that will continue to fuel their endeavours as they strive toward the 2002 Olympics in Salt Lake City. ◉

Lindsay Sparkes
September 1999

iii

Chapter One
WATERSHED

"**W**e both have this recurring dream we'll be wearing red and white. We know this dream can become a reality," a frustrated Joan McCusker and Marcia Gudereit muttered after a heartbreaking loss to Shannon Kleibrink's Alberta foursome.

Joan and Marcia's teammates – Sandra Schmirler and Jan Betker – joked that their dreams were a by-product of too much late-night fried chicken. But they were adamant their dream was more than that.

The Schmirler team had just suffered their second loss in three games. This loss to the Kleibrink team created a heated battle for first place at the 1993 Scott Tournament of Hearts in Brandon, Manitoba. Schmirler's team knew they had given the game away. They hadn't been out-curled, they just had not taken advantage of countless opportunities the game had presented.

Doubt began to gnaw at the Sandra Schmirler crew.

They found themselves in a lounge near downtown Brandon. Depression weighed heavily. Their first Canadian title appeared to be slipping away. They had curled with such consistency and control, starting 5-0 at the tournament, but now they seemed to be spiralling toward defeat.

The team was in a situation closely paralleling that of Chico Resch, a fellow Saskatchewanian. Thirteen years earlier, Chico and his New York Islander teammates had just suffered a loss to a team they should have beaten. Prior to the next game, Resch strode into the dressing room and slammed his goaltender's stick on the trainer's table. Taking a calming breath, he faced his teammates and then issued a challenge: "This game is up for sale. Who in here is willing to pay the price?"

According to many of the Islanders (after they won their first Stanley Cup a few weeks later), Resch's challenge re-sparked the fiery spirit of that talent-laden team. The Islanders refer to Resch's stick-slamming atten-

First national title – on the podium at the 1993 Scott. Sandra, Jan, Joan, Marcia and Anita.

tion-grabber as the watershed moment on their way to the first of four straight Stanley Cups.

A similar scenario was unfolding in a lounge in one of the world's greatest curling cities – the competitive drive just as intense, but no sweaty testosterone and no curling brooms slamming down on lounge tables.

Schmirler's team sat in stunned silence, the atmosphere thick with that "slipping away" sensation all good teams capable of becoming great sometimes feel.

And then into the lounge strode Anita Ford, the team's "fifth" (curling allows a fifth player at the national and international levels in case of sickness, injury, or a severe slump). The Ford name in Saskatchewan curling has been around for a long time. If you're from Saskatchewan and curl against a Ford, you know you're in for a battle. Gary Ford, Anita's husband, went to a handful of Briers with Bob "Pee Wee" Pickering, Canada's most famous curling bridesmaid. And Gary and Anita's daughters, Atina and Cindy, have been Canadian ladies junior champions. Anita has knocked on the door for years as one of Saskatchewan's top curlers.

Anita is a quiet lady who understands "the game." She seldom gives advice, but when Anita speaks, people listen.

The Schmirler team were crying into their drinks when Anita approached. She sensed the tension and emotion, understanding what this loss could do to a team.

Without a word, Anita pulled out a greeting card. She handed it to Sandra. Sandra read it out loud.

Simple and straight to the point, that card reminded Schmirler and her teammates that victory was still within their grasp. They must seize hold of it. Fear and doubt need not rule their game.

The card read, "Fulfill your dreams and never give up...Love, Anita." It helped break the funk the team was in.

The women began to talk and laugh.

The Schmirler team reaffirmed their belief they had the talent to win it all. In the past five years, they had beaten most of the former Canadian and world champions. They talked about Joan and Marcia's dreams about wearing red and white (the colours of Team Canada at the World Curling Championship). The conversation was intense, the commitment to win renewed. If they played as well as they were capable of, only an errant piece of horsehair (ice debris) and a near-perfect game by an opposing skip could beat them.

Lead Marcia Gudereit reflects on that watershed moment: "We refocussed on our goal of becoming Canadian champions. And you know what? None of us even finished our drinks!"

The team never had to drown their sorrows again. The next drink they took was a toast of celebration as the champagne cork popped a few days later. The Schmirler team had won their final two round robin games and beat hometown favourite Maureen Bonar in the final. Three weeks later, they won the first of three world championships, a feat unparalleled by any other Canadian ladies curling team.

That Brandon watershed could have sent this three-time championship team in many directions. But Sandra, Jan, Joan, and Marcia have often said that their commitment to win is rooted in their commitment to each other.

Winning a world championship is a major story any time it happens. But to win three within a five-year period makes for truly exceptional storytelling. In most sports, you play in a league with 20 to 30 teams. Maybe six or eight of those teams are serious contenders for the championship. In curling, over 1,000 teams a year compete for the right to go global. Realistically, about 75 teams around the world could be considered potential world champions. Considering these odds, to win one world championship is outstanding.

To win three...!

The Schmirler team tells a tale of dealing with adversity, of learning from mistakes. It's a tale of the evolution of team chemistry, team commitments, and goals. Of developing a common vision that sees red and white – Canadian, world, and Olympic champions. ◉

Laughing more often than not – Team Schmirler shares a chuckle with Regina Mayor Doug Archer at their send-off party to the 1993 Worlds.

3

Chapter Two
CURLING CHEMISTRY 101

One recurring theme emerges when one studies the Schmirler crew – the sense of team.

Team Schmirler was the first women's curling team in history to win three world championships with the same four curlers, and the only Canadian team to do so. Ernie Richardson won four men's Worlds (with his Regina-based family team), and three of his teams had the same four curlers. Ron Northcott of Calgary led the only other team to win at least three world curling titles – but not with the same roster.

What Team Schmirler has accomplished is unparalleled in the curling world. They have created a standard so high it may never be equalled – not just in women's curling, but in men's as well. And there are so many factors that influence women in athletics – marriage, child-bearing and rearing, career, injury – any of which could necessitate a team lineup change.

Joan took most of the 1995-96 season off when she gave birth to her little girl. The revamped squad made it all the way to the provincials, only to be defeated by the Sherry Scheirich team from Saskatoon in the final.

Sandra says, "It wasn't the same without Joan in the equation. We brought in Pamela Bryden, who is an outstanding curler, but the chemistry just wasn't the same. She curled well for us, but something was different. This isn't to knock Pamela. We're just not the same without our four regular teammates."

Walter Betker said, "They were making do with a new player and still came away one step from going to the Scott." He didn't say this as a put-down of Pamela or any other curler. Walter was commenting on the unique spiritual leadership that Joan brings to the team. "She has that ability to inspire the team to keep their confidence level high in such a believable way. It's an art she has. You can't expect someone else to just come in and replace that. Jan tried to be Joan for a while, but that's not who she is. Every player brings an

"They slay themselves" – somebody said something funny at the 1998 Scott in Regina.

internal gift to the team – it's not just talent."

Every team has an inner soul. Alter *that* and team effectiveness will diminish. Team soul is an ongoing renewal of overall values and fundamentals of the group. There are certain dynamics that sustain a healthy team soul.

Schmirler's main provincial rival in the beginning was Michelle Schneider. Schneider is a four-time Saskatchewan rep at the Scott. The *Canadian Curling News* once referred to her as the best skip to never win the Scott. Michelle says about Team Schmirler, "Their chemistry is the key to their long-term success. They aren't just a great curling team, they are a great *team*."

Ardith Stephanson covered curling for the Regina *Leader-Post* for most of the Schmirler years. "The key to their success is their obvious talent level, but their team dynamics are what make the difference," she says. "They get along so well. I like how they deal with a loss in a major event. They deal with it immediately. They talk about it. They are so open with each other. They get it out of the way and then they move on. It's like a healthy marriage.

"Each player brings something special to the relationship. Marcia appears quiet but is quite funny. Joan is the most verbal and gets the team talking through issues. Jan is just so even-keeled and poised. Sandra is so competitive and takes responsibility for her performance with little or no blame-shifting."

Anita Ford has had the best inner-circle view of anyone. As the fifth player or coach at all major events, her observations are well worth noting.

"The key to their success is the team chemistry. Part of this chemistry is that they are in the same stage of life in terms of marriage and family. The chemistry didn't just happen, although it may look that way. It was a growing thing. A team needs all four personalities to be themselves. Sometimes the spark comes from Joan's energy. Marcia is the glue that sustains friendship, the human element. Sandra's analytical approach solidifies a philosophy on the ice. She sets the tone of how the team will play each opponent. Jan's intensity is what keeps the team centred on their prime directive.

"A good example of this dynamic was in Geneva in 1993. There's a typical letdown that most teams struggle with at the Scott and the Worlds. It hits around Tuesday, halfway through the round robin.

"Sandra, Joan, and Marcia stayed out later than they normally would at a major competition. They had violated one of their own in-house rules. There was no morning game and they weren't scheduled until the afternoon versus Germany, followed by an evening game against the USA. These three thought that since there was no morning game they could maybe get away with it. They played terribly against Germany and lost in an extra end. It was obvious to everyone that Jan was not happy about the outcome of the German game. She felt it was a direct result of the previous night's activities. The team recognized there was a problem. Jan, along with Lindsay Sparkes and myself, pulled the team together to talk the tension through immediately after the game. The other three team members agreed with Jan – they needed her, and the focus she brings to the team."

Elisabet Gustafson, the four-time world champion from Sweden, says, "I have nothing but admiration for this Canadian team. They are such a strong team, and so tight-knit. They enjoy each other like no other team we've faced. These Canadians are so strong at each position. They are the envy of our sport for their togetherness."

So what's their secret? How is the soul of Team Schmirler sustained?

GENUINE FRIENDSHIP

Jan Betker says, "People ask us, if we start losing, would we break up the team. The first time I heard this question, I was caught off guard. Why would we break up? We like each other too much. We've invested so much time and energy and worked through so many issues on and off the ice. We really are best friends. I'd rather curl with my best friends than break up this rink."

The women readily admit their chemistry is unusual, to have "clicked" so quickly and so well. A competitive nature and a sense of humour are qualities they share. They never feel threatened by other team members; they can be honest with each other without ever feeling attacked. The acceptance of differences is a key component to their long-term friendships. They value and appreciate what each teammate brings to the table.

Marcia says, "We learn from one another. In many cases, we've adopted each other's philosophies of life and curling into our personal lives. We've learned from each other and have grown together. You can't help but grow in game focus and intensity from being around Jan. You need this quality to have a chance at winning at this level. Joan's ability to get us talking through team issues is something we can each adopt. Now it could be anyone being a Joan on

Humour goes way back – Joan, Marcia, Jan, and Sandra enjoy themselves more formally at the 1992 Provincials banquet in Yorkton.

Team Schmirler celebrated their 1993 World championship all over the province that summer, arriving at Cumberland House on the ceremonial York boat during the Northern Games celebrations.

the team. With Sandra you learn the need to be prepared and to cover all the possibilities. It's a great mix."

The women have shared many emotional off-ice experiences. When close family members have been hospitalized or have died, the women have supported each other. They've all had babies and understand the challenge of raising toddlers while curling competitively. Theirs is a natural empathy that only benefits on-ice performance, a friendship foundation that cannot be unduly affected by curling slumps. Indeed, their friendship and candor with one another accelerate their return to championship-winning levels of play.

FUN

Being multiple world champions brings added responsibilities. And it magnifies the "target" mentality with opposing teams.

But the intense Jan has said many times over the course of writing this book that curling is *fun*. Team Schmirler genuinely enjoys playing the game. They often talk about the fun aspect to keep joy in the game. This has become more difficult for the women in light of their many accomplishments. But if anything can take pressure off the moment, it's the simple pleasure of each other's company.

Sandra says, "Right from the start, we all had such a similar sense of humour. It helped us to have fun right away. It's like the oil that keeps the engine running."

Humour lends perspective. Sure it hurts to lose significant games or titles, but laughter can bring sunshine to the cloudiest days. And Team Schmirler laughs often.

They came to appreciate the value of humour in their first season together, when they went to the 1991 Autumn Gold Classic in Calgary, considered to be one of the best women's bonspiels. Most of the world's top teams compete, and the money is very good. The majority of cash 'spiels run a triple-knockout format – three losses and you're out – with only

eight teams out of 32 qualifying for the money.

Team Schmirler was almost down to their last chance. They decided to kick back and have some fun before taking their last shot at the money. Sandra relates the story: "We started joking – what's the worst thing possible each of us would have to do if we lost the game? It was all silly stuff, but Marcia's was the funniest. We were staying with relatives. They had this dog named Max. He likes to "hump" people's shoes. So, if we lost, Max would get to hump Marcia's slipper. It was really juvenile, but it broke the ice. We realized then that we could laugh with, and at, each other and still be friends."

Joan says: "It was so much fun in the beginning, getting to know one another. Marcia and myself, we're just happy to be there with such good curlers. Our first year together we didn't win many 'spiels, but we qualified in every event we entered. It was the year where we seemed to finish second in most events. We lost so many finals.

"But Marcia and I were so happy just to be curling in top-level competitions; it was the most success the two of us had ever experienced. We'd be high-fiving each other even after we lost. We couldn't believe we were winning money at curling.

"It drove Jan and Sandra nuts. They had been to a Scott and had done so well before we came along. They wanted it to be a break-out year where the team would go that extra step and start winning championships. They were accustomed to qualifying in these big 'spiels. So Marcia and I were happy and excited, and Jan and Sandra were walking off the ice depressed. They tolerated our enthusiasm, and it brought the four of us together. We brought perspective to Jan and Sandra that our accomplishments were pretty darn good, and they taught us to maybe crank it up a notch or two and not be satisfied with just qualifying."

COMMUNICATION

Joan tends to be the conflict resolution conscience of the team. She says, "You have to communicate. My theory is that this is a major problem with most men's teams. I talk to my husband a lot about this and he agrees. Men tend to not communicate. He's been to two Briers and says the main difference he's observed is that men's teams are weak in communication skills. He's almost envious of the communication level we've been fortunate to develop."

Marcia quips, "The men are cowards. They don't talk."

Marcia was joking, but former Oakland Raider coach (and now Fox TV football analyst) John Madden echoes her sentiment. He says communication is necessary to keep conflict to a minimum. Pent-up feelings can rot a team from the inside out. They can destroy the team's soul.

Joan says, "There are many top teams with four good shooters. But all too often there is one person on the team who is only there for herself; she doesn't put the team's interests ahead of her own. This is so destructive. The members of a consistently good team put the team ahead of themselves. This creates an atmosphere for open communication."

Jan says, "We're not guarded with each other. We can always be ourselves. No one is ever frowned upon if the tears come. We laugh a lot, cry a lot, and curl. There's a real atmosphere that we can be who we are. We have such an understanding of each other. Not many teams have this – believe me! Somehow we've created a genuine family-like atmosphere."

EGOS ON THE SHELF

Curling is a unique team sport. Most sports carry a lineup of dozens of players: hockey dresses 17 or 18 players and sits another five or six in the press box; baseball dresses 25 players; Canadian football dresses 36.

On most teams, if you don't get along with someone, you don't have to associate with them while off the playing field. In curling, you have only four players (five at the majors). You are in constant communication on the ice. You travel in one vehicle. You bunk together in hotels. You eat meals together. It's impossible to avoid your team members.

Through communication and putting their egos on the shelf, the members of Team Schmirler are able to fulfill the overall team mission. They are unwilling to succumb to the pettiness that can creep in. Team success is the main goal. No one person stands out over another. It's an intentional choice to put the team ahead of individual accomplishments.

Even in the Hot Shots compe-

9

Team Schmirler can hardly wait to chow down at the Brandon Scott Volunteer Night, with Scott Paper president Bob Stewart.

tition at the Scott – an individual skill event with a car as first prize – the deal is that if one team member wins, they sell the car and split the profits. The team shares all.

Jan says, "Too many talented teams don't reach the elite level because egos are put before the team."

DEALING WITH CONFLICT

Joan McCusker says, "We've had many conflicts, the kind that would break up most teams. It's part of life. So when a conflict happens, we are determined to work it through."

Sandra says, "We don't want to jeopardize what we've accomplished and the friendships we've developed. We understand that the good times and successes far outweigh any bad times we've had. It's evolved over time. Very few feelings of threat or intimidation exist among us."

Jan agrees. "One of us usually winds up crying, and that tends to put the brakes on. But it's easier to deal with conflict when the commitment level is high. When you've been successful, you see the value of what you have and fight for it."

Marcia says, "We've had a lot of fun together so we're willing to cut a lot of slack. We're at the point now where no one is afraid to be herself."

But this tightness and loyalty has grown over time. There have been significant obstacles along the way that had to be confronted and overcome.

Jan goes on to say, "It's similar to creating a happy marriage. A lot of energy and effort is put into the relationship. It would be awful hard to start this over again with other players. It's a lot of work, compromise, and patience to get where we're at. We may as well stay together, 'cause who wants to start from scratch?"

Joan comments, "We may let conflict go unresolved for a day or two sometimes, but not very often. Sometimes a little breathing time is needed to get one's perspective back. But we're at the point where we can't not deal with it. We value each other too much. Yeah, we can really get ticked off at each other

Jan: "Too many talented teams don't reach the elite level because egos are put before the team." Not this team.

occasionally. But it's the same in my marriage, and I think I've got an above-average marriage. Getting ticked is a part of life – not dealing with it in a healthy way is what erodes relationships."

The team tends to deal with internal conflicts quickly. The old adage of "not allowing the sun to go down on your anger" fits this team like a glove.

There aren't only internal conflicts to face; there are outside ones as well: the demands of high-level competition; expectations from organizers, curling officials and the press; family concerns.... The list is endless.

This is where the Fords (Anita, the current coach, and her daughter Atina, now the fifth player) have taken on an unsung role, often dealing with the outside conflicts, relieving the team of stress. Anita has been like a "curling mom" to the women. She understands the nature of competitive curling and has raised a family. Team Schmirler lauds her behind-the-scenes efforts. She's been their conflict buffer and defuser for almost a decade. She allows the team to focus their energies on the game. Anita, and now Atina as well, both help to minimize outside distractions. Their roles are as integral to Schmirler's game as throwing a last-rock draw to the four-foot.

SETTING GOALS

Sandra emphasizes, "You have to set team goals. If you don't set goals, you have no idea where you're going."

When Team Schmirler won back-to-back world championships in 1993-94, they were a new team and needed to clarify their direction. It was important to sit down and talk about their aspirations. Marcia says, "I think we meet more than other teams, formal meet-

Joan says, "We use this time to see how we're each feeling. It helps us to see and understand each other's mind space. We talk a lot about our curling, but also about family and careers."

Marcia adds, "I wonder if men's teams talk about their feelings as much as women's? It wouldn't hurt if they did!" she laughs.

Jan is very goal-oriented and highly focussed, and she often serves as navigator to keep the good ship

Curling talent and a whole lot more went into creating this gold medal victory leap at the Olympic Games.

ings two or three times a month. Sandra usually calls them. But we also meet informally a lot. After practice or club games, we usually get together; sometimes a coffee or drink after the game turns into a team meeting. Since the Olympic experience, we've had to increase the team meetings almost twofold."

The off-season sees them convening often, just to touch base or to talk about matters concerning the team. It's a good time to re-evaluate existing goals, or to set new goals.

Schmirler on course. "She's maybe the most intense one of the four," explains Anita, "although they are all competitive by nature. Jan seems to seldom, if ever, lose sight of what the team is trying to achieve. I've seen it a couple of times, Jan calling the team together to remind everyone what they are seeking to accomplish. Jan doesn't have to say a lot – her persona, her intensity, gives her, and the team, drive. You can't help staying focussed on the important task at hand if you're observing Jan."

ROLES

Two thousand years ago, the Chinese philosopher Sun Tzu expressed his ideas about the art of war. Sun Tzu taught that the effective military unit has no constant shape, just as water has no constant shape. Water adapts to the lay of the land. So an effective army, and an effective team, is founded on adaptability.

The members of Team Schmirler don't want to be boxed into a specific role or stereotype. Each is free to grow and evolve in the game, but also personally and in their relationships with each other. Each team member plays a specific position, but team dynamics allow for a lot of crossover. Marcia puts it best: "We all have our strengths and weaknesses. But we are given the freedom to change. As an example – Joan was the initiator of getting us to talk things through when we first started. It's still her strength, but we've all done 'the Joan thing' in recent years."

The team pursues very specific goals. Whoever achieves movement toward those goals is irrelevant. Jan may be the most consistently focussed, but even she wavers now and then; if that happens, any of the other women is willing to wear her shoes. They learn from each other, assimilate each other's strengths into their own lives.

SACRIFICE

Time off work. Year-long leaves of absence. Vacation days spent in places like Nipawin or Yorkton to play in cash bonspiels. Not too many Canadians book midwinter vacation days in cold Saskatchewan cities.

When this team first came together, sponsors had no idea who Schmirler was. There's always a financial commitment when you want to play better teams. Travel and entry fees were paid directly out of team members' pockets. However, international success has opened the doors to many sponsors.

Olympic stories are always tales of sacrifice – personal, social, and financial. Most Olympians retire from competition in their sport before they reach 25 years of age; any sacrifice happens over the short run, relatively speaking. The members of Team Schmirler are all in their mid-thirties. They paid the price long before anyone even dreamed curling would become an Olympic event.

Sacrifice is a part of their lifestyle. It's necessary to sustain excellence, and they don't view it as drudgery or hardship. Juggling home, career, and sport is not easy, but possible. The Schmirler women have proven that proper time management can ensure that no aspect of your life suffers. Of course, it helps if you've developed a strong support system.

During the Olympics in Nagano, Sandra said, "You must settle your affairs at home. If home is happy, you can concentrate fully on curling. If it's not, the game will suffer. We owe a lot to our husbands. All four of them have given up time to make sure our team works. Much of the sacrifice is theirs. We've all said that if our husbands tell us the family is suffering, then we'll give up the competitive part of curling. So far, they've never even hinted at this. They view it as a privilege and seem to enjoy it as much as we do."

Sandra and Sara – "You must settle your affairs at home. If home is happy, you can concentrate fully on curling."

Helping out pays off – Team Schmirler headed down east in the fall of 1993, to help promote the upcoming Scott Tournament in Kitchener-Waterloo. They wound up at an American League baseball championship series game, featuring the Toronto Blue Jays, with Kitchener committee member Murray Haase.

Such a strong support system is crucial to the team's success. It alleviates the ill feelings sacrifice can generate. Joan says, "I always feel guilty when I leave my kids. That's part of being a mom. I know my children are being well taken care of, but I still want to be with my kids. However, Brian and my immediate family always encourage me to fulfill the team's curling dreams. They almost get mad at me if I pull back. The good thing is the team is never away from home for more than a week, or sometimes two. And Brian brings the children to many of the events.

"In 1993, I was at the Scott, and Brian was representing Saskatchewan at the Brier. He missed our newborn son (Rory) while he was at the Brier, but it never once slowed down his competitive drive. It's different for me. Brian is a very liberated husband who helps in the child-rearing as much or more than most husbands. But he admits he didn't understand how stressful it was for me to leave Rory while I attended the Scott in Brandon. I was in the middle of breast-feeding – I enjoy that aspect of motherhood – and I had to give it up."

After winning the Canadian and then world titles in 1993, the team automatically got a berth to the 1994 Scott in Kitchener-Waterloo. They wore national colours as Team Canada. Jan and Marcia were hoping to start their families in 1994, but both put off child-bearing for another year.

Then the team repeated as Canadian and world champions and were afforded the same privilege in 1995. For two years, Jan and Marcia (and now Joan, who was planning a second child) had to wait to become mothers.

Finishing third in 1995 came as a relief to the team. Marcia, Joan, and Jan all got pregnant within the next year and a half – a short sabbatical from competitive curling. The women still curled, but baby time took precedence. These were the so-called "lean years" of 1995-96 when Team Schmirler did not curl at the Scott.

The glory years have seen the women's marriages grow stronger. But they've also become more intentional and guarded about family time. Sacrifice to the sport makes the women more aware of, and value more, the precious moments they share with husbands and children.

What about the parents of Team Schmirler?

Jan says, "My mom and dad are our biggest fans. And the four sets of parents really enjoy hanging out with each other. Our team success has deepened so many relationships. I think our parents enjoy curling competition even more than we do. Think about it. What a great way to spend your retirement. Travelling around Canada and the world cheering your children on. My husband and I would do the same."

Team Schmirler does whatever it takes to win, but never at the expense of family.

To a certain extent, the four team members meshed well right from the outset. But they have each admitted that the team could have blown apart on numerous occasions. Success takes hard work. While some may know the principles to make a team work, too few consistently practise those principles, and success remains elusive.

Sandra says, "We'd do it all again. The triumphs, the camaraderie, the experiences were all worth it. Our husbands and parents and brothers and sisters all agree, it's been the ride of our lives." ◉

13

Chapter Three
BUILDING THE FOUNDATION (1985-1992)

Back in 1985, Sandra Schmirler had just finished her studies at the University of Saskatchewan in Saskatoon. She then moved to Regina to take some summer classes at the University of Regina. She also went job hunting. "I begged every pool in town – I would have taken a part-time lifeguard instructor job at a waterslide," Sandra recalls. "It was tough, but eventually I found work."

Kathy Fahlman was one of Regina's hottest young curlers, and was looking to bolster her chances to win a berth to the Scott. Kathy asked Sandra to curl third for her newly-formed team. Jan Betker was the second. Sheila Schneider threw lead stones.

Their first year together (1985-86) brought moderate success. The team won a few games in the city play-downs, but were eliminated on the second-last day of competition. It was clear they could play with the best, but they needed to experience more consistent competition to win their first zone and advance to the south Saskatchewan playoffs. At this point, visions of world or national championships were nothing but fantasy for Sandra and Jan, and few could have foreseen Olympic gold.

Curling with Fahlman did a few things for Sandra and Jan. For one, a new friendship was begun, a unique bond that continues to this day. Both women possess the same drive and share a love for the game. It was as if they had discovered curling soulmates.

The 1986-87 season was the breakthrough year for Schmirler and Betker. Still curling for Kathy Fahlman, they went on to win their first Saskatchewan provincial title, beating Susan Lang's Regina team 8-3 in the provincial final, and winning the right to represent their home province at the Scott Tournament of Hearts being held in Lethbridge, Alberta. The Fahlman rink finished fourth, losing a tie-breaker to land in the last play-off spot. Quebéc's Helene Tousiquant's team beat them 9-3 – a disappointing conclusion to a good week.

The 1989 Kathy Fahlman team from Regina, including Sandra, Jan, and Joan.

Team Fahlman's record was a respectable 7-4.

Sandra, Jan, and Sheila Schneider all made the first all-star team. It was looking as if these curlers could make a name for themselves on the national scene. Sandra and Jan's confidence grew as they realized that, individually, they were as good as any other top-level curler in Canada. But did they have teammates who would jell and go all the way to a national championship? Maybe they could do it with Kathy Fahlman throwing the last brick. The team was considered one of Saskatchewan's best bets to lay claim to a Scott crown.

They had a terrific provincial run during the 1987-88 season and made it to their second straight provincial final, where they lost to Michelle Schneider 10-0 in the final game. Schneider had put together one of the best teams in recent Saskatchewan memory. This was Schneider's first of four Saskatchewan titles in five years, one of the best runs of any team in Saskatchewan curling history. Only the great Vera Pezer and Joyce McKee combination from Saskatoon did the same between 1969 and 1973.

Schneider's was also a Regina-based team. She became the new target for Saskatchewan curlers. Michelle was always in the hunt and was a pre-tournament favourite in all her appearances. In the twelve years since that 1987-88 season, Schneider has qualified for the provincials eleven times in the curling hotbed of Saskatchewan.

Practice, practice, and more practice – this is Michelle Schneider's curling ethic. Not many curlers were quite so diligent as Michelle during that era. But then others began to follow her example.

Schneider says, "My team practised almost daily during that five-year stretch. Not many of the contenders practised as much as us back then. Now most of them do. Schmirler's team obviously does. They have it all – work ethic, talent, passion. But especially team chemistry – you can't bottle that. They have something special and unique."

Sandra and Jan learned many valuable lessons during the 1987-88 season. It's tough to repeat as a champion – especially in a province like Saskatchewan.

The Fahlman team of 1988-89 was kept intact, except for a change at the lead position. Fahlman brought in a pair of sisters to fill the lead spot. Sandra and Jan were introduced to a school teacher named Joan Inglis and her sister Cathy Trowell – both solid curlers.

The Inglis sisters, Joan and Cathy, were from the small town of Saltcoats. This region of Saskatchewan had a reputation for tough hockey and baseball teams, but also produced many fine curlers. Their dad, Bruce, was one of the tougher curlers in the area, known for his big, accurate take-out weight.

Joan threw lead for Fahlman in the city and southern playdowns. The city playdown went well, but the south was another story. Disappointment followed by disappointment followed by yet more disappointment.

The south was a triple-knockout event. The Fahlman team lost the A final, B final, and C final. They curled more games than any other team, but couldn't gain a berth to the provincials.

Their final game was a 7-5 loss to Myrna Koch's team from the host community, Maple Creek. Koch was sick and couldn't even play. Her friend, Dena Weiss, curled the game of her life, rallying the team from being down 1-4 after five ends. She outscored Fahlman 6-1 down the stretch.

If anyone believes Team Schmirler hasn't experienced the despair of losing, they need only think of the 1988-89 season. Three chances to qualify, three

16

defeats. For Sandra and Jan, it was crushing.

Joan's reaction to her first southern playdowns taught her a valuable curling lesson. "I was devastated, depressed. From that experience, I learned that the best team doesn't always win. Never take games or playdowns for granted.

"That year with Fahlman and my two new friends showed me that I could curl at a high level and not embarrass myself. 1989 gave me a hunger to go competitive."

Sandra and Jan were ready for a change. They enjoyed curling with Kathy, but the on-ice chemistry just didn't seem to be there.

Along came the 1989-90 season. Kathy Fahlman disbanded her team. She was asked to curl third for her number-one rival, Michelle Schneider. In the minds of many curling fans, this could become a dream team in the Saskatchewan curling world. To prove the experts right, Schneider's new lineup went on to win the provincials that season.

Sandra Schmirler and Jan Betker approached Susan Lang. Could they form a team with her? Sure. Once again, Sandra curled third, Jan curled second, and a new teammate by the name of Gertie Pick curled lead. Joan and her sister went on to form their own team.

The 1989-90 curling season was significant for Sandra and Jan. They played well below expectations, winning their share of games in the Regina playdowns, but getting eliminated by Sharon Garratt on the final day. They fully expected to at least qualify and go to the southern playdowns.

Extreme disappointment led to soul-searching. Sandra and Jan drank a lot of coffee together and re-evaluated their curling goals. They knew in their hearts that they could compete and win against world-class curlers. Jan finally said it: "Either you skip or I skip, but let's get our own team together. One of us will skip, and the other play third. We're good enough. I really think we should be calling the shots and throwing the final four stones." Sandra's confidence had grown in the five years she'd spent curling third at the women's level. She decided to go for it.

She recalls, "Jan and I got along so well that I didn't want to curl with anyone else. She really didn't want to skip, so I won by default. I had confidence, but I was a little insecure. I had never thrown the last rocks, but I felt I could do it. I just had to prove to myself that I could.

"We had hit a plateau in our curling. We needed to do something to improve our chances of winning. If me as skip didn't work, we could always approach someone else the following year, or I could probably talk Jan into it. I had nothing to lose."

The new skipper: "If me as skip didn't work, we could always approach someone else the following year."

With a representative from Scott Paper, Team Schmirler celebrates the 1991 Provincials victory at their home club, the Callie in Regina.

Now they had to round out their team with a lead and second, something easier said than done. Too many good curlers want to curl third or skip. A lot of fine leads and seconds had started to move up and form their own teams. Some were very successful, but many others would never advance beyond their own clubs in playdowns.

Many good curlers are simply not content curling lead or second. Having a discontented front-end player can create bad chemistry, a problem that can affect the emotional health of the team, turning positive energy into negative. Teammates are either constantly trying to fix relationships or are turning inward to hide their true feelings. This is when the "who cares if we win" mentality can take over, creating a dysfunctional team in the true sense of the word. This was a major concern for Sandra and Jan. They needed talent to win, but they also needed four players who could get along. A solid "team" mentality breeds confidence. Confidence wins games. Teammates can build confidence in each other, in pressure situations or in slumps. The opposite is also true. When a team's confidence is eroded, they might as well mail in the "W" to the opposition. Sandra and Jan knew that finding a good front end could make or break the 1990-91 season.

Jan and Sandra were curling students who had followed the successful curling careers of Thunder Bay's Al Hackner and Rick Lang, who won two world championships in the 1980s. Jean Sonmor's excellent book, *Burned By the Rock*, chronicles the break-up of the 1985 world championship team they had formed. Like Schmirler and Betker, Hackner and Lang had spent almost their entire competitive careers with each other. Launching out on their own, they brought on two new front-end players who were a little younger, Ian Tetley and Pat Perroud.

Tetley and Perroud acknowledged the honour of curling with their mentors. As Tetley said, "it was like being asked to curl with a couple of curling gods." The 1986 season would prove to be the antithesis of 1985 for Team Hackner. Unfortunately, as Sonmer writes, "(Ian) Tetley was chomping at the bit, not only to reform the skip, but also to run the team's business." As Tetley said, "I thought maybe I could do a better job."

Team unity fizzled. Hackner vowed he'd never get into a situation like that again, with a front-end questioning his skipping to what he considered an extreme. The chemistry was gone. They've made up over the years, but there was a lesson to be learned.

Jan and Sandra were well aware of the potential pitfalls. Sandra doesn't mind being questioned. "I value input from all three players," she says. "It's a team game. All I ask is that when I make the final call, the team supports my decision and they play the shot-call with all their hearts. They know I'm not out to lose."

So Jan and Sandra began making phone calls.

"We called Joan and two other curlers," says Sandra. "It was pretty much whoever called back first." Joan called back in two weeks. Joan says, "Marcia and I were going to curl with my sister, Cathy Trowell, so I initially said no. Then Cathy found out she was pregnant and needed to take the season off.

We still didn't have a fourth curler, so it was just Marcia and me. I called Sandra back and said I was available, but could I bring along another girl I know named Marcia. They still needed a lead and second and Sandra said, 'Bring her along, we need a front end.' "

And so Team Schmirler was born.

The initial expectations weren't on the same page. Sandra and Jan were hoping to go to the provincials in their first year. Joan expected to win another zone; anything more would be a bonus. Marcia, who had only recently got back into the competitive side of the game, simply didn't want to embarrass herself; she would be happy curling above 50 per cent and not letting the team down.

A few things became obvious right from the start. They were all intensely competitive. They enjoyed the game and loved to win. The team chemistry was almost immediate. Everyone was content in their positions. This budding friendship seemed too good to be true. Even if the team didn't conquer Regina or Saskatchewan, they were going to enjoy themselves – in fact, they were going to have a blast!

Inwardly, all four were hoping there was no bubble about to burst.

Sandra proved to be a cool player under pressure. She seemed well-groomed to be throwing skip stones. Jan displayed flashes of becoming an outstanding third, not just in her shot-making, but in her complimentary personality to Sandra; Jan showed the highly-focussed, even-keeled style that gives a skip confidence. Joan and Marcia "just kept having a good time."

"We really enjoyed curling on such a good team," Joan says. "Marcia and I always felt that Jan and

Sylvia Fedoruk, former Saskatchewan lieutenant-governor, internationally-renowned physicist, and a Canadian curling champ herself, offers a word of congratulations at the 1991 Provincials banquet in Regina

Sandra could make any shot and pull us out of any kind of jam. It was exciting. But we still had no idea of our future successes. Like I said, we were just happy to be along for the ride."

The team entered the Regina playdowns. They curled solidly, winning a berth to the southerns – the 16 best teams in southern Saskatchewan. The top four would go on to the eight-team provincial finals.

Team Schmirler went quietly about their business, winning one of the four southern qualifying berths. They were on their way to the provincials.

Joan says, "The provincials were beyond my and Marcia's wildest dreams. What made it doubly exciting was that it was being hosted by our home curling club, the Callie, right in Regina. My favourite memory is walking out on the ice on centre sheet in front of our home fans. Just to be there was so exciting!"

Jan recalls, "Sandra and I knew deep inside that if we curled to our capabilities, we had an excellent shot at winning the province. I couldn't wait."

The team had an outstanding week. They made it to the final game versus the tough team of Kim Armbruster, the 1985 Canadian junior champion

skip. Sandra was a rookie skip. The final was a good test of her mettle. In a typically-tight, low-scoring final, Team Schmirler came through with an impressive, if somewhat nerve-wracking, 5-3 victory. In their first season together they were provincial champions.

Sandra had proven she could make the big pressure shots. Jan had made clutch shot after clutch shot. Joan was developing into one of the best take-out women in the business. Marcia had proven herself to be the most pleasant surprise of this new foursome. Few in the curling world knew who she was; this was only her second competitive season. All indications said she would become an outstanding lead, a great sweeper, and someone who set up an end like few leads could.

The team was jelling quickly. Saskatchewan was behind them. They were off to Saskatoon as the host province representative. Sandra recalls her second (but first as skip) Scott: "My biggest mistake was treating it as a learning experience. You don't win at that level if you don't fully expect to win."

The team curled a respectable 7-4, finishing fourth in Canada. They had lost the third and final playoff spot in a tie-breaker – Heather Houston's team from Thunder Bay beat them 6-3. Team Houston was the first repeat national champion (1988 and 1989) since Vera Pezer's three-year run from 1971 to 1973. Team Schmirler would become the next back-to-back foursome to win national titles.

Jan recalls the 1991 Scott. "I vowed if we ever made it back, we'd be back to win. I knew we had the team to do it. It was just a matter of time." "The 1991 Scott clearly showed me that I was on a team that could compete and win a major championship,"

Joan says. "I was no longer content just to be there. The Scott experience raised my winning expectations to the level of Sandra and Jan's. When I first got to Saskatoon, my mantra was, ' Just don't throw stupid.' When I left, it was more like, 'Let me at 'em!' "

Marcia comments, "That whole first year was unbelievable. I still remember Kerry (her husband) giving me some advice at the beginning of the year. He was telling me that it takes time for a good team to jell. You'll have lots of disappointments along the way, he said. Just hang in there and learn as much as you can.

"What he said was right in most cases. How many curlers go from recreational to a fourth-place finish at a national championship in less than two years? We

still laugh about his preseason pep talk. I was definitely in the right place at the right time with the right mix. I, too, now wanted the whole enchilada."

In 1991-92 Team Schmirler wanted to repeat as provincial champions. They couldn't wait to try. They all felt they could do better than just make an appearance at the Scott – they felt they could win. But they knew it wouldn't be easy.

Michelle Schneider, Kim Armbruster, Kathy Fahlman, Sheila Rowan, Lori McGeary, all these teams had legitimate shots at winning Saskatchewan. It would be a difficult year, but the Schmirler team was ready and psyched for defense of its province.

In preparation for 1991-92, the team committed to the cash bonspiel circuit. Club curling was fun, but playing the best curlers in Canada at bonspiels was the best training a team could get. "You only get better by playing against the best in your field," Sandra believes.

The team had high expectations. They had beaten most of the recent world, national, and provincial champions they had come up against. And when they had lost to these high-calibre teams, the scores had been close. The intimidation of playing against the very best teams was almost nonexistent. The anxiety about not embarrassing themselves had shifted to a

21

The 1991, team already including Anita Ford, marches in clapping for a draw at the 1991 Scott in Saskatoon.

nervous excitement. They felt their team could consistently beat the top teams in the curling world. And they could hardly wait for the new curling season to start.

Two-time Saskatchewan men's champion Randy Woytowich had watched this team emerge. He was not surprised at their newfound level of confidence. "I had curled with Jan and watched Sandra. Sandra was the most technically-sound woman curler I had ever seen. Her delivery was flawless. Her release was so textbook consistent. I had always thought Jan was one of the best curlers in Canada. Watching Joan and Marcia perform so well, you could see it coming. This was a team on the verge. It was just a matter of time."

One of the highlights of the 1991-92 season was when the Schmirler crew won their first major cash 'spiel at the Autumn Gold Classic in Calgary. It was the first big 'spiel of the year against most of the country's top rinks. In the early 1990s, there were only 10 or 12 big cash 'spiels in Canada. The largest purse was at the Autumn Gold Classic, and first prize was $6,000. Most of the entries are former provincial winners, national winners – usually six to eight American and European teams – and world champions.

Their lucky stars were shining as Team Schmirler rolled to their first major cash win, beating Calgary's Diane Foster in the final.

Winning the Autumn Gold deepened Team Schmirler's confidence level. Sandra and Jan always said they could compete at a world level – Calgary confirmed it for Joan and Marcia. It showed everyone that going to the Scott the previous year wasn't

The Saskatoon Scott, 1991: "You don't win at that level if you don't fully expect to win."

just a fluke or a lucky run, though competitive curling has had many one-year wonders.

"The win in Calgary gave us – especially the front end – the assurance that we had a very good competitive team," says Marcia. "We could contend at every 'spiel. We could win it all."

Their second bonspiel win was in the city of Yorkton, where Joan was born and went to high school. The field was small and each team highly competent. It wasn't considered a major 'spiel on the circuit, but a very competitive regional event. Yorkton is almost on the Saskatchewan-Manitoba border and this event attracted many of the regional zone winners from these two curling hotbeds. Sandra says, "It was good to know we could go out and win any 'spiel, no matter the size. It builds your confidence that little bit more."

The unique thing about that Yorkton win is that the team was not entered under the Schmirler name. Joan entered the team because it was close to her hometown of Saltcoats, where the team would be lodging. Curling trivia buffs take note. One of the first-ever cash bonspiels won by Team Schmirler was listed under the name of Joan Inglis.

The city playdowns began in early January. The Schmirler team went through undefeated and won the city's first berth, beating arch-rival Michelle Schneider in the A final.

On to the southern playdowns.

Once again, the team was undefeated. Their confidence level was extremely high. In the A final qualifier they again beat city-rival Michelle Schneider, forcing her for the second time down into one of the remaining berths through the B or C sides of the

Jan, Marcia, and Joan gather their wits about them prior to the start of a draw at the 1991 Scott.

draw. The Schmirler foursome were on to the provincials in Yorkton.

Eight teams qualified for the provincials. The curling pundits anticipated another Schmirler-Schneider final. Team Schmirler won one of the three qualifying events, and Schneider won the other two. In order for Sandra's rink to go to the Scott, they had to beat Schneider twice in a row. But Michelle and her teammates took control early and held the game firmly in hand, beating Team Schmirler 8-5; it was never really a close game. Sandra and crew felt like they were playing catch-up almost right from the start.

Incredible disappointment set in. Marcia says, "We were so confident at cities and southerns. Our psyche at provincials shifted. It's like we were playing scared – playing not to lose instead of playing to win. We subconsciously changed our approach and it cost us. Schneider was still the target."

It was Team Schneider's fourth Saskatchewan win in five years, and Michelle's team went to the Scott as one of the pre-tournament favourites.

The Yorkton provincials had marked the beginning of motherhood for Team Schmirler. Joan was pregnant with her first child, Rory. At all the fifth-end breaks, Joan had to eat a muffin to keep her energy up. This would be something the team would get used to.

The Schmirler foursome was hungry to get back to the top in Saskatchewan. The previous season had taught them much, and they were eager to put their knowledge to work. Sandra says, "Like all teams that win, we had to do some losing. It seems like you have to lose to learn the lessons of how to win. For some reason you learn more about the game this way. We were going to try and invest these lessons into some serious dividends." ◉

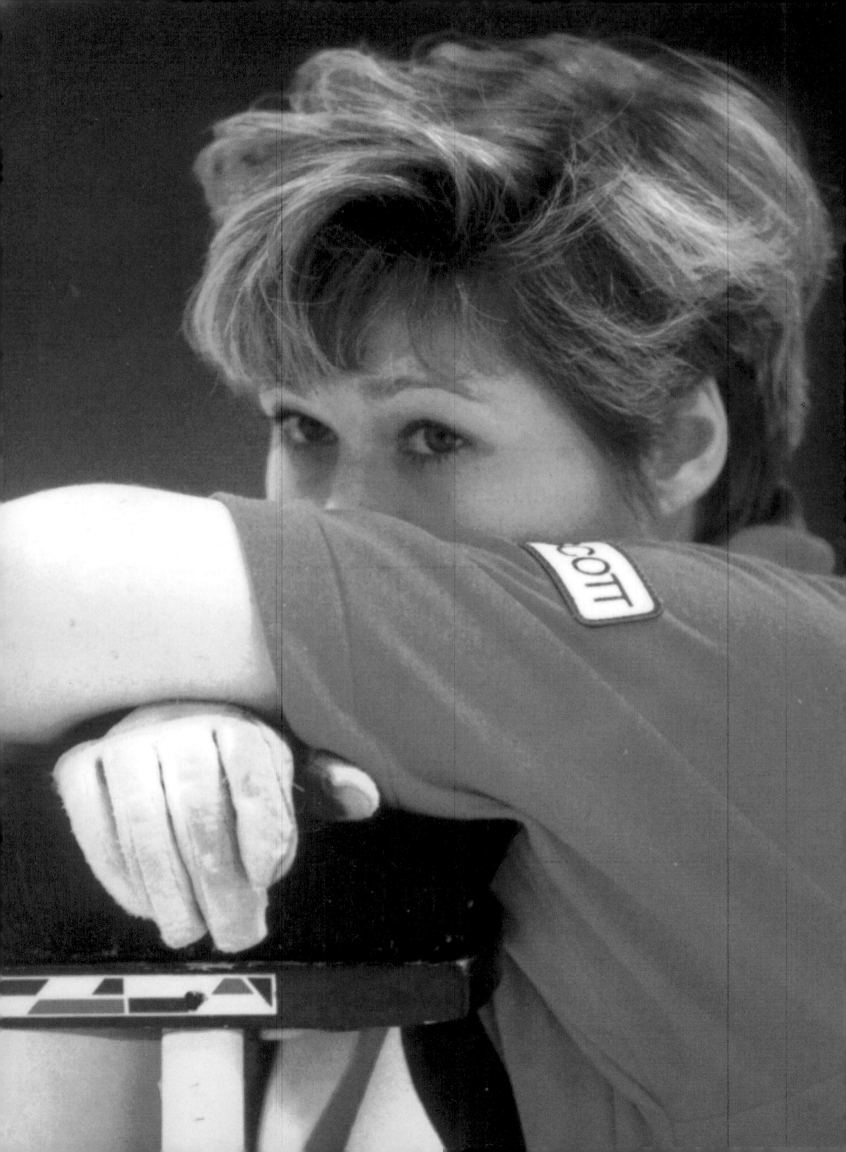

Chapter Four
MARCIA

"The FGZ (free guard zone) has Marcia's name written all over it," says Saskatchewan rival Kathy Fahlman. "Her drawing ability is so good and precise. She can single-handedly get an opposing team in trouble. Marcia is one of the smartest leads I have ever faced. With her and Joan playing front end, a mistake can never be counted on, especially in the sweeping game. If they ever did make a mistake, Ray Turnbull, TSN's curling commentator, would point it out very quickly, because they are so rare."

Quite a compliment coming from Fahlman, who had Sandra and Jan curl with her for over half a decade. Joan also roomed with Kathy for two years. If any opponent knows the Schmirler makeup, it's this respectful friend and rival.

Marcia Gudereit was a capable club curler, with her sights set on trying the competitive circuit. She knew in her heart she was capable of curling with the more elite competition of southern Saskatchewan, but had never had the opportunity to test the waters.

Winning Olympic gold and three world championships had never, ever, entered her thinking. Winning a city zone would have been enough to fulfill her curling dreams.

Marcia was the beneficiary of great timing. Her dad, Harvey Schiml, said, "Trevor (her brother) was the most avid curler in the family. Given the right set of circumstances, I would have bet on him getting on a highly competitive team with a realistic shot at going to the Brier. Marcia was a good curler who was fully capable and she got the opportunity of a lifetime."

Marcia is, as history is bearing out, a unique diamond in the rough. A competent curler – yes, but the world is full of decent competent curlers. Marcia is much more than that – a gifted young woman with intangible qualities not apparent at first glance. Her roots run deep into the heartland of curling.

"She was quite easy to raise...a bit of a tomboy."

Born on September 8, 1965, in her mom's hometown of Moose Jaw, Saskatchewan, Marcia Schiml lived her first three years in her dad's hometown of Avonlea.

Ten years earlier, a team from Avonlea won Saskatchewan's first Brier – the town was home to the well-known Campbell Brothers. Garnet, the skip of that team, would appear in a total of 10 Briers. He would go on to win 17 provincial titles including the men's, mixed, seniors, and masters, the most provincial titles by any Saskatchewan curler.

Harvey Schiml had curled with and against the famous Campbell brothers. Avonlea may possibly be Canada's most well-known small-town curling centre. With less than 500 people, this village has produced national-calibre curlers at every level of the game. The primary curling club in Toronto was started by the Campbell brothers and has remained known as the Avonlea Curling Club.

The Schiml family moved to Regina for six short months, until Harvey found a job as an electrician in the northeast Saskatchewan town of Hudson Bay. This would be home for the formative years of the three Schiml siblings – Trevor, Marcia, and Nomi. The family lived in a trailer just outside of town, beside the timber mill where Harvey worked.

"We were a close family that did a lot of things together," Marcia recalls with much fondness. "My mom and dad drove us to all our activities."

Being the middle child may have fostered her intense competitive spirit. "My brother Trevor really liked sports. So whether it was curling or board games, we both had to win. A lot of our family board games never officially ended because of the squabbles between my brother and me. But we'd go right back at it, in time."

Marcia was involved in many activities in her school and hometown. She figure skated for a few years, before curling took up most of her winter sports activities. School teams such as volleyball, basketball, and badminton filled up her schedule.

Harvey coached some of Trevor's baseball teams.

Marcia played on their mosquito league team. "She was the only girl on the team," her dad says. "I would say Marcia more than held her own. She turned out to be quite a good ball player."

Marcia still plays a modified form of fastball on a mixed team in Regina. Her husband, Kerry Gudereit, has been a part of this team for over a dozen years. "It's a fairly decent team, with only one player over five-six."

Her mom, Mary, comments on some of Marcia's other interests: "She was an outgoing kid who tried to get involved in as much as she could. Marcia spent some time in 4-H. She got involved in her school with the year book and SRC.

"She was quite easy to raise. We lived right near the woods, so she played in tree forts and houses the kids would make. A bit of a tomboy. They were always amusing themselves.

"Her marks were always up there at school. We tried to emphasize the importance of education. She wasn't a tough sell."

Harvey remembers his little tomboy: "She loved to motorbike. She had a 1975 Honda dirt bike. Of course in the winter there was always snowmobiling. Not just Marcia, but all three kids seemed to enjoy the outdoors."

Hudson Bay had three timber mills that among them hosted the annual Cordwood Bonspiel for the area's children. "This was my first experience at curling," Marcia recalls. "The hockey arena was converted to curling ice. To get extra sheets in, they'd shorten the playing surface and go width-wise. We'd have 12 sheets of ice and a million kids ready to curl. It was just grades three to six who were allowed to curl. They just finished their 32nd annual bonspiel this year.

"The older kids would skip and the grade threes and fours would play the front end. Mom and Dad would try to persuade us not to go, because it was such mayhem with all those kids. Actually, I think all the parents tried to convince their children to stay home. But whatever we children wanted to do, our parents would take us. It was a lot of fun and I loved it right from the start."

Marcia's earliest childhood memories are associated with local curling clubs. "Even before I threw a curling rock, I remember playing in and around curling rinks. Hudson Bay also had the Simpson Timber Bonspiel, which was sponsored by the company my dad worked for. It was a whole family event, with the older kids and parents curling. It was a fun 'spiel that curlers took seriously when they were out on the ice.

"I would watch my parents for about two minutes, then go play with my friends. It was a great atmosphere. I naturally associated curling with having a good time. Often many of us younger kids would sit on the stairs leading up to the lounge where our parents went after their games. Whether adults drank or not, they went to the lounge to visit. Of course, you had to be over 18 to go up the stairs. So we'd play on the stairs and wait for our parents."

Marcia started curling at the age of 10 in Clemenceau, a small hamlet 13 miles south of Hudson Bay, where there was a two-sheet rink with natural ice. All three children learned to curl there, and it became the Schiml family's home club.

Marcia cherishes the memories. "It was natural ice, so it was keen when the temperature was below freezing. When it got above freezing, us kids had to put both feet in the hack to try and get our rocks down to the other end. Sometimes if it was too warm there would be a film of water on the ice. I was lucky to get it to the first hog line in those conditions.

"We sometimes threw against negative ice, because of the ground the rink was built on. You got used to curling under the worst of ice conditions.

"The waiting room was often as cold as out on the ice. But my Dad hated to cancel a game, so

Marcia Schiml started curling at the age of 10, in Clemenceau, a hamlet 13 miles south of Hudson Bay.

27

we'd drive to the rink in a blizzard or -40 degrees. We thought nothing of it, especially my Dad and Trevor."

"Trevor would build a curling rink behind our trailer in the back yard," Marcia recalls. "We'd use jam cans or cordwood for rocks. He'd even make us homemade sliders out of cut-up Javex bottles. We would glue them on our sliding foot and curl. He was fanatical. I remember Mom getting annoyed with him when he practised his sweeping on the kitchen floor. He'd get an old rink rat or corn broom

her dad's standard – she started to curl with the adults. Her first big test was to enter the Simpson Timber Bonspiel. Her second year in the Simpson Timber, her team won the event. It was big-time stuff for a kid. Her team's picture made the local newspaper, and she won a trophy and a winter jacket. Marcia still isn't sure if she ever wore the jacket, because it was about three sizes too big. Events like this continued to build a love for curling and its social culture in Marcia's life.

As the children got older, the Schiml family

The extended Schiml family at home. As the children got older, the family started to curl as a mixed team at the Clemenceau curling club.

and sweep for twenty minutes straight.

"Trevor still curls, up in Thompson, Manitoba. He's always one of the best in his club. He's just never gotten the break of a solid team behind him. It's still his favourite sport.

"He's supported me all the way. He drove by himself to Saskatoon in 1991 to watch my first Hearts. It's a long way from northern Manitoba to Saskatoon. He came for the first weekend to watch. The only problem was that he came a week early. It was such a long way to come, he never did see me in person in that first event."

When Marcia was old enough – 11 years old by

started to curl mixed at the Clemenceau Curling Club. Harvey skipped, with his wife, Mary, at third. Trevor curled second and Marcia lead. As Nomi grew up, she moved into the lead spot and Mom became the fifth. Everyone else moved up a position.

Harvey says, "In the first year we got beat pretty bad in the first part of the season. Then the kids got a little confidence and style, and we started to win a few. Our family team was always in the running after that.

"We'd go to a few bonspiels every year. Places like Weekes, Hudson Bay, Prairie River, and our home club. The highlight for us Schimls was winning the Prairie River 'spiel one year.

"Marcia was the most polite of the three children on the ice. She never questioned the skip. Trevor and Nomi would always ask why. I didn't mind because they asked in such a way as to learn. You could tell Marcia was listening. She's always been quick to the little nuances of sports. I would say she's got sports smarts, because she caught on to things so quickly."

One of the most important curling lessons for Marcia was taught to her by her dad, on their mixed family team. Marcia recalls this fundamental of curling, especially for a lead. "I always had a reasonable feel for draw weight, all the way back to those days in Clemenceau. My dad would always tell me he couldn't do anything with a rock behind the back line. As long as it was in play, he could use it, whether it was out front, close to the rings, or even two inches from the boards. A rock in play always gives you a chance, it can always come in handy. He was happy as long as I could draw close to the house, that was a good thing."

Marcia curled every year in junior and senior high school, making the school team all three years she was eligible. They weren't especially strong teams, but the competition was fun and the experience invaluable.

In her final year of high school, she and some friends decided to enter the Saskatchewan junior playdowns. The team was skipped by Gwen Anderson, with Patricia Harris at third, Marcia second, and Tammy Anderson throwing lead rocks.

The success of this team was the first clue for Marcia that she could maybe play at a higher level. They won their regional zone and went on to play in the northern playdowns. The team lost the B final, but only two teams from the North went to the four-team provincial final. To finish third in northern Saskatchewan was quite a feat.

Marcia graduated from high school shortly after that curling season and moved to Moose Jaw. She attended the former Saskatchewan Technical Institute, now Palliser campus of SIAST, and graduated with a two-year data processing certificate.

In her first year at STI, she tried out for the women's curling team. The team competed against other western Canadian post-secondary schools. Marcia made the first round of cuts and then was released from the team, as the final selections were chosen. It was a very discouraging time for Marcia. Her curling consisted of a few fun bonspiels over the next two seasons.

The thought of curling competitively was now a remote thought at best in her mind. She would curl, but mostly for the exercise. The social side of the game was always a good release from school and work. And it was a terrific way to meet new people and sustain lasting friendships.

After graduation from STI, she was offered a job in Regina at Co-operators Data Services Ltd. Marcia remained with CDSL from May, 1985, until October, 1997. Since October of 1997, she has worked for Co-operators Life Insurance Company.

Marcia curled in her company's recreational league for her first two years in Regina. One person she got to know was Brian McCusker (Joan's future husband), who also worked at CDSL. Every now and then Marcia's "fun" team needed a spare and Brian would graciously fill in. For Brian, who was on Randy Woytowich's Brier contender, it was a kind gesture, and an extra game or two to throw rocks. For Brian to curl at a recreational level would be akin to Steve Yzerman filling in for a local beer league hockey team. But once again, Brian's gesture is not unheard of in curling. The overall spirit of the sport is the social nature of the game.

In the 1986-87 season, Marcia's junior skip from Hudson Bay moved to Regina. Gwen Anderson, along with her sister Tammy, asked Marcia if she wanted to enter a regular ladies' club team. Marcia was excited to get back into a higher level of curling and immediately agreed to join the team. They curled out of Regina's Wheat City Curling Club, picking up Kerri-Lynn Haas to curl second.

Another highlight from the 1986-87 season was being asked into the mixed playdowns. She curled against Al Trowell, who was married to Cathy, Joan's sister. This was another connection to a provincial contender. Cathy was beginning to make a name for herself in Regina curling circles. She liked the way Marcia played and filed it away for future reference.

Marcia joined Patti Peters for the 1987-88 season for club play. Marcia was enjoying the competition of club play more and more and kept her options open to curl at a more serious level. They entered city playdowns but had little success.

During these two seasons of getting back into regular club play, Marcia met Kerry Gudereit, who would become her future husband. Kerry was curling front end for Brad Hebert's team, which would even-

Kerry Gudereit, a top-level curler himself, proposed to Marcia at the Scott Tournament of Hearts.

tually capture the 1992 Saskatchewan men's Brier berth.

The 1989-90 season was the year Marcia got back into curling's competitive ranks in full force. Cathy Trowell and Joan Inglis were putting together a new team to contend at the playdown level. Cathy mentally pulled out the Marcia Schiml file and considered asking her to join the team's front end. Cathy consulted with Brian McCusker, who felt that Marcia would be a very healthy addition to Trowell's team.

Marcia was excited at the opportunity, but was a little apprehensive as well. This would mean more bonspiels, practices, and an overall higher priority for curling in her schedule. She decided to talk to Kerry and get his opinion on the matter. Kerry had been committed to the competitive circuit since his high-school days and knew of the frustrations this level of curling could bring. Kerry offered this advice to Marcia: "I don't know if you want to start into competitive curling. It's really frustrating. The first few years, you probably won't have a lot of success. Maybe it's not for you."

She says, "Kerry's words were pretty accurate for that first year. We entered a lot of 'spiels and never qualified in any. We entered playdowns and won a couple of games. We always felt we were close at having some success in Saskatchewan playdowns, but it just wasn't clicking yet."

As that season wound down, the team was invited to curl at the Medicine Hat, Alberta, women's cash 'spiel. Most of the top teams from the prairies would be there. Cathy Trowell couldn't attend, so Joan asked Kathy Fahlman – her roommate at the time – to join them. Marcia moved to second, Joan was curling third, and Sharon Bachmeier was lead.

This was to become the biggest curling success to date in Marcia's curling life. The team curled extremely well and won the bonspiel. Marcia reflects back, "Joan and I were so happy. Joan had tasted a little bit more curling success than me, but not that much more. Here we were, a couple of no-names winning a pretty major bonspiel. Kathy, of course, was used to it, but it was exciting for all, fun. We had beaten top-notch teams to win in Medicine Hat. It

was a huge confidence-booster for myself and Joan that we could hold our own against the best. It was simply a matter of jelling as a team – that was the fine line so many of us were seeking."

The 1990-91 season brought some significant team juggling on the Saskatchewan scene. Michelle Schneider and Kathy Fahlman would stick together. Sandra and Jan were looking for a new front end. Cathy Trowell wanted to keep Marcia and Joan and look for a fourth curler to possibly take over as skip. The biggest alteration to Saskatchewan teams happened when Cathy Trowell found out she was expecting. Cathy would choose to sit out the year, leaving Joan and Marcia looking for two new curlers to fill in the gap.

Meanwhile Sandra and Jan were without a front end. This was when Joan was contacted by Sandra and asked if she was interested and if she knew of a good lead. This was the first year of Schmirler's new team and it would remain this way until present…and counting.

Kerry's prediction of it taking years to become successful was accelerated beyond Marcia's wildest imagination. Two years into serious competitive curling and she was on a provincial champion team that would finish fourth in all of Canada, at the Saskatoon Scott Tournament of Hearts.

Harvey and Mary Schiml knew that Marcia had worked her way up to a pretty good team, but had no idea how serious a contender it was becoming. The parents' comment on that 1990-91 run: "Marcia would phone us in Hinton, Alberta, where we were living at the time. She called after they won their city zone. Then she called a few weeks later when they were curling quite well at the south.

"Then we get this phone call that her team had won the provincials and were going to the Scott, so we never really realized they were in provincials until they had won it. As Saskatchewan-raised curlers, we realized how tough it was to win our home province. We were so excited. We made sure we were in Saskatoon for the Scott. In Saskatoon, it was so exciting to watch Marcia curl at the highest level. When she walked on to the ice the first time wearing her province's colours, we were filled with so much pride."

Marcia's mom and dad have attended every Scott Tournament of Hearts Team Schmirler has curled in. They have enjoyed the bond that has developed with all the players' parents and families.

Marcia's mom, Mary, says, "I'm a little like my son-in-law, Kerry, when watching their games. Especially on television, curling a Worlds or Olympics. I start to walk around, my heart is pounding, I feel pretty tense. It's hard to watch, you want them to win so bad. I sometimes walk into the other room and peek from around the corner.

"Harvey sits there looking calm, but he does bite his nails.

"We usually watch the big games in our living room, all by ourselves. I can remember where I was on the real big shots. That famous seventh end wick-and-roll by Sandra in the Olympic trials, I was hiding around a cupboard, just off the living room in our home on Denman Island in BC."

Harvey admires this team tremendously. When asked what sets it apart, he offers these insights from his years of cheering them on: "Sandra is so steady, she seldom gets overly excited. Her head is always in the game. Jan is the spark plug. She keeps the intensity level up for everyone, just by her presence. Joan is definitely the conciliator, both off and on the ice. She has that way about her, that if a miss occurs, to encourage the player back on track.

"Marcia is the quiet one – on the ice. Our family admires that so much about her. She's become so steady in her shot making; second to none. Her dedication to the game and what it takes to stay compet-

31

Mary and Harvey Schiml share a smile with their gold medallist daughter at the 1998 Scott opening banquet in Regina.

At home with Colin – with both parents committed to his care, curling schedules get juggled.

itive. The way both her and Kerry keep family as the top priority. She's always been a quick learner in sports and I see it so clearly after a miss, because you seldom see her make the same mistake twice. The mental side of her game is so strong and it's continually developing. Marcia has learned to pick herself up, if her game is off a bit. We've watched her develop into one of the best curlers in the world."

Marcia and Kerry's romance began at the Callie Curling Club in Regina, where Kerry's parents, Ron and Dawn Gudereit, were the managers. A bit of a romantic, Kerry thought it would be appropriate to ask for Marcia's hand at her first Scott Tournament of Hearts.

Near the end of the closing banquet, Kerry gave a little jewelry box to each member of the team. He had a pin for each of the women. When it got to Marcia, she said, "This had better be an engagement ring!"

Kerry got down on his knees and made the formal presentation. Sure enough, it was an engagement ring. Overcome with emotion, Marcia closed the box and started to cry, then got up and ran out of the hall. Like any nervous fiancé-to-be, Kerry thought the worst, but they were only tears of joy. They were married the following year.

Kerry and Marcia became the proud parents of Colin on December 1, 1996. Marcia had taken the fall of 1996 off from curling. When she resumed curling in early January of 1997, her personal win-loss record for the rest of the year was "something like 45-3." Curlers can usually give ballpark numbers to their statistics, but don't often document all their games. Added to that was a third provincial crown, a third

Scott title, and a third world championship. Not too shabby for only curling half of a season.

Colin has become the central focus of the Gudereit family. With both parents committed to his care as the highest priority, curling schedules are juggled with his needs in mind.

Kerry has been a calming influence and sounding-board for Marcia since the beginning of their courting days. She comments on her husband's undying support: "He's always been there, he tries to go to all my playdown events, whether they're in small-town Saskatchewan or our favourite location of Berne, Switzerland. Kerry is my shoulder to lean on. Whenever I'm struggling in a big game or just need to calm down a bit, I look for my pacing husband in the crowd. Just looking at him makes me feel better. His support sort of oozes out of him.

"I'd love to see him get back to the Brier. He enjoyed the Brier so much when he was there, but it was in Regina, which brings added pressure. At this point in my career, I'd give up some of my success for him to experience a portion of success too."

Marcia has always been among the percentage leaders for leads at all the major events she's curled in, consistently curling in the mid-to-high 80s with her averages. The amazing part of those statistics is that most of her curling has taken place since the advent of the free guard zone, and leads have had to become a little more precise with their shooting. The take-out game isn't as common for Canadian leads, because of the great number of draws the leads have to throw. But Marcia's take-out game remains steady. She has also developed a reputation for the very tough split on an opponent's stone without removing it from play, which may be the most difficult shot in curling – next to a high-pressure late-in-the-game freeze for a third or skip.

In the days before the FGZ, a high-level team could sometimes get away with an average lead. The game was more wide open, so a second and third could usually compensate for a lead who was a bit off. These days a lead must be a better-than-average curler or a team is quickly put behind the proverbial eight ball.

As Trevor Schiml has said on many occasions, "They are the best put-together team in the world at each position."

The curling world, which often overlooks the accomplishments of a lead or second, gave Marcia a long-overdue award at the 1997 Scott. Marcia was twice overlooked as the all-star lead at the Scott when her averages were higher than all other leads. Her high averages alone should have been enough to qualify her, but she also has an uncanny ability to judge rocks and better-than-average sweeping skills, which might be missed by the casual sportswriter or fan.

Marcia received the Scott Tournament of Hearts playoff MVP award. Her obvious talents and intangibles really came to the forefront during those two 1997 playoff games. End after end, her stones set up the strategy for the team and made everyone else's shots a little easier. To date, she is the only lead to win this honour.

Marcia has kept her head over all the successes of the 1990s. "It's so hard to view myself as a world champion, let alone a three-time world champion and Olympic gold medallist. I almost have to pinch myself with all of our success – it's almost embarrassing to me sometimes. I'm so grateful for the opportunities I've had, the lifetime friendships I've made with Sandra, Jan, and Joan, among many others I've met through curling."

Pat Reid of the Canadian Curling Association, who travelled with the team to all the world championships and Nagano, tells the following story that captures the inner character and thoughtfulness of Marcia. "I was coaching the Kirsten Harmark team from Ottawa. In a team meeting I asked each player who their hero was and why, in the game of curling. Our lead, Andra Harmark, said it was Marcia Gudereit from Regina. She explained that Marcia was her ideal role model and that she wants to be a career lead, because of Marcia's example of the position's significance. I mentioned this to Marcia and she sent the most personal, insightful, encouraging letter with an autographed picture. She also sent Andra one of her Team Canada championship jerseys with Gudereit on the back, and Marcia asked that I arrange to have it placed anonymously under her Christmas tree. Her parents told me it was the treasured moment of their Christmas when Andra opened the mystery gift.

"Andra wore the shirt under her curling jacket for her entire junior career and still carries it around in her curling bag for inspiration.

"Andra admires Marcia – for her skill, sense of teamwork, and for being a career woman, a wife, and a mother. But what she remembers most is how much she cared for a young impressionable 17-year-old who she had never met. She is Andra's hero and I think Andra has chosen well." ◉

"I'm so grateful for the opportunities I've had, the lifetime friendships I've made with Sandra, Jan, and Joan, among many others."

Chapter Five

THE HUSBANDS

Walter Betker, Jan's dad, described the team as an entourage. Team Schmirler has an incredible supporting cast: parents, in-laws, brothers, sisters, co-workers, friends, and children. But Walter said the husbands are the major players in this troupe.

It would be a mistake to underestimate the important role of these four men. A married woman struggles to compete at a high level of athletics when she has children. As much as we would like to believe modern parents share equally the task of child-rearing, the reality shows us otherwise.

Doug Dias illustrates this point well. He is married to Claire Carver, a member of Canada's national synchronized swimming team (headed to the 2000 Olympics in Sydney, Australia). Dias – a liberated male thinker – puts it this way: "I've always firmly believed in equality between men and women. But in our culture, it's easier said than done. In practice, I'm probably 60 per cent liberated and 40 per cent not – and it frustrates me. We live in a culture that makes it much easier for men to compete in high-level athletics and to go at it for a long time. It's much harder for a married woman – especially one with children – to compete over an extended period of time."

Team Schmirler's husbands strive to do everything in their power to give their wives the chance to pursue world championships. But it's not a cakewalk. The husbands are athletes as well, and hold down demanding jobs. For Team Schmirler, family comes first.

Brian McCusker focusses on the positive. "I don't think I'd have gotten to know my two children as well as I do. I want to be the main caregiver when Joan is working on her game and at competitions. We've both turned this into an opportunity, and the kids are the ones benefitting. Joan is currently a stay-at-home mom – especially since our children are both under 10. She'll probably go back to teaching at some stage, but our family is still

Brian McCusker, Frank Macera, and Shannon England, as exhausted as their Olympic champion wives, take part in the homecoming reception at the Regina airport.

the main priority. It's a win-win situation, or at least we try to make it that way.

"Many times in local club play, one of us has the children during the early draw and we make the quick switch for the later draw. And it's not just Joan and me – I see Marcia and Kerry doing the same juggling act."

All four women have mentioned that having children and aiming to keep family a priority helps keep the pressures of the game in perspective. Marv Levy, the long-time professional coach of the Montréal Alouettes, the Kansas City Chiefs, and the Buffalo Bills, always looked for the "Schmirler" type of athlete. He says the athlete who consistently performs well under pressure is the one with one or two healthy outside interests. The player who tends to let you down in the clutch is the obsessed athlete whose whole being is wrapped up in their sport. Levy looks for athletes who take family seriously and/or who are competent in outside business ventures.

Each of the husbands is, or has been, involved in high-level competitive sports. Shannon England (Sandra's husband), Brian McCusker, and Kerry Gudereit are skilled curlers, all on Brier-contending teams in Regina. Frank Macera, Jan's husband, is the only non-curler, but he is no stranger to national competition. He played on the Regina Rams junior football team for four years and was an integral player in two national championships.

Brian has been the most successful curler. He's been to two Canadian mixed championships. Jan curled lead and Brian second as they won the 1984 mixed with Randy Woytowich throwing skip rocks. In 1992, they finished in the middle of the field. Brian says jokingly that the problem in 1992 "was our two ladies," referring to his wife, Joan, and Sandra, who was the third for Woytowich. They had won only one provincial title up to that stage.

Brian also curled for Woytowich at two Briers, the first in 1991, a heartbreaker as they lost the national final to Alberta's Kevin Martin team. In his next Brier appearance, Brian's team finished 6-5, so didn't qualify for the Brier's three-team playoff.

Kerry curled in the 1992 Brier in his hometown, Regina. He was lead for Brad Hebert's Regina foursome. Being the home province's team brings added pressure. When Kerry first stepped out on the ice, he tasted real fear – 7,000 people in the stands, the media, the big-name opponents. On top of all this, the very real possibility that he could humiliate himself in one of Canada's most avid curling cities. "We just didn't want to be the first Saskatchewan team to go 0-11. We were respectable at 6-5."

Shannon is on a very competitive team, curling for Troy Robinson in Regina's Super League. One of his goals is to get to the Brier and add to the family's trophy case.

Like all of the husbands, Frank has a sincere respect for his wife's talent and accomplishments. Frank coaches high school football at Martin Collegiate. He encourages his team to adopt some of Team Schmirler's competitiveness. "I tell my teams all the time – at appropriate moments – that they need to have the same ambition and desire to win as Team Schmirler. I wish my team would get a little more upset after a loss. Not to be poor sports, but to have that Team Schmirler-like quality that won't accept losing. Team Schmirler wants to do whatever it takes to win.

"My students are big Schmirler fans. When the Scott or Worlds are on TV, they will watch. We have an annual sports banquet at the school. One of the biggest turnouts in the school's history was when Sandra and her team were the honoured guests."

The men rave about the dynamics that make Team Schmirler so successful: their wives' competitive natures; their drive to be number one. As Kerry points out, "None of them like to lose. Their desire to win is all-powerful, but not just in curling. I see this in Marcia at work. She sets goals and does everything within reason to reach those goals."

The team can accept and live with losing, but like all great athletes, they find losing distasteful. Brian says, "The team is driven to catch their rivals – a challenge worth chasing. They have incredibly high standards. But they should, because they've proven they can play with the best the world has to offer. They would only be cheating themselves if they dropped their standards."

They are simply trying to be the best at their craft; however, it's not a single-minded obsession. Shannon says, "Curling is their main hobby; they have an almost pure love for the game. They're amateurs in their sport – they just happen to be the best."

The men all have stories about learning to live with women who are highly competitive athletes. Shannon comments on Sandra's drive to win: "It eats Sandra up when she loses. Not just playdown losses, but even in Super League or club curling. She gets over it, but she can't wait to redeem herself.

"We play lots of games together. Ping-pong, cribbage, even practise curling, just the two of us! We practise a lot together. We always finish it off with a mini two-end game. It gets really fun if we're tied. Then we have a draw to the button to determine the winner. I try to forget that I'm curling against a world champ. The loser has to buy dessert or do some chore at home. I do win the odd time!"

Frank thought he was ultra-competitive until he met Jan. He says, "Jan is so determined to get back out there after an off night or a team loss. Being a non-curler, I never realized how serious Jan was about the game. In one of our first few dates together, we sat down to watch a Scott on TV. I told her she couldn't possibly be that calibre of player. She gave me 'the glare.' She said, 'I've been on teams that have beaten most of those teams!'"

Brian tells a story of Joan's competitiveness. Brian's team (skipped by Randy Woytowich) and the Schmirler women's team got together for a season-ending party. "We were having a good time and decided to play *Pictionary* and *Trivial Pursuit*. Of course it was men against women. We were killing them. They couldn't take it. They started to cheat.

Kerry, Shannon, and Frank with Marcia at the 1994 Worlds. All four husbands have been high-level athletes in their own right.

Mike Farquharson's (upper left) skill in ordering authentic Japanese cuisine for (clockwise from centre) Brian, Gary Ford, Frank, and Kerry in Nagano, led to Gary's talking in his sleep.

It was good-natured, of course, but it proves the depth of their competitive natures."

Marcia is no exception. To outside observers, she seems like the quiet one. "She's always been a good athlete who tries her hardest to excel," explains Kerry. "Marcia is a better-than-average fastball player. She's a perfectionist who always strives to improve. She still has a hard time believing she's part of the best ladies team in the world."

Curling has a high incidence of players switching teams. It's unusual for a team to stay intact for more than a handful of years. Part of the reason is that non-skips start to grow in confidence and want to try their hand at the tee-line. The other reason is that it takes a lot of work to maintain team harmony over a long period of time.

Anita's husband, Gary, curled for a decade with Bob "Pee Wee" Pickering. Gary says, "The Schmirler team is a lot like our old team, in a way. We were content to play our positions; egos weren't a big thing. I curled lead for Pee Wee and went to four straight Briers. I'd rather have curled front end and gone to the Brier than play skip my whole life and never get a shot. The Schmirler girls are this way. They realize that each position is vital and understand that each contributes in different ways."

"It's one of their big keys," echoes Shannon. "Marcia is maybe the best lead in the game with her

steady draw weight. She sets the tone of each end with her shots. She gives the team the opportunity to play out their philosophy. Joan can throw the key hits at second. She has to hit and peel. Jan always makes the big shot when the pressure's on. Sandra calls such a smart game and is so consistent with her own game."

Brian believes Sandra is such a good skip because she values the importance of each position. He puts it like this: "Sandra played third most of her life, or front-end in her early days. She never skipped until putting this team together in the fall of 1991. Sandra knows you can't win without a good front end and their many hours of sweeping. She values Jan as her third. Curling history has taught that every championship team has a third who is equal in shot-making to the skip."

Frank (the non-curler among the men) loves the strategy of the sport. He says, "Sandra really understands the game. They all do. What impresses me about the team is that they hardly ever give up the big end. Sandra's maybe the best skip out there at damage control. She knows when to cut her losses and give up one or two points rather than gamble and give up three or four."

All of the women know how to play a cerebral game. Brian was impressed in 1993 after Team Schmirler had won their first Scott. "In Canada, we were one year away from the new free guard zone rule. The Europeans already had the rule in effect and had lobbied successfully for the FGZ to be played at all future world championships. Our girls were concerned because they were a typical prairie team. Hit first, draw second. The FGZ favours a strong draw game with quiet tap-backs.

"They knew they had to change their philosophy to compete with the Nordbys, Gustafsons, and Schopps of Europe. Sandra consulted with my skip, Randy Woytowich. He always favoured the draw game and was studying the FGZ because he knew it was coming. We played a few practice games and the team had a few coffees with Randy. Sandra's team prepared themselves well."

The husbands see first-hand how their wives deal with the stress of striving to be world champions. Frank says, "I think they like the pressure. It's not a negative thing; it's an opportunity to play with the best."

Team Schmirler always has a target to aim for. Brian explains, "In 1991, the target was to win Saskatchewan, to upset the four-time defending provincial champ Michelle Schneider. In 1993, the target was Canada's most consistent ladies team, Connie Laliberte of Winnipeg. At Worlds, the target was two-time defending champion Dordi Nordby of Norway. Then the target shifted from chasing teams to chasing history!

"In 1994, the target was to become Canada's first back-to-back world champions. In 1997, it was to become the first three-time world champions. Then it was to win the first Olympic gold medal as a fully sanctioned sport. And there's still fellow Reginan Ernie Richardson's four-time world champion record."

Kerry feels the secret to handling so much pressure is the team's longevity: "They know each other and their strengths so well that confidence naturally evolves. You can see them pulling for each other. It comes from working through all the team dynamics over the years."

Brian says the team has developed respect for the demands of high-level competition. "They become appropriately nervous. I've never seen them take any team lightly, ever. They're never overconfident with an opponent. The team is so aware of how tough each opponent can be. All it takes is a red-hot skip to cancel out four consistent curlers. They prepare so well.

They concentrate on what gives them the best chance to win."

Team cohesiveness minimizes pressure. The fewer squabbles among team members, the more they are able to put their energy into the game. Team Schmirler and their husbands are the best of friends on and off the ice. It's a natural support system.

If losing became a habit, would they break up?

All eight agree no such thing could happen – it would mean not spending as much time together. They genuinely enjoy socializing together, whether it's curling season or in the thick of a scorching Saskatchewan summer. The Schmirler women are not the only ones to spend time together. The men enjoy golfing, barbecues, and showing their support for the local Canadian Football League team, the Roughriders.

Teammates and mates – these are friendships that would be hard to duplicate.

There is a deep-rooted commingling of the Schmirler crew, a kismet-connection obvious to all who know them well. Many exciting mutual experiences have brought them close together, and humour is another element that has helped solidify their relationships. Team Schmirler and their men love to laugh together and to recount the many funny situations curling life has presented them.

Frank and Shannon love to tell "The Nipawin Golf Story." Nipawin is a good-sized Saskatchewan community northeast of Saskatoon, famous for its 1950s and 60s car 'spiels and now home to one of Canada's richer cash 'spiels.

Sandra and Jan, along with their husbands, were invited to form a foursome for a big charity golf tournament, shortly after Team Schmirler won their second straight world title in 1994.

Frank is a low-handicap golfer and Shannon can hold his own. "Frank is hot, sharper than even his normal, consistent game," Shannon says. "We are in contention after the first round, so we think we'd better take the second and final rounds seriously. We hardly ever dip into the complimentary cooler in the golf cart. Frank gets hurt on the second hole. Sandra and Jan realize their dream of winning the tournament is about as likely as Jamaica entering a curling team at the Worlds and winning it."

Sandra and Jan discover the complimentary cooler....

"They totally give up, these two-time world champions. Of course they realize they'll never make the LPGA.

So, after every hole, they keep shouting, 'Juice me! Juice me!' It kind of became the phrase for the rest of the festivities in Nipawin. People would look at these two and wonder what in the world 'Juice me' was all about. It obviously wasn't 5-Alive getting them all happy.

"For the rest of the year, 'Juice me' was the rallying cry whenever things got dicey, whether it was on the curling ice or at a function where things got a little uncomfortable."

When the team mentions Geneva 1993, the first thing that comes to mind is the first world championship. Running a close second, however, is "the row 65 story."

Early in the week, before a game, the committee for the 1994 Worlds in Obertsdorf, Germany, had a wine promotion. All the teams and their close friends were invited. It was supposed to be just a simple wine-and-cheese ice-breaker for everyone. Brian and Kerry were engrossed in conversation when they finally noticed everyone had left to watch the evening draw. Three open bottles of wine sat on the table. The wine was free and the French-speaking hosts kept encouraging Brian and Kerry to drink it up. Not wanting to appear rude, they obliged. To put the story in its proper context, you have to understand that Team Schmirler and entourage are moderate social drinkers at best.

Brian and Kerry managed to polish off every drop, and then headed out to the stands to watch their wives. The fans had filled most of the bottom rows, so Brian and Kerry ventured up to the higher seats in what is a large and steep venue. Around the third or fourth end, the women noticed Kerry hanging over the boards trying to get Marcia's attention.

This was a tight game versus the Americans, one of those must-win affairs to create a cushion in the standings.

Kerry was laughing and shouting to the team, "You should see Brian!"

They look up, way up, and Brian had passed out all by himself in row 65. It turned out to be perfect tension-relief for the women. They went on to win the game, but it was the only time Brian slept through one of his wife's victories.

The husbands of Team Schmirler all agree they've benefitted from their wives' successes. Getting to travel across North America and Europe, and now Asia, to cheer their wives on, they've met many interesting

people both in curling and outside the game. Achieving the status of world champion creates many spin-offs in attending formal and civic functions around the globe.

The husbands each have their own way of coping during game time. It's not easy sitting in the stands, or behind the glass at a local club, cheering for your wife. The more significant the event, the more dense and agitated the swarm of bees buzzing in husbands' stomachs.

"We all find it tough to sleep the night before a big game," Shannon says. "I think the men are more nervous than their wives, because we don't get to throw the rocks. As curlers, we know that most of the jitters leave after you've thrown a rock or two or swept some rocks down the ice. It's tough being on the sidelines.

"I prefer watching the game by myself or with Frank. Each of us husbands have our own routines. But it's hard on the parents, too. Sandra's dad, Art, almost gets sick, but he won't miss a shot. One time he actually threw up before a final, and his stomach never settled until Sandra threw her final stone."

Frank says, "It's hard to sleep the night before a Scott or world playoff game. At those stages, it's one loss and you're out – no second chance. Shannon and I sit together in most games, but I'll get up and pace around a bit."

When it comes to pacing, Kerry is known as "the Pace King." "I've got a fair amount of nervous energy," says Kerry. "I *need* to get up and pace. I'll sit or stand in many locations throughout the arena.

"It's not that I'm superstitious, I just don't want to take any chances. I create superstitions as I go. If they got a two- or three-ender while I was sitting in a certain seat, I'll go back to that seat hoping they'll score another big end. I'll avoid places where disaster has struck."

Brian prefers to watch the games alone: "I don't mind sitting with family, but I like my own watching-space. I also like to get up and watch the game from various locations. I don't pace a whole lot, but I like to move around. It's the same when I watch our Roughriders on TV. I may invite someone over to watch the game with me, but they need to understand that the game is the priority. Some people think game time is visiting time. I meet people like this at curling championships. I want to watch the game. The bigger the game, the more I want to be alone or with someone with the same game focus."

40

A Worlds tradition is the Grand Transatlantic Match. In 1994, Canada was represented by Kerry, Shannon, Frank, and Ardith Stephenson, curling reporter extraordinaire.

The husbands are obviously among their wives' greatest admirers. But this admiration transcends the curling ice. And it originated long before Team Schmirler had achieved so much success.

"I'm amazed how Sandra has remained the same down-to-earth person," Shannon says. "Sure, she is more confident in the public forum, but I see her as staying humble and fun-loving. She's maintained an even keel and tries to keep family as her main priority."

Frank says, "I have to remind myself that I'm married to a world champion. But I so admire how Jan and each of the ladies have stayed in the game. Their personalities have remained and blossomed more fully. How they maintain their level of curling competence while all starting families is astonishing. They've each had babies and were back on the ice in three to five weeks, competing in major 'spiels."

Brian says that if he gave his wife, Joan, and the other women a toast, it would go like this: "This team has been successful without drawing attention to itself. To Team Schmirler, the game is the issue, not status-seeking. Of course, they appreciate most of the accolades that come their way. Deep down, they simply want to curl and see how far they can go each year. They honestly love the game.

"Joan plays the same role on the team as she plays in our marriage. She's the catalyst to maintain team chemistry, the one who gets everyone talking through the issues. I didn't realize just how important her role was until the 1995-96 season. Joan took most of this curling season off. They brought in a very good replacement as far as curling goes, but there was a missing dynamic as far as the team was concerned. The chemistry wasn't the same, and the team wasn't the dominant Schmirler unit.

"This quality that Joan has is the same one she brings to our home. And it's definitely made our family closer and richer."

Kerry echoes many of these observations. His admiration for Marcia is evident: "She's remained very humble through the team's achievements. It's almost like she's a little embarrassed to say she's a world champion, let alone a three-time champion and now an Olympic gold medallist! I'm amazed how she's gone from a recreational curler to possibly the best lead in the world. She's constantly looking for ways to improve her game. I've learned so much from observing Marcia, and the entire team."

Team Schmirler may be the envy of any female competitive sports team. So many successful male athletes say that one of the keys to their success is a supportive wife. The flip side of this is Team Schmirler. Sandra acknowledged the team's husbands after winning the Olympic trials in Brandon in November, 1997. With tears streaming down her cheeks, she thanked the husbands on national television: "We'd never have won this event and had the opportunity to represent Canada at the Olympics. We have a huge support system, and our husbands are the key. Thanks, guys, and especially Shannon, who's holding our nine-week-old little girl."

When was the last time a mother of nine weeks won a berth at the Olympics? Then only three months later travelled halfway around the world to win Olympic gold? ◉

Chapter Six

THE FIRST ONE
(1992-1993)

The 1992-93 curling season started out with high hopes for the Schmirler team. The goal was to get back to the Scott Tournament of Hearts in nearby Brandon, Manitoba, and win their first Canadian women's title.

The 1992 half of their season would be considered a rousing success for most competitive teams. They had qualified in every bonspiel they had entered. In reality it was a frustrating exercise in near misses and not closing out the deal, as Sandra said to Murray McCormick in a *Leader-Post* article. "If someone told you before the season started that you would make every semi-final, you would say that's a pretty good year. With a shot here or there, we might have been in the finals. But we lost four semi-finals in a row."

The team qualified through the A side in each 'spiel, which means they got a few extra draws off to rest. This was a bonus, as Joan took Rory along to each bonspiel. He was born in August, so she had to breast-feed in between games. The more free time the better.

The team knew they were capable, but there was still a hurdle to jump. They were winning well over 80 per cent of their games on the competitive circuit. But some doubts were starting to trickle into their psyches.

Just before Christmas, the team was wrapping up the Regina Wheat City all-star curling league. The team came through with a convincing win over the Jenn Jordan team in the final. It was a bit of a confidence-booster to finally get through a semi-final and go on to win a final. This was the team's second consecutive Wheat City title.

After a short Christmas break, there was one more 'spiel before the city playdowns, the Regina Ladies Bonspiel, 1993 edition. In most years, the cream of Regina's women's curling rises to the top. The 1993 'spiel was no exception, as Schmirler met long-time rival Nancy Kerr in the final. It was a classic nail-biter, with Kerr winning 6

This would be the last final the team would lose for the next while. Sandra couldn't take the blame. C way to the game, she was the victim of a hit-and-run car accident, and didn't make it to the rink until th

The Brandon Scott – Marcia encourages her sweepers, as the front end of the Julie Sutton rink from BC looks on.

end. Though unhurt, she was obviously shaken up. So Sandra curled second, as Joan had started the game at skip. Darlene Kidd was already filling in for Jan at third, as she had to miss this bonspiel. The team was jumbled right from the start, but still almost pulled off the victory.

Ardith Stephanson of the *Leader-Post* sat down with Sandra after the game and got her comments. "I was a little shaken up, I didn't need to think. I have a hard enough time thinking when I'm not shaken up, never mind when someone just crashed into my car."

As Stephanson reported, "McCusker did an

admirable job at skip, but she didn't necessarily enjoy holding the broom rather than using it."

"I came to sweep," McCusker said, "I didn't come to skip. I felt like an ice cube. We told Sandra not to play, but she wanted to sweep it off."

At least Sandra could laugh after the game. She reminded Joan in a joking way about the responsibility of skipping and throwing the last stones. "We didn't leave her very much and left her with some pretty tough shots. I asked her after the game, 'How does it feel?'"

The teams had a five-day rest to get ready for the

city playdowns. Four out of 26 rinks would qualify out of Regina for southerns.

The team was feeling pretty optimistic about their game. They were throwing consistently well and had qualified in five out of five bonspiels. They won the Regina All-Star league. Could they win consistently when their last life was on the line?

As Sandra has said, "I don't know if there is a curling god out there, but it seems like sometimes he's with you and sometimes he's not. Sometimes you go through a stretch of curling well but coming up short over and over. Wicks, ticks, a hair, a sweeping error, an ounce too much weight and you lose a few. Then for some unknown reason the gods smile and you come around the guard by an eighth of an inch, you become unconscious with your draw weight, and everything works and you start winning the games you have to win. Whether there is a curling god or not, I always hope and sometimes even pray he's on our side."

Little did these four young women realize that they were beginning a journey towards their first Canadian and world titles and would go on to become possibly the most recognized female team in the history of the sport.

The gods must have been smiling at the city playdowns. Schmirler went undefeated, winning four straight to advance to the southerns. The A Event final was at their home Callie Curling Club and the foe was perennial target Michelle Schneider. The team won it 6-4.

Weyburn hosted the southern playdowns. Only four out of 16 teams would qualify for the eight-team provincial finals. Team Schmirler went 4-0, again beating "the target," Schneider, in the A final. They were now 8-0 in the playdowns.

The provincial final was held in Shaunavon in the Cypress Hills region of southwestern Saskatchewan. The format was the usual triple-knockout

The Honourable Sylvia Fedoruk poses with Team Schmirler in Brandon. After congratulating their feisty spirit, she became one of the team's most avid supporters.

45

tournament. With their A-B-C style, a team could qualify for the finals by winning any of the three events. Any team that won all three events would be the champion.

Team Schmirler won their first three games to claim a playoff spot. They beat Saskatoon's Sherry Scheirich 6-4 in the A final, which dropped both teams down to the B semi-finals and a chance to claim the second playoff berth. Here Team Schmirler would suffer their only defeat of the playdowns. The veteran Merle Kopach foursome, another Saskatoon entry, beat them 8-7 in an extra end. Scheirich eventually won the B side to claim a spot in the playoffs.

Down in the C Event, Schmirler had to start in the quarter-finals because of their B semi-final loss, though the Kopach defeat was a minor blip. The team went on to win the C final against Michelle Schneider's foursome. It was probably the most excit-

ing game of the whole provincials, with Schmirler winning 7-6 in an extra end. It officially eliminated Michelle's team, as this was their third loss.

Sandra's team had won both the A and C Events, meaning Sherry Scheirich would have to beat her twice to win the province.

The team came out firing on all cylinders and soundly defeated Scheirich 7-2 to claim their second Saskatchewan title in three years. This put the team's record at 15-1 in playdown competition, the only loss being an extra-end game.

Winning the province was not a surprise to the Schmirler team. They knew it wouldn't be easy, but that if they played up to their potential it would be possible. Jan expressed the team's thoughts. "This would be my third trip to the Scott. The first provincial win with Sandra skipping was a bit of a surprise because we jelled so quickly. This one was in our grasp

Left: The final game of the Brandon Scott in 1993 – Jan and Sandra keep hawk eyes on a shot called by Lois Fowler, third for the hometown Maureen Bonar rink.

and we knew it. We would have been disappointed not to have won."

The Shaunavon *Standard's* Fred Farnworth interviewed Sandra after the championship. Schmirler commented, "We were hungry and played with a lot of confidence, we got in a groove and off we went. You think about going to Brandon when you get here and I believe we have as good a chance as anyone at the nationals."

It was quite a week for Joan as she curled nine games in three days, breast-feeding Rory in between. "It was an interesting weekend for our family," she reflected. "Brian was in Yorkton winning the men's provincials on Randy Woytowich's team. My mom roomed with me to help take care of Rory. The other three all roomed together. I thoroughly enjoyed the curling, but now I realized that I'd have to wean my baby to go to the Scott in Brandon. As a mom, I was finding that part very tough. He was only about six months old. I considered that a bit of a sacrifice for the team. I know other mothers would understand my dilemma. Thank God my support system was so good. Rory was going to be in very capable hands with my mom and sister."

The team was getting excited about their preparations for Brandon. They knew their chances to win were outstanding. Marcia told the *Leader-Post*, "Everybody is saying, 'You're going to do well' or 'You're going to win.' In sport, you can only do the best you can do. We have to be consistent.

"This time we have a really good feeling, but you can't win on feelings."

The team recruited Anita Ford to be their fifth player, coach, and team driver. They rented a mini-van and headed east down the Trans-Canada Highway to Brandon, a four- to five-hour drive from Regina.

Joan describes their departure: "We pretty well all live in the south part of Regina, so we met at the Golden Mile Plaza on Albert Street. Our journey was fun from the word go. We had a good-bye breakfast at Smitty's and loaded up the van.

"Marcia decided she would be the flight attendant and gave us each complimentary chocolate M&Ms for the flight. All the other teams flew into Brandon, but we lived so close we thought it would be more fun to drive."

The team arrived in Brandon a couple of days before the start of the tournament, which gave them a chance to get acclimatized to the hotel, the Keystone Centre, and to the general atmosphere of the Scott.

The field in Brandon was one of the strongest ever – defending champion Connie Laliberte from Winnipeg, Maureen Bonar from the host city of Brandon, Ottawa's Anne Merklinger, perennial Nova Scotia champion Colleen Jones, and former World Junior and Scott champion Julie Sutton from Victoria. There was also Alberta's up-and-comer Shannon Kleibrink, one of the best teams in Canada without a Canadian championship to her name, and the wily Québec quartet of Agnes Charette. Rounding out the field were provincial champion Maria Thomas from Newfoundland, New Brunswick's Nancy McConnery, Prince Edward Island's Angela Roberts, and Yellowknife's always-dangerous Kelly Kaylo.

Game one of the eleven-game round robin was against New Brunswick's Nancy McConnery, and Schmirler was heavily favoured. The team was revved up for it. Upsets traditionally happen in the opening draw, and there are a few reasons for this. Number one is the ice conditions that a team hasn't yet mastered. Then there are the butterflies, which can usually be kept in check but are more like cocky ravens, ready to feed on every positive thought. If a player allows the ravens into her head, all that's left is magnified self-doubt. By the time these metaphorical birds have had their way, the player feels like the only league they can curl in is the dentist's league at 4:30 on Friday afternoons down at the local club.

The crowd at these games has expanded from the 500 or so at a provincial championship to 5,000-plus. And there is Canada's sports network, TSN, with their cameras and curling experts ready to point out all the strategy mistakes and the hitches in everyone's delivery.

As the teams are lined up for the national anthem, the curlers can't help but notice all the former deserving Canadian and world champions they have to curl against in the week to come. Then the anthem winds down and the players notice the huge media section, there to critique the upcoming games. The players vow never to read the sports section again.

The anthem is over and it's time for the practice slides before the opening rock is thrown. What comes so naturally and has been performed literally thousands of times leaves the second-nature part of the brain and

47

it becomes very mechanical. The player at this stage may actually pray that they can slide down the ice without tripping over the tee-line. All these thoughts are common, from Scott veterans to rookies. If the normal butterflies are allowed to evolve into a flock of ravens, an upset is inevitable.

Jan says, "I don't know why, but boy were we nervous for that first game. Probably because all the experts, ourselves included, picked us as one of the final three playoff teams."

The Saskatchewan reps started out decently. They seized control from the start but were not playing their "A-game." It was an adequate performance, a typical opening-round game. The upset almost happened.

Jan recalls that opening game "was ugly, very ugly. We won it but almost gave it away. We weren't great but had control until the tenth and final end. We won it 7-6 and Sandra had to throw her last stone to win it. But she never should have been put in that position. It was like we didn't want to win or something. I was just glad it was over and the butterflies were gone. It was time to get down to business."

They played two games the next day, regaining their personal shooting averages in a 5-4 win over Ottawa's Anne Merklinger. In the evening draw, Team Schmirler was left as the only undefeated team with a very convincing 8-3 win over Prince Edward Island's Angela Roberts.

After two more wins on Monday, the Brandon *Sun's* reporter Jim Bender said, "Brandon has been caught in the throes of a Saskatchewan storm with a curled coiffure."

He was quite accurate, as Team Schmirler beat two of the pre-Scott favourites, Julie Sutton of British Columbia and the host province's Maureen Bonar. Their record kept them on top of the standings at 5-0. But breathing down their necks were defending champion Connie Laliberte and her formidable Winnipeg team and Colleen Jones of Halifax, who were both 4-1. Alberta, Ontario, and Manitoba were also still in the hunt.

This particular Scott was breaking all kinds of attendance records, and Brandon was setting a standard for future Scotts. The curlers loved it, and their profile was on the verge of exploding. TSN television ratings were better than ever, with some of the draws even out-rating the NHL games of the week.

Tuesday brought another two games. Win number six was a key game against Halifax's Colleen Jones. A loss would have created a three-way tie for first with Nova Scotia, Team Canada, and Saskatchewan. Schmirler and company moved two games ahead of Nova Scotia with their hard-fought 6-4 triumph.

Up next was the cagey Québec veteran, Agnes Charette. Charette was having an up-and-down week, playing well against the favourites but struggling with the weaker teams. Sandra knew she'd be tough. Charette's team was true to form, playing easily their best game of the week. The Québec champions controlled most of the game to win 8-6. It improved Charette's team record to only 2-5 and gave Saskatchewan their first loss of the week. Not many teams go undefeated at a nationals, so the team took the loss in stride. Ardith Stephanson of the *Leader-Post* huddled with the team after the setback and got their comments.

"You don't come here thinking you can go undefeated. You really don't want to lose games you probably have a chance of winning, but we just didn't have that good of a game," Sandra commented.

Joan saw it this way: "There it is – our loss. I thought we did really well to hang in there and come back. Québec played very well and they deserved every point.

"It was a real see-saw game. They'd have control and it would look bad for us. The next end we'd be in control and things looked bad for them. They weren't making their shots, either. The nice thing is nobody got down. We said, we're still in this and there's lots of time left."

Team Schmirler's goal at the beginning of the week was to go 9-2. Their logic was that nine wins would most likely give a team first place and the bye to Sunday's final. At 6-1 it was looking realistic.

Sandra was glad the team played in the first draw at 10:00 a.m. the next day. "If we lose on the last draw the night before, I can't wait to get out on the ice the next morning. Especially if my last shot the night before was a miss that could have helped the outcome of the game. I'd prefer losing, if I had to, in a morning draw and then have a quicker chance at redemption. I don't usually sleep too well if we lose an evening draw."

Sandra would get her chance against the team from the Rock, Newfoundland's Maria Thomas. The Islanders had the lead for a while, but the

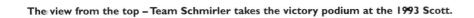

The view from the top – Team Schmirler takes the victory podium at the 1993 Scott.

Saskatchewanians mounted a 7-6 comeback win. The team was now 7-1 and assured of at least a tie-breaker to get in the playoffs. One more win would clinch one of the final three playoff spots. Up next was Alberta's Shannon Kleibrink.

It was about this time that the media and fans picked up on the Regina team's mascot. A replacement for a former teddy bear mascot, they called it the lucky "curling rat from hell." A co-worker of Sandra's had given her the flat, black rubber rat with a tiny curling broom around its neck.

Sandra tells the story. "It's a disgusting-looking thing, but he seems to help us curl our games. We scrapped the cute little teddy bear and brought in the curling rat from hell. We stuck it under the scoreboard. Even our fans are buying those squeaky ugly little things." Maybe the rat would work against them with their upcoming opponent – Alberta claims to be Canada's only rat-free province.

Saskatchewan versus Alberta in curling is viewed by many fans as "the rivalry" in the sport.

So this match wasn't hard to emotionally get up for. The rivalry is generally quite friendly, but these teams love to beat each other, and more often than not the game determines the winner's chances of making the playoffs.

The 7-4 loss to Alberta was the watershed moment for Team Schmirler. Kleibrink's win would be the wake-up call for these Regina women. It's ironic that five years later in this very same venue, at the Olympic trials, these same two teams would hook up in possibly the most exciting final of any sort at a women's major championship.

Sandra felt they had given the game away. "We basically shot ourselves in the foot. We had chances, but the shots we made just weren't good enough." Then she added with a chuckle, "You're never lonely at the top. We're just trying to make the crowd happy."

A win over Alberta would have made the playoff picture fairly simple. Schmirler was still alone in first at 7-2. But now there was a three-way tie for second with Alberta, Manitoba, and Scott favourite Connie Laliberte's Team Canada all at 6-3. Ontario and Nova Scotia were still alive at 5-4. The team could conceivably slip from first to fourth if they lost their final two games. The dream wasn't exactly a nightmare as yet, but it was getting as tense as a good X-Files episode.

Thursday would bring an end to the round robin.

Why rush the long drive home? Saskatchewan fans stick around to celebrate the win in Brandon.

First up was Kelly Kaylo and her Yellowknife shot-makers. Team Schmirler came out with guns ablazing and won 10-4, clinching their first-ever playoff spot at a Scott.

The final game of the round robin could be a possible passing of the torch. A win over Team Canada and Team Schmirler would accomplish two things. Number one – go straight to the Saturday final by clinching first overall. Two – eliminate Laliberte's team. Connie's crew lost to BC's Sutton team earlier in the day. A win for Laliberte and she was in the playoffs and a loss would kill her dream of repeating. Sandra says, "We felt that if we didn't eliminate Connie, we would see her again in the final, having the psychological edge of beating us in the round robin. That's why we wanted to beat her. We were loose – had nothing to lose!"

The final game of the round robin was a classic match-up. The experts had been saying it all week – "Laliberte and Schmirler, the two best teams, not just in Canada but probably the world."

"I honestly felt that player for player we were a slightly better team," commented Sandra. "We had always played Connie tough and had reasonable success against her. Connie could do it all herself. I really believed, we all believed, that if we could play up to our standard, we should be able to win. As a team, we could beat her. They were a consistent team, but I felt our whole team together were just a little bit steadier. We knew it would be real tough, but we had an excited confidence going in. The game was huge for both teams."

Brandon was focussed on curling, with that evening draw attracting 4,999 curling fanatics and establishing a new weekly attendance record. The only people in Brandon not aware that this championship was in their town were probably spending their final days at the morgue. The game came down to last rock with Sandra delivering the final stone. Laliberte was up 6-5 coming home. It had been an outstanding game, with the lead changing hands on five different occasions.

Connie put Sandra in a pickle for her last shot. Jan, holding the broom for the last stone, recalls the situation: "Connie had one buried behind cover. Her guard came in a little deeper than she wanted it to. Sandra had a couple of options, her best being a raise take-out and chip-out of the Laliberte stone. We weren't exactly sure what to do, so Sandra asked the crowd. It seemed to ease the tension as the crowd got a kick out of Sandra's consulting them. Everybody laughed.

"If anyone ever questioned her ability to make a clutch shot with a huge game on the line, they won't anymore. It was an absolute thing of beauty. She threw it perfect. On the stick, perfect weight, dead on. We scored two."

Team Schmirler was on its way to the final with that 7-6 victory. The pundits were wondering if the torch was being passed.

The team got a well-deserved day off during the semi-final, which pitted Ontario's Anne Merklinger against hometown heroine Maureen Bonar. Bonar beat the Ontario team 8-4 to set up the prairie showdown.

A day and a half between games is a long time when you've been playing two games a day. Jan acknowledges that their nerves were starting to get to them: "It was the worst case of nerves I've ever had. The waiting didn't help matters. I wasn't afraid of losing. I couldn't wait to get the game going. I knew we were on a roll and had a great chance to win it all.

"I think all of us sat down and cried somewhere on the Friday. Maybe it's a woman thing, but it sure helped to calm down and get our worries out of our systems."

Joan appreciated all the support from their home

province: "Saskatchewan hadn't won the Scott since Marj Mitchell's team in 1980. It had been a long time for our province. It seemed like Saskatchewan was always close and couldn't finish. I'd be lying if I said we never felt the pressure to win for all the curling fans back home.

"The support was unbelievable. Faxes from every corner of Saskatchewan. Our family and friends were all coming for the final. The media who came from back home were some of our biggest fans. Sandy Rutherford and Warren Woods from STV (now Global) stayed on the same floor as us and always had timely jokes and humour. The pressure was there, but the support was even greater."

Sandra said if she could do it over again, she'd only change one thing: "I never would have gone to the Keystone Centre to watch the semi-final. Everyone wanted to talk to us, especially with me being the skip. The media wanted me to do some TV interviews. I just wanted to watch the opposition, see what the ice was like, and sit back and enjoy the game. It was just the opposite.

"On Saturday morning, after getting very little sleep, we all went for a walk to clear our heads. My memory kind of leaves me once we get to the arena for our pre-game preparations. I remember being so focussed on the game and what we'd have to do to be successful. For some reason I was able to block out most of the potential distractions."

5,331 fans filled the Keystone Centre. The obvious fan favourite was the hometown team of skip Maureen Bonar, third Lois Fowler, second Allyson Bell, and Lois's daughter Rhonda throwing lead rocks.

It was a cranked-up crowd. Loud, excited, and boisterous doesn't even capture the atmosphere. Team Schmirler had more than a handful of supporters, since the Saskatchewan border was only a couple of hours from Brandon. But it was clearly a pro-Manitoba crowd.

The first end began as a typical conservative final game. Nothing fancy by either team. Just throw your two rocks, sweep a few stones, and get rid of the nerves.

Sandra remembers that first end well. "I was pleasantly surprised how quickly the nerves were kept in check. Manitoba missed a hit, which probably settled us down in the process. They were just as nervous as we were, if not worse, playing in front of a home crowd. The little sleep I got the night before did produce a dream. I dreamt we'd score two in the first end and that's exactly what happened. It was a great way to start."

Manitoba wasn't going to give up. They fought back with three singles over the next four ends to take a 3-2 lead at the fifth-end break. The crowd was really getting into it. Saskatchewan fans were fewer in number, but, being raised on Rider Pride, got quite vocal. Joan says it was appreciated. "Every time we heard a 'Go Sask' yell it put us on cloud nine. At one point in

51

The Canadian teams' coaches in Geneva – Lindsay Sparkes and Jim Waite – flanked by Anita Ford and Joan.

the game we all had to laugh. My brother, Hudson Walker, went and sat in this all-Manitoba section of the arena and was getting into it. There he was, sitting with no front teeth, his baseball cap, and smiling. The fans on both sides were good-natured!"

Going into the sixth end, Schmirler had the hammer and was only down by one point. They played an almost flawless eight shots and scored the crucial two they needed to go ahead 4-3 with four ends to go.

Sandra says the seventh end was probably the turning point. It wasn't either skip who threw the key stone, but Jan. "She threw an absolute pistol on her final shot. It was an out-turn draw to the four-foot, behind a guard. It may sound like a routine shot, but considering the circumstances it was very tough. Manitoba peeled the guard and, on my next two, I threw up perfect guards.

"Bonar tried a double take-out to blank, but was just a whisker off and we stole one to go up two going into the eighth. We had our two-point lead and control of the even ends."

In that eighth end, Jan made a comment over national television that got a lot of coast-to-coast chuckles. The skips and thirds of the two competing teams are "miked" for feature games and playoff games. Jan was oblivious to literally a million-plus viewers. She had just missed a hack-weight shot, badly. The fans ooohed when she missed and started cheering. Jan says, "Of course you hear it more when you've just missed a key shot. Because I was upset with myself at missing, it probably sounded louder than it really was." That's when Jan mumbled to Sandra, "These fans are starting to piss me off."

Manitoba came back to tie the game with two in the eighth. Team Schmirler went ahead with a single in the ninth. Sandra describes Bonar's shot to tie the game in ten and send it to an extra end – "She had to hit the rings anywhere to force the game to the eleventh. Right out of her hand, she yells for sweep. The sweepers pound it – the fans were going crazy. The noise in the arena was deafening – everyone was urging them to sweep harder.

"Our team thought she pulled the string, it seemed so light. Miraculously, it made the rings. We were shocked. The place went nuts and it was definitely a test of character that we were able to regroup for the extra end. We really thought we had it won when Maureen let it go."

The Schmirler team, having hammer, played a textbook extra end. Manitoba tried to throw up guards to force Schmirler's team to hit on the nose to create the necessary junk to steal the final point. Manitoba hogged two guards, so Marcia and Joan had one peel each, the other two were simple throw-throughs.

Jan also had two routine shots. "I wouldn't call them routine considering the circumstances. My hands were literally shaking, and as I released my final stone, I thought, just let go, then I thought, I'm finished, it's up to Sandra."

When it was time for Sandra's final shot, the only serious rock in play was Bonar's last stone sitting alone at the top of the twelve-foot.

Sandra's final strategy call reveals their philosophy to the core. Sandra likes to play the percentages and keep the damage to a minimum. She's aggressive, depending on circumstances, the score, ice conditions, how the team is throwing, and who the opposition is. She had two choices. She could try and draw the eight-foot for a win, but if she came up short or threw too much weight, Manitoba would win. Her second choice was to try the open hit and slight roll for the win.

The team chose the second option. Sandra's reasoning: "I wanted to make sure I threw easy control weight in order to have the shooter stick around. If you make a half shot with a draw you lose. Make a half shot with a hit and you at least get a second chance with the extra end. To me it was a no-brainer. I wasn't trying to impress anyone and dazzle them. I wanted the best opportunity to win the Scott."

Sandra started down to the far end to throw her final stone. The crowd gave a better-than-polite ovation to show their appreciation for the great entertainment of the week and to encourage Sandra. Sandra gives us her thoughts as she sat in the hack – "I never thought about the results of winning the Canadian championship. I reminded myself not to overthrow the take-out. I simply tried to remind myself to throw it like I always have. Throw it clean, don't overthrow, don't get wide, and let the sweepers keep it clean."

Sandra pushed out of the hack, was dead on the broom, and her weight was near perfect. As soon as she released the rock, she knew they would be Canadian champions. It was perfect, with a slight roll into the rings to win 7-6.

Sandra tossed her broom and ran down the ice weeping. To win their first Canadian championship on last rock in an extra-end was almost overwhelming.

Jan jumped about four feet in the air and ran towards Sandra. The four of them met at the near hog line and leapt into each other's arms. The crowd gave them a standing ovation.

Sandra's comments in the *Leader-Post* describe the release of emotion. "We weren't thinking about the consequences if we won this thing. We were just focussed on the shots. That's why it was such a shock when it was all over. It was like, holy smokes, what have we done?

"It got a little scary in the extra end, because you know someone is going to win that end, so it's pretty nerve wracking, but we pulled through.

"Someone really smart sent us a fax that said 'a kite flies higher against the wind.' To us, that meant a lot. It's not going to be near as sweet unless it's hard to get, and this was hard to get."

The smart person Sandra was talking about was Saskatchewan curling legend Vera Pezer.

The fantasy that became a dream was now reality. The Sandra Schmirler curling team from the Caledonian Curling Club in Regina, Saskatchewan, were Canadian women's curling champions. It seemed too good to be true.

First there was the on-ice presentation of the Scott championship trophy, with medals and rings. Then over the PA system it was announced that the new Team Canada was the team from Regina, Saskatchewan.

For Sandra, this was a moment to remember. "It hadn't sunk in yet, but when Bob Stewart, the CEO of Scott Paper, announced us as the new Team Canada, which would represent our country in Geneva, Switzerland, it hit me that we're off to the world championship. The job wasn't totally finished. What a neat feeling to be called Team Canada. I couldn't wait to wear our country's colours and Maple Leaf."

After the presentations, there was a short break and then they were off to the closing banquet. Finally, after the banquet, the team could go to the hotel to celebrate in a more private way.

"The first thing I did was order a pizza," Sandra recalls. "The banquet was very classy, but wild boar and buffalo steak didn't quite do it for me. I needed some food I was more used to."

Prior to the Worlds – As the world would soon find out, the big guns had arrived in Geneva.

So the post-game festivities were more of a savouring of the huge win as they spent time with each other and their families. There would be a week-long celebration waiting in Regina – city functions, celebrations at work – plus their new fame with the Canadian media.

The ride home was a lot quieter than the ride to Brandon. Joan found some boxes to lie on in the back of the mini-van and crashed. It was quiet contentment.

As they crossed the Manitoba-Saskatchewan border, they decided to gas up in Moosomin. Out of the van appeared these five, bleary-eyed exhausted women, to face the first hint of their new-found fame. People at the service station recognized the team and congratulated them on their title. Then one of Joan's hundreds of relatives, who just happened to be passing through Moosomin, spotted her and came over to congratulate her and the team. Being Canadian champions was becoming a whole new experience.

The city of Regina rolled out the red carpet for

53

The calm before the free guard zone storm – Jan and Marcia check out the rink in Geneva prior to the start of the 1993 Worlds.

their new heroines. The women appreciated the show of affection but knew Geneva was only a few short weeks away. Going to the Worlds wearing the Maple Leaf always meant you were one of the pre-tournament favourites, but there were three obvious roadblocks in trying to win Geneva.

Sweden's Elisabet Gustafson was the defending champion. Over the years this Swedish juggernaut had been the most successful European in the Canadian cash bonspiel circuit. And Dordi Nordby was back. Her team was the first women's back-to-back world champions in 1990 and 1991 – always tough and very aggressive. Finally, there was the free guard zone rule. The eight non-North American teams were playing the four-rock free guard rule. No rock could be removed from play until the fifth overall rock of the end, which created a lot of "junk." The North Americans wouldn't adopt the FGZ in regular play for another year. They were going into the heart of Europe playing "their rules."

"We were paranoid, to put it bluntly," Sandra says. "We knew the Gustafsons and Nordbys were so efficient at the FGZ. We were a typical Saskatchewan hitting machine. Hit first, draw second was the general rule. We had always been able to play a strong draw

game, but the FGZ was to the extreme for a Canadian team, especially from the hit-happy prairies. We knew we'd have to adjust to be effective.

"This was a time I watched tape after tape. I had no life but curling; this worked to our advantage, because I could devote my whole existence to learning the four-rock FGZ.

"We had a great resource at our disposal," says Sandra. "Randy Woytowich was one of the few Saskatchewan teams looking forward to the FGZ. His game had also been to throw up guards and be very aggressive. He agreed to sit down with us and talk about the FGZ . We also played a few practice games against his team.

"One other resource was that the Russ Howard team from Ontario was the Canadian men's rep at Geneva. Russ was the inventor of the FGZ, to create more fun when his teams practiced. We knew he would be more than happy to help us out, if needed."

The nine-game round robin in Geneva started out against the feisty Norwegians.

Joan comments on the unforeseen outcome of their first game ever in representing Canada. "We were nervous but so pumped. We couldn't wait to throw those first few stones. Our strategy was simple. With the FGZ we wanted to throw up our few guards and get rocks in the house first. It's almost like we were oblivious to the score. We beat Nordby 12-3. Looking back, we could have played more conservative at the end of the game, because it was over so early. But we were so paranoid of giving up a big end that we stayed on the offensive the whole game. We felt we got a decent handle on the FGZ after that game. We knew we could be in the running to win the worlds."

On day two they had a couple of games, first beating Janet Hurliman from the host nation 6-2 to go to 2-0 in the standings. The evening draw was against the defending champs from Sweden. Team Schmirler has never gone undefeated at a Scott or Worlds, so the inevitable loss had to happen somewhere. Gustafson finished off the Regina foursome in seven ends, with a final score of 10-3.

Tuesday brought games against the upcoming curling nations of England and Finland. These two countries qualified but realistically knew the playoffs were a long shot.

Sandra comments, "Maybe the Monday night loss was good in the sense to get us back on track. We were about to face two nations who were there mostly for the experience. But we all knew from experience that curling is one of the few games where a weak team with a red-hot skip could pull off a big upset. We weren't taking any chances."

Team Canada made it look easy with a 13-3 win over England and an 11-3 win over Finland. They were tied for second at 4-1. Only Scotland was undefeated, and they would be Canada's last game of the round robin.

Japan was on the menu for their only game on Wednesday, and was in the same situation as England and Finland – at the Worlds to learn – and Team

Two grinning dads, Bruce Inglis and Walter Betker, like the numbers they see on the standings board in Geneva.

Schmirler beat them 12-3.

The Japanese team of Mayumi Seguchi had just won their first game ever at a Worlds. They attributed their first win to Joan's dad, Bruce Inglis, a friendly man who liked to visit with the other curling fans in the stands.

Bruce was standing beside the Japanese coach, Hiroshi Kobayashi, during one of their earlier games. Kobayashi realized that this Canadian man must know the game. Bruce was a very competent curler in his day and knew the game well.

Kobayashi started to quiz Bruce on his approach to the game. He wondered what his women's team could do to improve their chances. The Japanese team was very sound mechanically, but they knew that strategically they were well behind the elite curling countries.

Bruce's main advice was, "Start hitting a little more, because the team is getting into too much trouble by gambling so much."

Kobayashi suggested this minor change in strategy and they promptly went out and won their first game ever at a Worlds. Kobayashi was so excited he sought Bruce out to thank him for his sage advice. Joan says, "He literally lifted my dad up with his bear hug and in his polite Japanese custom kept bowing to my dad."

Bruce was wise enough not to give away all his curling savvy, as his daughter's team clinched a tie-breaker spot with the 12-3 win.

Sandra assessed the Japanese team in a Saskatoon *Star-Phoenix* report after the win: "We've watched enough world curling on TV to know what would happen. They throw a really good stone, but they need a few years to develop strategy and some confidence."

Coach Hiroshi Kobayashi agreed. "We have little experience in the sport. Our strategies are poor compared to Canada. In the near future we have to learn

55

Top: How can you tell who these guys are cheering for in the final game of the 1993 Geneva Worlds?

Bottom: Celebrating the Geneva victory with nine-time Norwegian men's curling champion, Eigel Ramsfjell

how to beat Canada." The Japanese went on to finish sixth, their highest finish ever.

There was now a four-way tie for first with three games remaining – Team Schmirler, Sweden, the Scots, and Germany, skipped by Regina-born-and-raised Janet Clews-Strayer.

Thursday's first draw would be the showdown against Germany. Clews-Strayer married a Canadian military serviceman, James Strayer, and was stationed in Germany. Janet knew of Schmirler because they were both members of the Caledonian Curling Club in Regina.

Clews-Strayer was a respected curler in her home province. Outsiders may have wondered if she had lucked out moving to Germany. The old story – a decent Canadian curler inheriting an internationally competitive team that valued her Canadian birth certificate.

Janet had put together an impressive curling résumé on her way to the Worlds. She wasn't just another competent Canadian shot-maker. As a Saskatchewan junior, she skipped her team to two straight Regina Youth Bonspiel wins in 1987 and 1988. This is one of western Canada's most competitive junior bonspiels.

In 1987 her team finished fourth at the Saskatchewan junior provincials. She got a little revenge on the top three finishers by winning Saskatchewan's winter games berth to Sydney, Nova Scotia. Her team earned the bronze at this edition of the Canadian Winter Games.

Clews-Strayer fell off the Canadian curling map and arrived in Lahr, Germany, with her husband. She couldn't enter German national competitions for two years. After that an international curler could keep their citizenship but could represent Germany as an "auslander" (German for "foreigner"), as long as the other players were German citizens.

Janet was excited to face Team Schmirler. She

respected their team but thought her one advantage would be her three years' worth of the four-rock FGZ rule.

This would be Janet's one and only time to represent Germany, as she was preparing to move to Calgary with her husband's upcoming transfer. They moved to Calgary two days after the Worlds. She was also seven months pregnant. To be in Geneva at all was an amazing accomplishment.

The German team won 8-7 in an extra end. It dropped Schmirler to 5-2 and out of first place. Sandra was disappointed. "We had so many chances to take control, I just blew it. Janet's obviously a good curler, but I didn't have to help the cause."

The team rebounded in the evening with a relatively easy 9-3 victory over their American rivals.

Going into their final round robin game, Canada was in danger of settling for a tie-breaker or, worse yet, missing the playoffs. Christine Cannon's Scottish team was their final opposition in the round robin. It was a battle. Team Schmirler stole two in the ninth end to break a 5-5 tie. They ran the Scots out of rocks in the final end to win 7-5.

Mission accomplished. They were in the playoffs, finishing third at 7-2. Janet Clews-Strayer's team finished first at 8-1, her only loss coming against Norway. Sweden was second at 7-2, which set up a Canada-Sweden semi-final.

Schmirler would have to play both teams that beat them in the round robin to win their first world championship.

Elisabet Gustafson was step number one, in the semi-final. The Canadian women put together a convincing 10-7 win over the defending champions. The final would put them back up against Germany and Janet Clews-Strayer. The Germans knocked off the former two-time world champions from Norway in their semi-final. This Canadian-skipped Deutschland entry had now defeated three former world champions to advance to the final – they also had defeated Andrea Schopp twice in the German nationals to advance to Geneva.

All of Regina was excited. Both competing skips from the same city, a curling first. The television ratings in curling-mad Saskatchewan would easily match numbers in a Roughrider playoff game.

Clews-Strayer went from a euphoric semi-final

victory to the depths of depression in the Pondhopper Lounge immediately after the team's win. She revealed, "I was the new kid on the team and was never one to rock the boat. It took me a long time before I told the team I was pregnant, because I thought they might let me go. Our coach made all the personnel decisions. Our fifth player rotated in the lead position all season. My preference was Karin Fischer, because she brought an emotional edge to the team that elevated our performance, and she had played all the contending teams in Geneva. Both leads were technically sound performers, but Karin brought an attitude to the ice that gave the team extra fight. The intangibles permeate a team and their performance. I assumed in the playoff round we'd go with our best lineup.

"Then I found out from the coach that he had spoken to the team previous to the semi-final game without me. He said they made the decision that it's only fair we play Lisa Landle in the final. But here's the clincher – he says, 'You're the skip, so the final decision is up to you.'

"I thought, oh my god, I can't make that decision! I wanted to leave the team on a positive note. It was our last game together as Germany. I was the *auslander*. We had gotten along so well that I felt if I

57

First stop after winning the 1993 world championship in Geneva – the Callie club reception in Regina.

Right: Flashing the hardware in Saltcoats, Joan's old stomping grounds, as part of the hometown tour in the summer of 1993.

spoke out it would sour a great year.

"The coach is a nice man but was more concerned with personal feelings than winning. How could I cause waves?

"We needed Karin to have a legitimate chance in the final. But I felt the coach was just happy to play in the final and settle for silver. It seemed like it was more important to be nice than to play to win.

"We were always so careful to not offend our coach or hurt each other's feelings. In hindsight, I was only 24, I liked all four curlers, and I didn't want to leave the team on a bad note. I was fearful of causing waves and losing good friends.

"I reluctantly went along with the decision but determined to curl the game of my life in spite of the circumstances. It took me about three years to come to terms with it."

McCusker says the emotional state of Team Canada was "one of relief and excitement. We had an unusual sense of calm. Sure, we were nervous, but our confidence was soaring. We finally felt like we understood the ice and were all throwing so well. The four-rock rule wasn't this huge mystery anymore. We were ready!"

The final was a hard-fought, close game. Team Schmirler put the pressure on right from the first end. Sandra would curl 91 per cent. The team would curl a very high 79 per cent. Germany curled only at 61 per cent on that day. Normally that would be a gloves-off seven- or eight-end blow-out.

The Canadians stole one in the second to go up 1-0 after the Germans blanked the first end. Germany tied it at 1-1 after four. Having hammer for the first time in the fifth, Team Schmirler took advantage by scoring two to go ahead 3-1 at the halfway point.

Betker remembers, "This game should have been over early. Janet was incredible. Her team struggled. Once she had to draw against three, another time against four. If she missed either shot, it's over quick. She was unbelievable. When you face a skip making all the clutch shots, sometimes your best isn't good enough. I'll be honest, that was in the back of our minds."

Germany got one in the sixth to make it a one-point game. The rest of the way the teams traded single points. Canada went up 4-2, then it was 4-3, and after nine it was 5-3. Clews-Strayer was trying to win

the final, in spite of her coach's controversial decision-making.

Looking back at the final, the opposing skip had this to say. "I knew we could beat Canada. We had beaten them once already. But we needed our best four in the lineup to have a realistic chance. After the Pondhopper meeting, I resigned myself to just keeping it close. Whether we had played Fischer or not, Sandra and her team were the class of Geneva. They were on a mission."

Playing the tenth, all Schmirler wanted was to keep it clean and run the Germans out of rocks. They met their objective and were crowned world champions for the first time. It was an incredible feeling of relief mixed with ecstasy.

Sandra explains, "Canada is expected to win. Only once has a women's team missed the playoffs. Canada wins about 50 per cent of women's championships. That Maple Leaf in curling is a sign of representing the most successful curling nation in the world. You are so proud to wear it, and don't want to let the curling fans back home down."

All the women said standing on the podium to receive the gold medal and world trophy was both a humbling and a proud feeling.

The losing skip was also very emotional. "It was the hardest thing receiving our silver medals for Germany and then listening to my home country's national anthem. The weirdest part was seeing my Canadian military friends from Lahr waving Canadian flags, yet I knew most of them had cheered for me in the final. It was like they wanted Canada or me to win, but not Germany. In spite of it all, hearing "O Canada" was good although I knew it wasn't for me."

The team was ready to celebrate. They went back to the arena to support Russ Howard's team. He beat the tuck-sliding Scottish dynamo David Smith 8-4 to win the double for Canada. It was the first time in four years that Canada had won both men's and women's world titles.

The two teams supported each other during the week. Marcia says Russ Howard paid them a huge compliment after their women's win. "He said he was surprised a Saskatchewan team was the first Canadian team to win a Worlds using the new FGZ rule. He knew Saskatchewan teams favoured the conservative hit game compared to the finesse of the FGZ. That game works well, but with the FGZ the times or rules are now

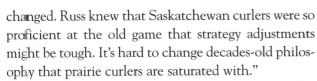

changed. Russ knew that Saskatchewan curlers were so proficient at the old game that strategy adjustments might be tough. It's hard to change decades-old philosophy that prairie curlers are saturated with."

The hard work and adjustments had paid the ultimate dividend – world champions! They were only the second team from the Wheat Province to claim this crown at the women's level.

The women were looking forward to some time off to let this championship sink in. In only four months, curling rinks would reopen and the thought of defending would challenge this team.

The off-season was akin to their Roughriders' two Grey Cup wins. When the Riders won cups, they visited every little nook and cranny of this appreciative province. Team Schmirler did the same with their two gold medals. Saskatchewan may only be the sixth-largest province in Canada by population, but because it's a farming mecca there are more actual communities than in any other province in the country.

The off-season turned out to be much busier than they had anticipated. It began with a horse-drawn carriage from the airport to thousands of people lined up along the drive to the Caledonian Curling Club for a big welcome home. The team was invited to so

many communities in the off season that they had to learn how to say no. This was very tough for four women who understand the culture of prairie curling. They made sure they went to their four towns of family origin – Biggar, Saltcoats, Hudson Bay, and Regina.

Joan, the energetic spark plug, says, "We simply burned out that off-season. We didn't know it would happen again, so we were determined to take advantage of as many invitations as possible. This province had supported us so well. We had faxes and letters from almost every community, places some of us had never heard of. I had shut-in seniors tell me that we were so much fun to watch, that it made their winter go by that much quicker. Things like that make you appreciate all the fans out there."

No Canadian team had ever repeated in women's curling at the world level. The team had a new challenge ahead of it. Sports enthusiasts had been saying for decades that the toughest thing in sports is not winning a championship, but repeating. 1993 was a dream season – could lightning strike twice?

Saskatchewan is home to some of the world's most spectacular thunderstorms. Rumour has it that those struck twice by lightning are usually Saskatchewan residents. ◉

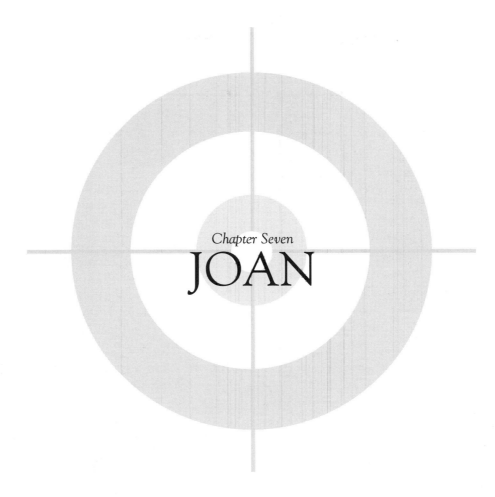

Chapter Seven

JOAN

"Hate will open the door to the dark side of the force," Yoda warned aspiring Jedi Knight Luke Skywalker.

If Yoda had been a curling sage, he would have taught young Joan McCusker, "Negative thoughts will open the door to the dark side of the game that is played on pebbled ice." After a few years, Yoda could have died in peace, saying, "Young Joanie, you have learned the lessons of the game well."

Her teammates, husband Brian McCusker, fellow competitors like Kathy Fahlman, Team Canada personnel director Pat Reid, and Lindsay Sparkes, have all echoed the reality of Joan's being the inspirational or spiritual leader of Team Schmirler.

Joan is the glue that keeps the three-time world champions together, the motivator who keeps her teammates believing in the power of their abilities. Sandra has said on many occasions, "When I'm sitting in the hack and the doubts begin to build, Joan has the ability to make me believe I can do anything, make any shot, come from behind any lead or obstacle. We are a different team without her presence and the attitude she brings. Joan is the most positive person I have ever been associated with. She's a realist but finds that silver lining, no matter how thin it may be in the overcast clouds."

Kathy Fahlman echoes Sandra's observations: "Joan and I were roommates for two years. I've never met a more positive person in my life. She has that gift to make a person believe you can accomplish anything in life. She's like a built-in sports psychologist for her team. Never say never with Joan around."

Just as Yoda (the wisest being in the known Star Wars universe) was found on some obscure planet in the middle of nowhere, Joan has discovered many Yodas along the way to develop her inspirational and shot-making abilities.

Joan is gracious in acknowledging the influences who have shaped her view of life and curling, those sages

The 1983 Provincial High School champions – Joan, Donna Burkell, Sandy Krasowski, and Heather Torrie.

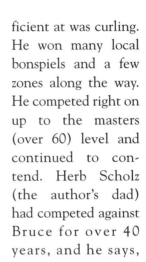

who can be found in many curling outbacks like Tonkin, Saskatchewan. One can learn a lot from these sages, who may be obscure on the national curling map but not in the hearts of many nationally ranked curlers.

The Pearce brothers ran the Tonkin Curling Club. Tonkin's population is under 100. Joan's mom, Joyce, says, "These two jolly little elves loved curling and were so good with children. They taught our kids that curling is a game and a game that should be fun."

Gordon and Irving Pearce organized the children's league for ages 12 to 17. Tonkin had a two-sheet rink with natural ice. Joan recalls fondly, "When it got warm, the ice was unbelievably heavy. Under normal conditions the ice was often slanted and very tricky. But what great memories – we had so much fun. The Pearce brothers kept it in perspective. It was a great way to start in the sport.

"There was a big sign in the rink that said no one under 12 could curl. So I couldn't wait until I could curl, I was counting down the years until I could start. I was the fourth one in my family to join the Tonkin league. The older kids would skip and teach us younger ones the very basics of the game. As you got older you were moved up to third or skip."

Joan was born to a curling family. Her dad, Bruce, and mom, Joyce, were both avid, successful players. Joan's earliest memories are of curling rinks. "I loved it, going to watch my parents curl. It was a chance to visit cousins and friends. We grew up seven-and-a-half miles from my hometown of Saltcoats and it was a chance to get off the farm and socialize. We'd travel to Tonkin, Saltcoats, or Yorkton to watch games."

Joan comes from a family of six, plus foster brother Hudson Walker. Rob is the oldest, followed by Cathy, Lloyd, then Joan. Karen and Nancy, both outstanding curlers, come next. Hudson was from Toronto. His mom had died when he was 13. His dad was in a wheelchair and wrote a letter to the family to see if Hudson could get a summer job at the farm.

"My parents are very generous people and never hesitated," explains Joan. "Hudson enjoyed it so much, he wanted to stay. My parents became his legal guardians from that point on."

Bruce (who died in the fall of 1998) loved all sports, but his favourite and the one he was most pro-

ficient at was curling. He won many local bonspiels and a few zones along the way. He competed right on up to the masters (over 60) level and continued to contend. Herb Scholz (the author's dad) had competed against Bruce for over 40 years, and he says, "He was one of the best in the area. He could throw bullets. He'd fire a take-out and hit it on the nose and next shot he'd draw the four-foot. Bruce was always tough to beat. You always had to be at your best to beat him – make a mistake and his teams would be all over you. I can see where the Inglis girls got their savvy from."

Joan curled with her parents from a very young age. Besides curling in Tonkin, she curled with her mom and dad and Karen in a family league in Saltcoats. It was a constant learning experience for Joan. "We were taught sportsmanship, accuracy, and a real affection for the game. Karen and I were young and curled front end. We would try to sweep Mom and Dad's rocks. It got to be a bit of a standing joke when it came to their take-outs. My mom was nicknamed 'killer' because she could throw the big weight like my dad. When Dad called for a take-out, Karen and I would start running down the ice before Mom delivered her stone. If we were lucky we'd get a couple of swipes in with our sweeping."

The whole family learned to play the game and were taught by their parents. Cathy says, "Dad would get us in the hack and say, if you're going to learn the game you might as well learn it right. We were never allowed to put both feet in the hack like some of the other kids our age. That was lesson number one for all of us.

"He was a very good strategist and taught us to be

62

fearless. Never to be afraid to try any shot. Not ridiculous gambles, but being able to play both turns and all the different weights. To have a well-rounded game and to get in our heads that we could make all the makeable shots."

Bruce never hesitated in using his children whenever he needed a substitute for his regular men's or mixed teams. The family seldom turned him down. He was a natural teacher who would explain the game and its various strategies. He would talk about whys and not just play the game ignoring his teammates. These lessons serve Joan and her brothers and sisters to this day.

Joan's mom Joyce is an ongoing influence and support in her life, having taught and reinforced much of Joan's approach to curling. In grade 10, Joan tried out for the women's team at Yorkton Regional High School. She was sick with the flu and had to miss a tryout, and as a result was cut from the team. When Joan found out, she was absolutely devastated and cried all the way home on the school bus.

Her mom naturally inquired what was wrong with her daughter. Joyce's response is something Joan will never forget. "Well, what are you going to do about it? You can't just quit. What other teams can you get involved with? Are there any intramural teams or a school mixed team?"

With renewed determination, Joan decided to talk to the mixed coach, Mr. Mitchell. Joan says, "I talked my friend Barb Miller into going with me. So before school even started we marched into his office. I managed to bluster out that he should let us try out. I said we could help his team even though it was probably already set. He saw that we were eager to play and took us on. He wound up rotating us four girls the entire season. We ended up doing pretty well, eventually losing a zone final that would have qualified us for provincials."

In grade 11, Joan made the girls' team as the third; Leslie Westburg, also of Saltcoats, was the skip. Sandy Krasowski and Donna Burkell rounded out the team. They played a lot of games, but they didn't do that well in high school playdowns.

The coach of that girls' team was another inspiration for Joan. Flo Sanna had curled with Marj Mitchell's 1975 Saskatchewan women's champions. Flo curled with Mitchell until she moved to Yorkton. Marj went on to become the first Canadian world women's curling champion.

Joan learned some valuable foundation lessons from Flo. "She was such a good coach, an excellent curler who understood what made a good team, not just a good curler. She taught us mostly about attitude and how to play the game as a team. She emphasized

Highway sign celebrating one of Saltcoats' most famous former residents

The Inglis extended family – 30 people and still growing. They're a curling family through and through.

positive communication for on-ice play. We were taught to relate to each other and to constantly encourage our teammates. Flo was good in basic strategy as well. We didn't just throw rocks and hope for the best, but analyzed things and looked for ways to work on an opponent's weaknesses.

"She didn't mess with the technical that much, unless there was something obviously out of whack. She let us work out our own styles. Flo worked very hard at keeping the game fun and made sure we were getting along. She knew that negative thoughts could destroy any talented team."

In grade 12, Joan took over as skip. Flo was still the coach, and Joan's parents and family supported her all the way to a high school provincial championship in 1983. The team added Saltcoats cousin Heather Torrie to replace Leslie Westburg, who had graduated the year before.

Joan nearly had to sit out the year, as the 1982-83 season started. Joyce wasn't impressed with her daughter's attitude on the ice. The team was struggling a bit and Joan was showing her frustration by pouting, yelling, slamming her broom, and being an all-round general poor sport.

Joan recalls her mom's words: "My mom laid down the law. She could do that. I still lived under my parents' roof and their word was still final. No arguments.

"Mom said, 'That's it. Your attitude stinks. It's absolutely terrible. I will not have you doing that. If you can't start smiling and enjoy yourself and become a team out there, I cannot allow you to curl.' I respected my mom, knew she was right, but hated to hear those words.

"Next game, my mom was sitting in her usual spot behind the glass. After every shot, good or bad, all of us would turn and look at my mom with these big Cheshire Cat fake smiles. We did it for my mom's benefit.

"We began by 'faking it' that we were enjoying ourselves, but before you knew it, the smiles and fun were genuine. Our year took off, all the way to that provincial title. It's amazing how a changed attitude will take you a long way."

Joan fulfilled her first curling dream by winning the high school provincials. Her sister Cathy had won it five years earlier. "Cathy's success was a huge influence in my life," Joan says. "I always loved curling, and watching Cathy win it all made me want to go after it hard. I was so proud of her accomplishments. I wanted to be as good as her."

Joyce adds, "I really believe that Cathy's success showed Joan and other rural women curlers that you didn't have to be from the cities to have success. It didn't matter where you were from as long as you dedicated yourself and worked hard at the game."

Joan has always had a strong family support system. Her four grandparents, the Torries and the Inglises, attended as many grandchildren's sporting or social endeavours as they could manage.

Grandpa Inglis, who lived in nearby Yorkton, was initially a tough sell that high school girls' curling was worth watching. He was converted shortly after Cathy started to have success representing the Yorkton Regional High School team. He would go down to his favourite coffee shop and hear about this hot-shot entertaining girls team from the high school.

Joyce said, "It was kind of funny because my husband and two grandfathers would always say, 'Girls can't curl.' So Grandpa Inglis went down to watch Cathy's team. He was amazed and told Bruce, 'You better go down and watch your daughters, they're pretty good.' All of a sudden the biggest supporters were the men in the family. Then they cheered on Joan, Karen, and Nancy when they started competing."

The Inglises are a tightly-knit unit that supports each other in their curling.

When Team Schmirler was struggling at the 1995 Scott in Calgary, Cathy hopped in her car and headed west to support Joan and the team. She knew things weren't looking that great and wanted to be there. Cathy says, "They still had a chance, but I wanted to visibly be there for Joan, even though she knows we're 100 per cent behind her whether we are there or not."

During the 1991 playdowns, the Inglis support system may have set an unofficial record for playdown participation in one weekend. Joan, Cathy, and Karen were on three separate teams at the women's southern playdowns. Nancy was in northern women's playdowns. Brothers Rob and Lloyd were in men's zone playdowns with their Saltcoats team. Bruce was in senior men's zones in Kamsack. Only Hudson and Joyce were available to cheer their family members on.

After graduating from high school, Joan left home to attend the University of Saskatchewan in Saskatoon. She had always been an above-average student and looked forward to pursuing her education. She would graduate with a BEd with majors in math, science, and phys ed, specializing in elementary education.

Joan made the U of S women's team, curling third for Dena Birtram (now Weiss). They were still young enough for junior women's and played at both levels.

"My university years were great years, but not very successful on the curling front," recalls Joan.

"We had our moments, but couldn't advance along the playdown trail. People would say, 'Your team is the best losers, you take losses so well.' My mom's lesson was implanted pretty deep, but don't ever misinterpret my intense desire to win as not caring. I've always cared about winning and have hurt deeply over losses, but those early lessons help me keep priority on the big picture.

"The benefit of my U of S days was being coached by another sage – Lee Morrison. She was on Vera Pezer's front end for four Canadian championship wins. Her experiences were inspirational.

"One thing I do remember is watching Sandra Schmirler curl with Carol Davis's team. I remember thinking how far Sandra could slide and her high-pitched yell at the sweepers. I never knew her, but was in awe of the whole team. They were curling at a level I could only dream of, at the time."

After graduation, Joan applied for various teaching jobs. Her preference was to teach in a rural area, and she was accepted in Raymore – about an hour's drive north of Regina. She was a grade 9 home room teacher. It was an obvious stretch from her desire to teach younger children.

Joan spent two years in Raymore, "and loved every minute of it. I enjoyed the town and we had a great staff in the school. I learned a lot.

"Curling was not what I expected. Raymore is a hockey town and curling plays second or even third fiddle. I curled in the local club, but it was a recreational focus. Inwardly I wanted to get back into the competitive circuit. I did coach all the school curling teams. It was a lot of fun and loads of work. I started to realize how much work and effort my former coaches must have put into it."

After her first year at Raymore, Joan knew she needed to upgrade her special ed classes. Cathy now lived in Regina, so Joan boarded with her family over the summer and took a couple of classes at the University of Regina.

Cathy and Joan decided to create their own team and play at a Regina club. This would mean a one-hour drive from Raymore, but Joan thought it would be fun to curl with her sister. As they were brainstorming about who to get to round out their team, Cathy got the call from Sandra Schmirler inviting her to play lead on their team. This was Kathy Fahlman's team with Jan Betker and Sheila

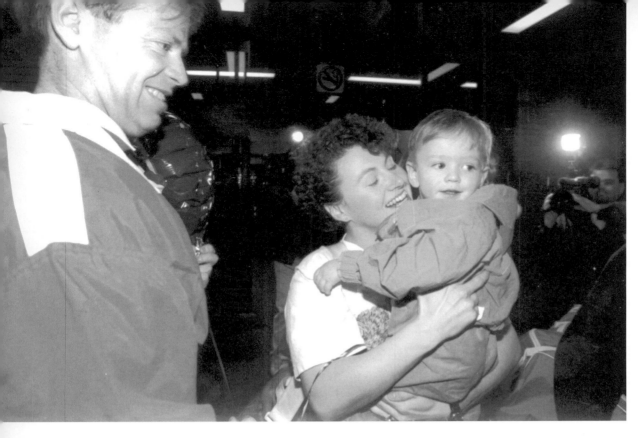

and he suggested Marcia, a co-worker who was very eager and threw well, but who had never had the opportunity to break into the Regina competitive scene. Brian was impressed with her potential.

This was one of the best learning-curve years in Joan's curling career. "We decided to go big time. It wasn't as easy as we thought. To curl competitively on a regular basis, you need experience. We went to Calgary, Kelowna, Saskatoon, and all over the Regina area and never made a dime. We learned a lot. I skipped for a while when Cathy struggled, then she'd skip again. It was fun but not very successful in terms of qualifying. Yet we were determined to stick it out as a team. We weren't that far off, we just needed the games against the big-name teams."

In that spring of 1990, Sandra and Jan were looking to form a new team and called Joan to see if she'd join them. Her initial answer was no, because she wanted to stay with her sister. In the meantime, Cathy found out she was pregnant with her third child and would have to take the year off from curling. Joan tried to find a replacement skip for Cathy, but to no avail.

After a few weeks she phoned Sandra back and asked if she still needed a curler or two. They did. Joan said she would join the team only if she could bring Marcia along, because she was also without a team. Their lead from Trowell's team, Sharon Bachmeier, understood the frustrations Joan was having finding a replacement for her sister and was happy for Joan and Marcia's opportunity.

"Part of the reason I wanted Marcia along is that we get along so well. We are soul mates. Traditionally the skip and third hang out together, and the lead and second spend time with each other. So I wanted someone I would have a little fun with. Who would have thought at this stage that our future would be so unbelievable together?"

Schneider. Sheila was starting a family and they needed a new lead.

Also throwing a wrench into their planning was Cathy's finding out she was pregnant with her second child and thus only being able to curl half a season. Cathy suggested to Joan that maybe the Fahlman team would take on both Inglis girls. Cathy phoned Sandra back and they said the team would be willing to alternate Cathy and Joan as lead. Cathy and Joan scrapped their plans to form a team and went with the Fahlman rink.

Joan was excited at the possibilities of this new team. "I was thrilled to curl with one of the best teams in Canada. They had been to a Hearts, and now I had a legitimate chance in playdowns.

"We advanced out of the cities and went to the southern playdowns. This is the one where we made it to the A, B, and C Event qualifiers and lost all three. Our last loss was a game we were in control of and then gave it away to my former U of S skip Dena Weiss.

"I was just devastated. I never knew if I'd ever get that close to the provincials again. It was another curling lesson learned the hard way. The best team doesn't always win. All these other factors and distractions are involved and sometimes the underdog makes more shots."

After that curling season, the Fahlman team disbanded. Joan moved to Regina and renewed the dream of curling third for sister Cathy Trowell. They decided to take a run at the competitive circuit and enter as many major cash bonspiels as their schedules would allow. They felt they were ready to curl with the best. All they needed was a front end.

Joan was dating future husband Brian McCusker

Joan's husband Brian McCusker is originally from Saskatoon and moved to Regina shortly after university. Brian has curled the bulk of his competitive career with Randy Woytowich, and he is considered one of the best male curlers in Saskatchewan. He's been to three Briers and to two Canadian mixed championships.

It was through the mixed that Joan met Brian, and in July of 1991 they tied the matrimonial knot.

"The marriage was tested at the next provincial finals in a game against Kindersley's Grant McGrath," Brian remembers. "Up until this time Joan had never verbally expressed her opinions of my skipping calls. It was a last shot with the game on the line. I had to make a quiet tap-back to win.

"As I settled in the hack she said, 'You don't have enough ice.'

"I said, 'We do. Sandra (the third) and I talked about it and we think it is.'

"But she wouldn't let up. Even in my backswing she kept telling me, it's not enough ice. I wound up throwing the right weight and hitting the broom and I missed. Joan was right. I was still mad, anyway. It's an unwritten rule in curling not to plant negative thoughts into the thrower's head when he or she is in the hack, especially during delivery. And Joan is probably one of the best, if not the best, at *never* violating this rule. But we were married, and you always take more liberties with your spouse for some reason.

"After the game Sandra came in to save the day and maybe even our marriage," Brian recalls jokingly. "Sandra took Joan aside and told her, 'Don't ever do that again, you never do it with me.' Joan felt bad and she knew better. She's usually the one doing the relationship mending. We recovered and went on to win the province, which was a real thrill, especially with your spouse."

Joan values her husband immensely. She realizes she has a very supportive partner in life and in her curling career. "Brian more than understands the sacrifices and demands that our success has brought," she says. "His parents are on board, as well. They come to as many of our events as possible, whether it's Brian or me. They've helped with our children and all the other little things that enhance our opportunities in curling."

Brian says, "I don't view it as a sacrifice. I wouldn't want to hold Joan back from curling and her chances to compete. I mean, how many chances do you have to win a national or world championship or go to the Olympics?"

The McCuskers have two children: Rory Bruce, born in 1992, and Christina Mary, born in 1996. Joan was the first Team Schmirler player to become a mom, allowing the others to view first-hand the dicey juggling act of parent, career, and favourite hobby. "It's been a real ordeal at times," she says. "I've experienced a lot of anguish and guilt at wanting to be with my kids when they needed me and I wasn't there. I've been very fortunate with my support system, but it's still hard as a mom.

"We're usually only away for a week or two at a time but I always, to a degree, feel torn between curling and parenting. There's been a couple of times where I wondered if it was worth the sacrifices.

"The first year we won the Hearts and Worlds, Rory was a newborn and I was breastfeeding. We hit the major 'spiel circuit and our motivation was to qualify as fast as we could so

Bruce and Joyce Inglis – they could both throw the big, big take-out weight.

The McCuskers at home – Rory, Bruce, Christina, and Joan. "If we honestly felt our children were getting cheated, I'd quit in a nanosecond."

I could have the time I needed with Rory. We took him to all our 'spiels. It was quite an adventure to get his feedings in. I knew when we won Saskatchewan that I'd have to wean him, because of the demands of the Scott. It was so hard because he absolutely refused to take a bottle. Believe me, I tried. So when we left for Brandon I had a lot of mixed feelings about leaving my six-month-old little boy. Both sets of parents reassured me that he'd adjust and that he was in good hands with his Auntie Cathy and his grandparents. They were right, but as any mom knows, you still feel terrible on the inside.

"Then the night before flying to Europe for the 1993 Worlds, I felt like I was going to lose it. I was lying in bed fretting about everything and turned to Brian and said, 'I can't swing all this.' He thought some and gave me timely advice that really helped get my perspective back. He encouraged me to eliminate the things I had no control over and focus on the things I did have control over. We had capable child care for Rory, and I needed to fulfill my commitment to the team. Marcia also helped over in Europe as my roommate. I could share my frustrations and she'd help me align back on the task at hand.

"My number-one priority is our family. If we honestly felt our children were getting cheated, I'd quit in a nanosecond. My support people have always encouraged me to keep at the curling and not give it up. I've had to take some necessary time off. Almost the entire 1995-96 season. I would have taken the entire year off if not for the Olympic trial berth in Thunder Bay.

"I'm currently a full-time stay-at-home mom. That was tough because I enjoy teaching so much. I kept slashing back my hours to the point where I am now. I've always been fortunate to have a good boss or bosses to give me time off for curling. My former job-share partner, Norma Millard, was very supportive and flexible. "The closest I ever came to a breakdown was the day after winning the 1994 Scott. I had to get back to work, job-sharing, but I knew what lay ahead – more curling, more sacrifice. I needed more time at home. I sat with my principal, my V.P. and my job-sharing partner and worked out an arrangement that I could work part time until after Worlds so that I could focus on family and curling. I had cried my eyes out, and those three listened and helped me through a tough time. At some stage, I probably will get back into the profession. But I love the extra time with Rory and

Christina, so it's been worth it. I totally enjoy being a mom."

Joan is the first to acknowledge the influences in her life. She was honoured in June, 1998, by her hometown of Saltcoats, which declared a 'Joan McCusker Day.' The full day included the unveiling of a large sign on the Yellowhead Highway at the entrance to Saltcoats, as well as a supper and community dance.

The essence of her appreciation speech was to thank all the influences in her life. She acknowledged her parents, brothers, sisters, grandparents, and her husband, concluding by saying, "I've often thought that all of the lessons that my team has learned and needed to learn to win the Olympic gold medal were learned here, here in my hometown and my home community.

"It's all a big circle, the lessons learned from my many teammates, coaches, family members, and other local curling hands – it is appropriate that the circle

should now be completed by this return to Saltcoats where it all began.

"You all earned a piece of that gold medal. You should claim it and be proud of it – I salute you."

Joan's sister, Karen, who was part of the festivities, says, "Joan is one of my heroes. It was amazing how she conducted herself on her appreciation day. She had a marathon autograph session that lasted for more than three hours. Anyone who wanted to could wear the medal and get a picture with Joan. She was so patient and accommodating. She believes that medal was made possible by all the role models and support from her grass roots.

"The town threw this huge banquet and had to turn away about 300 people. As a family we didn't know how big the event would get. It was quite a day."

Joan is known for the curling smarts she brings to Canada's most successful women's curling team, but what cannot be overlooked is her talent for consistently high averages. She will go down in history as one of the best take-out artists in the sport. Her draw game is more than adequate, usually complementing Marcia's two stones which help set up those big turning-point ends.

Her sweeping ability is *par excellence*. She can move a stone with the best of them and her ability to judge the weight of the rocks is among the best in competitive curling. When Marcia and Joan are on the ice, it's taken for granted that few mistakes will be made in this crucial aspect of the game.

Joan understands that the game is won on a sheet of ice, but the talent and execution begins with how one's thoughts are working. Her philosophy is to tackle the negatives in practical ways and turn them into something good. As she says, "What's the worst thing that can happen in a curling game? You lose! So now you have time for what's really important, anyway – your family and significant relationships. It keeps things in perspective.

"This is not to downplay losing. I don't like it and it hurts, but I know I'll get over it and get to try again. No matter what happens, I've been part of three world championships and an Olympic gold medal. That's more than I ever dreamed. The success is all gravy. It's been a wonderful ride. Curling is my hobby; family is my life." ☉

A rare pensive moment at the 1994 Worlds. Joan's gift to the team is getting them to talk everything out.

69

Chapter Eight

THE PRIME DIRECTIVE

Team Schmirler follows the grind of Canada's four grueling phases that lead to a world championship. The first three phases are in their home province. They must qualify in the city playdowns, then in their regional district, and then in provincials. The fourth phase is the Scott Tournament of Hearts – the national championship.

To represent Canada at the Worlds, a team curls 30 to 50 highly competitive games, which does not include the 50 or 60 club and bonspiel games in preparation for playdowns. A team must win 80 to 90 per cent of those games to have any chance of qualifying for the Worlds.

Teams in Europe are stunned to hear this. In some European countries, a team could curl only eight or ten playdown games and emerge as a national champion!

Curling fans in Europe may have occasion to wonder, if they don't hear the name "Schmirler" at a Scott: "Whatever happened to Team Schmirler?" What may have happened was a miss in Shaunavon, Swift Current, Estevan, or Melville. It's an irony that a team can win the world championship in one of the world's leading metropolises, watched by millions on international television, and less than a year later, the season may end in a place like Elbow, Saskatchewan (which, by the way, is just down the road from Eyebrow).

Over the course of the decade, the Schmirler crew has developed a solid team philosophy that consistently makes for champions. Their *prime directive* is to win major championships: the provincials, the Scott, and the Worlds.

Holding their breath – A crucial eighth-end measurement in the Olympic final against Denmark goes Team Canada's way.

CURLING IS A TEAM GAME

Sandra strongly emphasizes that this foursome is a team, in a team game. She may throw the last brick, but she says, "We'll do whatever it takes to win. Orthodox strategy or unorthodox, whatever will work to give us the advantage. My favourite question to the girls is, 'Now what do we do?'"

Sandra praises her teammates for their competence and knowledge. She considers them three of the top curling consultants. She says, "Why not use the resources at your disposal?" Then jokingly adds, "I'm too chicken to take the full responsibility."

But Joan and Marcia are quick to interject that Sandra can make the final call when necessary. When the game is on the line, Sandra Schmirler is one of the top shot-makers. Jan clearly states, "Sandra is the skip. She calls the game. But you really feel a part of the strategy process. We always feel we can give input, but we know too many fishermen muddy the water. In reality, Sandra calls at least 90 per cent of the game. We trust Sandra, and we know she values our insights."

It can be humorous at times. The team recalls a game against Finland at the 1997 Worlds in Berne, Switzerland. Sandra was looking over the situation for her final shot of the end, trying to figure out a way to draw for two. The other team members looked at each other as if to say, "Where's Sandra's head at?" Finally, Jan spoke up: "Sandra, why don't you make the wide-open hit for four? Then we can seal the win and go home early."

Sandra laughed. "Good choice, Jan. Let's hit for four."

THE LAST SHOT

A common topic around curling tables after a game has to do with the "last shot." The game is on the line and it's up to your skip to win it or lose it. Some curlers never want to face this situation, others relish the moment.

Sandra had never skipped until 1990, having mainly played third for various teams. Throwing the last stone with the game on the line was not something she grew up with in her formative curling years. "On a team as talented as ours, it's really not that tough," she says. "Everyone usually curls so well that many of my last shots are high-percentage shots. Open hits, free draws, mopping up in many cases. I don't think about the consequences of making or missing the shot. I try to concentrate on simply hitting the broom and throwing the correct weight – like every other shot I take."

Sandra admits to being slow sometimes in thinking through strategy. This goes back to her first year of full-time skipping, when she missed a last rock victory at a major cash 'spiel in Kelowna, British Columbia. She overlooked a shot that could have at the very worst forced an extra end. Another 30 seconds of thinking was all it would have taken. That losing shot is a constant reminder to Sandra, and in tight situations she now knows to take a few extra moments to make sure of her shot.

However, missing the odd last shot is part of this slippery game. Sandra deals with it as an occupational hazard. Usually, she has one bad night's sleep and then lets it go, although tournament games are tougher because there's more at stake. She comments, "I hate missing a crucial shot, or any important shot in a night game, because then I've got to sleep on it. If a bad shot has to happen, I hope it's in a day game, so I can redeem myself later that night."

COPING WITH PRESSURE

To win three world titles, a team must learn to handle pressure. Joan says, "We're always on the lookout for something to lighten the moment. Like in our 1997 Scott final versus Allison Goring of Ontario. It's Sandra's last shot of the first end. Marcia notices Sandra's fly is down. She points this

out to Sandra. We all crack up. The timing was perfect – it calmed us all down, and Sandra went on to make her shot."

According to Jan, "We laugh a lot; we cry a lot; we talk a lot. The crying thing is something men's teams may not understand. We cry to wash away our worries. When there is so much emotion, you go to extremes – laughing or crying. We have freedom to express our emotions, but that didn't happen overnight. The trust has developed over time."

Team Schmirler's trust transcends curling-rink walls. Barely a week goes by, even in the off-season, when the team members aren't visiting, barbecuing, or chatting on the phone. They genuinely enjoy each other's company, and this closeness is a tremendous help when the pressure situations occur.

OVERCOMING SLUMPS

The team finds technical slumps easiest to work through. They've been together long enough to be

73

"Now what do we do?" Sandra draws extensively on the three "consultants" she always has at hand.

candid with each other, to point out those mechanical weaknesses every curler has to be aware of. They are patient and know that, in most cases, a mechanical flaw will work itself out.

The VCR comes in handy. Sandra says, "If I have a bad game – maybe it's something in my release – we put on tapes and watch what I was doing."

The mental slumps are more effort. The key here is open communication: positive reinforcement;

team meetings to talk issues through; or maybe an extra practice session with a teammate. Jan says, "This team has too much on the line to let it go for a long period of time. You don't want to let the other girls down. You almost force yourself to mentally get into it."

The birth of Marcia's first baby broke Joan's early-season mental slump in 1996. Joan recalls the turning point: "My game was in the tank for the first two months of the season. Mechanically, I was okay, but my consistency was just not happening. Marcia couldn't join us until halfway through the season because of her new baby. Her first game back she curled about 96 per cent. Maybe she missed a few half shots – that's it. I started thinking, if Marcia can curl this good after her long layoff, I'd better get my act together. I bore down in my mind to just keep up with Marcia. It was the turning point in my season."

CONQUERING COMPLACENCY

Schmirler's team has to contend with a unique problem. They are "the target" every time they curl. All teams would love to say, "We beat a three-time world champion!"

Joan comments, "We get psyched simply because we know teams want to knock us off. Doesn't matter if it's playdowns or a fun club bonspiel. It can get a little lonely on this side of the fence." She's quick to add, "But we enjoy being world champions; it's a constant challenge to perform well."

As different in temperament as each woman is, they share a common attitude: a highly competitive spirit to succeed. Complacency often topples successful teams once they've reached

"You don't want to let the others down. You force yourself to mentally get into it."

"They don't do complacency! Somehow they maintain their high focus and drive."

the pinnacle, but not this crew. They would feel they were cheating each other if they allowed complacency to take root.

Joan recounts the first bonspiel they attended the year after winning their first Worlds. "It was an open, fun 'spiel. You know, men's teams, mixed, juniors, seniors, whoever. We got kicked! Three straight losses! Some to a couple of 'B square' (semi-competitive to recreational) teams. Lose a few games like that and complacency isn't even in your thinking anymore."

As Kathy Fahlman says, "They don't do complacency! Somehow they maintain their high focus and drive. They genuinely love the game and the culture of curling. Curling with Sandra and Jan for so long, and now against them, they never feel like they've arrived and conquered the game. They keep the challenge fresh. Every year is a new year."

PRACTICE

In the bygone days of curling, not every high-level team devoted a lot of time to practice. The mentality was often, "Join a club, hit a few big 'spiels, and away we go." Those days of winging it are long gone.

When it comes to practice, Schmirler's team follows the adage of "No commitment, no progression." They credit much of their practice routine to former Vancouver world champion Lindsay Sparkes, Canada's coaching representative to the team that qualifies for the Worlds, and a good friend of Team Schmirler.

Lindsay's philosophy on the importance of practice is "You achieve what you emphasize." The Regina foursome has taken this philosophy to heart. When they practice, it is with goals in mind: to work on consistency in their deliveries; to work on turn-glitches; to practice some of the nuances of the free-guard zone; to simulate the many different game situations.

Much of their practice is off the ice – sitting around after a game or an on-ice practice. They talk about their tendencies and about on-ice communication. They ask each other how they are feeling about their game and about what's happening in their personal lives that may affect performance. They also have their personal workouts or jogging and swimming times.

They call themselves "crammers" – constantly

working on their game to maintain consistency. There are times when they pace themselves, and other times when they crank it up – loads of practice ice-time to work off summer rust before major bonspiels, and, of course, on the playdown trail.

The "slow times" may see them practice only once or twice a week plus normal club games. Sometimes individual team members will visit the rink during lunch hours, but everyone prefers practising with someone else. As Joan says, "It's lonely practising by yourself."

Practice to Team Schmirler is a lifestyle. Formal ice times, minor bonspiels, club games. More often than not, informal dynamics are the key to team improvement: relationship-building among teammates; post-game discussions; watching game videos; reading motivational materials; and constant observation of other curlers and other teams.

PSYCHOLOGY

When it comes to the mental gymnastics of sport, curling is similar to golf or pitching in baseball. Physical skills are needed, but athletes who excel are those who can out-think their opposition.

Curling has often been called chess on ice, although chess may be easier because players don't have to contend with changing ice conditions, mismatched rocks, or an errant straw. Whether it be chess or curling, the brain works double-time.

No official degrees are granted, but members of Team Schmirler should be granted honourary degrees in psychology of sport and life. Each member of Team Schmirler says a key to their success has been the ability to keep in the forefront of their thoughts the understanding that the number-one opponent doesn't throw a different-coloured rock – most of their

76

A key to Team Schmirler's success is their understanding that their number-one opponent doesn't throw different-coloured rocks. Most of their big-game losses come when they've beaten themselves.

big-game losses have come when they've beaten themselves. They know well the time-worn curling cliché that a D-level team with a hot skip can occasionally beat a world champion. That's the beauty of this frustrating game.

Some teams will treat opposing teams as "the enemy." Team Schmirler prefers to acknowledge good shots made by their opponents. Sandra says, "For us, kindness takes the negative away, especially after the other team has made a piss-cutter of a shot. I feel when we tell the opposition they've made a good shot, we're simply giving credit where it is due, and thus it becomes easier to forget about so we can get back to our game."

When all things are equal, and the women are on top of their game, few teams can beat them. They know this, but it's not arrogance. Most world-class teams have that same inner conviction. Winners centre their concentration on the team's destiny – you must play to win. This philosophy guides each team member's shot-making. Joan comments, "We each focus on our individual 20 shots, *not* the opposition's stones."

The Schmirler crew taps into Sparkes for this psychological approach as well. Lindsay asks the girls to visualize "the ideal performance state." The day starts well before the first rock is thrown. While stretching before a game, each team member reminds herself of the task at hand. As Joan puts it, "I remind myself of my potential. I leave my concerns at home. I take responsibility for my game. I don't feel good because I've played well – I play well because I feel good. I choose to execute because I know I'm capable. I don't let any emotional baggage control my performance."

Each player says they've learned to fake themselves out: "Fake it until you make it." This minimizes the "playing not to lose" syndrome, and has helped them overcome outside distractions, and negative thoughts and emotions. It's the art of mastering the opposition between your own ears. Ever since the game was invented, curling gurus have always emphasized that successful curling is 80 to 90 per cent a cerebral challenge. For Schmirler, many of the games they've won were decided while stretching, long before the first game rock was even thrown.

The ultimate sports psychological state is being in "the zone," that state where Zen curlers say they are "one with the ice" – an elusive state of mind. You can't get into the zone by flipping some magical switch, and few, if any, have been able to explain it.

Sandra has tried, and you can tell she wanted to capture its essence and define it.

"Although there is much more, because so much of the sport is played in your head. However, if you can't execute consistently, the zone will always remain elusive.

Team Schmirler focusses on its prime directive and is constantly trying to master the nuances of curling.

"A lot of the zone is about faking yourself into believing you're in it. You have to take responsibility for achieving it. Waiting for it to happen is allowing yourself to be influenced more by your emotions than by your will.

"You have to be comfortable in your surroundings. Part of our problem at the Scott in Calgary in 1995 (if *third* in Canada is a problem) was that we never properly got used to the venue. It was a cozy arena, but we didn't spend the proper time before the tournament making it our own.

"A lot of the zone is finding a comfort level in your game and your surroundings. You must cover all your bases: your individual game, the venue, TV, and the crowd. You have to keep fun in the game and maintain team harmony.

"This comfort level creates confidence. Confidence gives you a chance to be successful. Once success is happening on the ice, something clicks, and you're in the zone. It's almost impossible to lose the game once you're in the zone.

"You can be successful without being in the zone. But, oh, if you are in the zone, you really do feel invincible. The normal adversities of the game are mere distractions."

Whether in the zone or out, it takes Team Schmirler at least three playdown months each year to achieve champion status. Canadian teams generally start their club playdowns in early January. If they are fortunate enough to win the Scott and go on to the Worlds, their season will wrap up sometime around Easter.

Curling Canucks lose track of how many must-win situations they encounter. So often, games come down to one crucial shot, or to which team does the little things best. As TSN's Ray Turnbull (a former Brier winner) has observed, "At this level the athletes are so good that it's the little things that divide the top teams from the rest. Like Sandra Schmirler and her team. They do so many of the little things so well, like judging rocks as soon as they're released."

Team Schmirler focuses on its prime directive and is constantly trying to master the nuances of curling. In their quest, the team is consistently in the running for championships.

Opposite: "If you are in the zone, you really do feel invincible. The normal adversities of the game are mere distractions."

Chapter Nine
REPEATING
(1993-1994)

Winning one world championship is a rare
achievement. There are scores of dominant athletes who have never won a childhood
championship, let alone one on the world stage. To attempt to win a second one and reach
that goal can feel akin to discovering the Holy Grail.

Ray Bourque, the great Boston Bruin defenceman, a 17-time NHL all-star, has never won a championship
at any level.

Roger Clemens, arguably the best pitcher in the big leagues in the last 15 years, has never been a World
Series champion.

Reggie White, the all-time NFL sack leader of the Green Bay Packers, won his first football championship
of any sort in the 1997 Super Bowl.

In curling, Edmonton's Kevin Martin, a two-time Brier winner, Canadian junior champion, and Canada's
representative at the 1994 Albertville Olympics, is still actively pursuing his first world crown. Martin may be
the best male curler on this planet. Sports enthusiasts sometimes forget that to win a team title you must jell
as a team. Great talent doesn't always guarantee championships. Outstanding performers who are matched with
the proper supporting cast are those who tend to win it all. To win back-to-back championships, the greatest
obstacle, according to coaching experts like Bill Walsh (San Francisco 49ers – three Super Bowl wins), Phil
Jackson (six-time NBA champion with the Chicago Bulls), and Toe Blake (10 Stanley Cups – Montréal
Canadiens), is complacency.

It is normal to experience a letdown after achieving a difficult goal, and, to duplicate the feat, teams often
talk about needing one or two motivators to keep complacency at bay.

Often one of the cures can be found within. Drawing upon one's cultural upbringing can be a starting point.

Of the three aforementioned coaches, Phil Jackson stresses one of the stronger messages against the disease of complacency in his book *Sacred Hoops*. Maybe it's his western Canadian parents and Williston, North Dakota roots that make him so passionate about guarding against this potential team killer.

Growing up on the Prairies is not very conducive to the "We've finally made it" mentality. That mindset is awfully hard to adopt when raised in or around agriculture. A bumper-crop year can be followed by trying to survive on a hail-insurance cheque.

The Schmirler women weren't fooled by their success. They knew that to repeat would be an enormous task. Complacency was a potential obstacle they were able to manage. The farming lessons of the wheat province were subliminally planted in their approach to the game. The second motivator was the game itself.

All four members of this team have observed the uniqueness of curling, which unmercifully exposes the pitfalls of becoming satisfied with your accomplishments.

Early in the 1993-94 curling season, the team entered a local warm-up bonspiel to get the feel for the game back. It would be the equivalent to other sports' preseasons. Winning was more of a side benefit; working on basic fundamentals of curling was primary.

Joan explains how this bonspiel was a key motivator: "I guess everybody wants to beat a world champion. I know I would. We didn't curl particularly well, but it was good to work on our deliveries and just get back out on the ice.

"This bonspiel had every level of curler from Brier and Scott contenders to your average club curler. Some of these teams would never win a zone and really aren't highly motivated to anyway. To some of them it's just a fun game to play, which to me is the beauty of curling.

"We played three games and lost them all. We weren't brutal, we just weren't sharp. You could see the intensity in the eyes of the teams we were drawn against. It might be their only time to be on the same sheet as a world champion team, let alone beat one.

"It reminded all of us very quickly how an average club team could knock off the best team in the world on any given day. Any decent team is capable of curling 80 to 90 per cent every now and then. The secret of course is to sustain high averages over the course of the season. We realized after that fun 'spiel that every team we would face from now on wanted to say, 'Hey, we beat a world champion.' This experience seemed to be a healthy wake-up call. You must maintain the elements that make your team successful, because if you don't, your chances of contending forsake you pretty darn quick."

Sandra says, "About the only positive I got from that 'spiel was meeting Shannon – my future husband."

That 'spiel was another reminder of how curling is possibly the only sport in the world where a semi-competitive local team could conceivably win a game versus the number-one-seeded team in the world. What makes it even more unique is that followers of the sport aren't surprised when it happens.

Ernie Richardson and his Regina-based four-time men's world champions used to say, "The toughest part of getting back to the Brier was often winning a berth in our own local club. Everybody there knew us and weren't intimidated by our team. They'd all seen us lose some club games. We lost our share of games to teams that couldn't advance out of their own local clubs."

The Schmirler team was off to a slow start for the new standards they were setting. They entered two more smaller local 'spiels, winning one and not even qualifying in the other. In late October, they accepted an invitation to curl in the ninth annual Canadian Regional Airlines Double Cashspiel in Kelowna, British Columbia. This was the first of four major 'spiels they would curl in, in preparation for the 1994 Scott.

Sandra reflects on getting out of Regina and finding their collective game. "It's hard to pinpoint why we curled so well in Kelowna, other than the fact we were out of Regina and away from all the normal distractions. We could finally go out and just curl. We could go back to our motel and sleep and concentrate on the task at hand."

Brian McCusker has an insider's view. "I don't know of any other curling team that can turn it on so well when the stakes are so high. They really zero in on the events that matter. A club game or a local 'spiel doesn't bring out the best in them. They do well at the smaller events, but there's not as much on the line.

"When it's crunch time, look out. All four of them. Club play and smaller regional 'spiels are more for toning their deliveries and staying reasonably sharp. It's almost like they pace themselves for the real big events."

This goes against conventional sporting wisdom, which teaches competitors to give their all every time, because it is so hard to conjure up an A-game by simply showing up when it matters.

Sandra says pacing themselves is part of their approach to focussing on what really matters to them. "To our team, winning the Scott and the Worlds has become our ultimate goal. Who remembers the teams who win major cash 'spiels, let alone the local or regional ones? History remembers national and world champions. We prepare ourselves in the major cash 'spiels because our national and world competition are at these events. It's not that we don't care about club play or smaller 'spiels; we like to win them all. But the local events are more like competitive practice. That's not meant in a disrespectful way at all. Our emotional energy is preserved as we try to focus on the major events."

The Kelowna 'spiel was the correct prescription for the team to get back on track. They flew back to the Queen City $9,000 richer, beating Calgary's Diane Foster 9-2 in the final.

In a Kelowna *Capital* news article by sportswriter Al Peterson, Sandra talks about the tough field they faced, but also of the realities of the high financial cost of playing the major cash 'spiel circuit.

Team Canada confers at the 1994 Scott at Kitchener-Waterloo. They had to get emergency stitchery done on their jackets to outline the maple leaf, which was originally just red-on-red.

At the opening ceremonies for the 1994 Scott in Kitchener-Waterloo. Al Badley, who was to be their driver for the week, carries the Team Canada flag for them.

"Schmirler may, however, not be back to defend next year," Peterson wrote. "It's very expensive, about $2,500 plus the $800 entry fee, she said. 'It's not too bad because we have a partial sponsorship (SaskPower) now that we have won the Worlds, but unless they get a better deal on hotels and flights, I don't know.'"

Of the 32 teams in cash 'spiels, only four or five will come out ahead financially. The average curling fan tends to forget that less than 20 per cent of competitive teams will make money or break even on the major cash circuit.

One week later the team won the Sun Life Grand Prix of Curling in Thunder Bay, Ontario. The first-place money was $7,000.

Their last major 'spiel before the short Christmas break was the Sun Life Ladies Classic in Saskatoon. They lost to northern provincial rival, Sherry Scheirich, in their opening draw, then reeled off seven straight wins to reach the final, where they faced Karen Powell's team from Grande Prairie, Alberta. Team Schmirler completed the three-week championship hat-trick, downing Powell's team to win $9,000, plus another $1,000 for winning the two Sun Life sponsored events.

The final preparation for the Scott was their first-

ever bonspiel outside of Canada. While their provincial rivals were starting out on the playdown trail, Team Schmirler was facing most of the top European rinks at the Berner Damen Cup in Berne, Switzerland.

"Berne was our reward for winning the Worlds and for our successful cash 'spiel run in the fall," Joan observed. "These out-of-town bonspiels were key bonding times. No work, no kids, no men, just the four of us. Switzerland was one of the best times our team ever had. It became a huge motivator for other years."

Sandra says Berne was a tremendous amount of fun, and essential. "We needed the high level of competition because all the competitive teams back in Canada were in the middle of playdowns. We had to pay our own expenses except for the accommodations, but it was well worth it.

"It was a tough field. Most of the big-name European teams were there. We won the 'spiel, which of course gave us a lot of confidence going back home."

Marcia says it was the best holiday of her life. "We kept phoning home and telling our husbands or boyfriends how much we missed them and wished they were here. Then we'd get off the phone and roll with laughter. How do you tell them, you don't really miss

1. On the gold medal podium at Nagano. "How do you describe getting a gold medal and watching your flag rise as you sing your national anthem? Unbelievable...unforgettable."

2. Anita, Marcia, Joan, Jan, and Sandra take a formal moment with Saskatchewan Premier Roy Romanow, after winning their first world championship in 1993.

3. The 1994 Worlds – "Jan's intensity is what keeps the team centred on their prime directive."

4. The Skipper at the 1994 Worlds – "Sandra's analytical approach solidifies a philosophy on the ice. She sets the tone of how the team will play each opponent."

5. Joan at the 1994 Worlds – Sandra says "She could make me feel like I was the best skip in the world."

6. The 1993 Worlds - "Marcia is the glue that sustains friendship, the human element."

7. Atina Ford, pinch-hitting again at the 1997 Scott. "She'd done so much for us," the team subbed her in in Nagano, so she too would receive a medal.

8. Anita Ford - Anita has been there with Team Schmirler through national and international competitions for all of the 1990s.

9. Jan and Sandra watch a Scottish skip-rock make its way during the 1994 Worlds in Obertsdorf, Germany.

10. Curling in kilts is rare these days; Team Schmirler tried it out at the 1994 Worlds in Obertsdorf, Germany

11. The grand opening ceremonies at the 1998 Nagano Olympics. Team Schmirler in the front row, with coach and mentor Lindsay Sparkes, second from right.

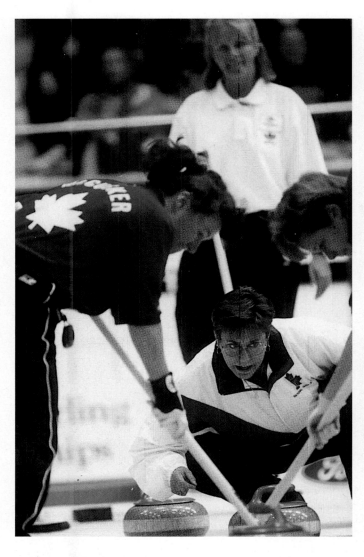

12. Joan and Marcia, the hardest-working front end in the game, put the finishing touches on a shot, as Sandra and a Norwegian opponent look on.

13. Lindsay Sparkes - She got Team Schmirler back to winning form to track down Olympic Gold.

14. Team Moms take a break with the gang, right before leaving for the Olympic trials in Brandon in Fall, 1997.

15. Who knew what this would be the start of? At Team Schmirler's first Worlds triumph in 1993, along with men's world champion Russ Howard rink.

16. Team Schmirler, wearing Saskatchewan green for the first time at the opening ceremonies of the 1991 Scott Tournament of Hearts.

17. Team Schmirler on the victors' podium again, at the 1997 Worlds in Berne. The Danish team is on their left, the Norwegians on their right.

18. The exquisite World Championship trophy, rarely sent anywhere, had an exhibition at the SaskSport Hall of Fame in Regina after Team Schmirler's 1993 Worlds victory. The team makes the most of the...exposure.

19. Joan, Marcia, and Jan ham it up with Wayne, Theo Fleury, and Brendan Shanahan. "We're trying not to freak, because these people are so *famous*."

20. Just hanging around Canada House in Nagano, wearing the hardware. Atina and Elvis Stoyko cut the cake, while members of the Mike Harris men's curling team look on.

them and you're having the best time of your life?"

Joan says it was a little bit of Camelot. "It was two weeks of jam-packed fun. I knew reality would hit when we got back to Regina."

The team had the red carpet rolled out for them by Werner Beck, a Swiss hotel owner who loves curling and enjoys being a good host. The team took trips to various parts of Switzerland during their two-week stay, going to places like Zurich and Grindelwald for sightseeing, skiing, skating, and sledding.

Jan tells a story of how she almost wound up being the skip for the upcoming Canadian championships. "We went to Grindelwald. We saw that you could sled down this mountain. We really didn't bother to get a lot of instructions, like what the track route would be. We just hopped on our sleds and headed down the mountain. Four prairie girls with no clue. The track was incredibly windy. On our first run, Sandra lost control and went off the track, flew off the embankment, right off the mountain into a snowbank. We're laughing hysterically. I mean Sandra could have been hurt. She was covered in bruises. She brushes herself off and says, 'Let's go again.' We went down three times.

"I don't know what we were thinking. The Scott was only a month away."

The team had a high level of confidence going into the Kitchener-Waterloo, Ontario, Scott Tournament of Hearts. They had just curled four major bonspiels against the best competition in the world and won all four. Not since the 1970s and Paul Gowsell's young Calgarians had a team been so dominant on the cash 'spiel circuit on either side of the gender line.

The Callie Curling Club sent the team east with a light-hearted gathering, advertised as a toast, but which in reality was a good-natured roast.

The *Leader-Post* captured the evening well: "It was a night of secrets revealed. For example, the Inglis sisters – McCusker's siblings, Karen Inglis and Cathy Trowell – let it slip out that McCusker, Schmirler's second, had whined for years about being the middle child and not getting attention, and is now complaining that she is in the middle of a curling team and not getting recognition.

"The sisters also dropped the spicy tidbit that Brian McCusker met his wife by placing a classified ad in the *Leader-Post*. Some of our more careful readers may have seen it. It was something along the lines of 'tall curling stud' is looking for a woman who 'can't cook, can't clean, can't curl, but loves to talk.'"

The evening was full of good humour, and finished with an appropriate toast from Callie president Kenda Richards. "We hope we'll be back here a little bit later, having another sendoff."

Kitchener-Waterloo is Canada's Oktoberfest city. The team had been there in the fall to help promote the event, and they knew the tournament

85

Victory hug after winning the 1994 Scott. The media, as usual, was right on top of them.

was going to be well run.

"The committee was so good," Sandra says. "Audrey Cook was the chairperson and put together one of the best Scott tournaments we ever attended. They are to be commended on such a super job. It was one of the intangibles that helped us keep any distractions to a minimum."

The 1994 Scott was probably the most dominant they have ever been at any event. Sandra, referring again to her favourite sporting concept, says, "In all my years of curling it was the most classic case of *being in the zone*. From the very first rock Marcia threw in game one to my final stone in the championship – it was awesome how we all curled. We lost one game – to Connie Laliberte. It was an extra-end loss decided by two incredibly close shots."

The team sustained high averages throughout the week. If anybody doubted their ability to repeat their Canadian title, those thoughts evaporated as the week wore on. The sense in Kitchener-Waterloo was that Team Schmirler was the only team capable of

beating itself. An extreme off day appeared to be the only hope for a new champion to be crowned.

The final standings and game scores looked like this:

FINAL STANDINGS	W	L
Team Canada	10	1
Manitoba	8	3
Saskatchewan	7	4
Newfoundland	7	4
P.E.I.	7	4
British Columbia	6	5
Ontario	4	7
Quebéc	4	7
Nova Scotia	4	7
New Brunswick	4	7
Territories	4	7
Alberta	0	11

TEAM CANADA OPPONENTS & SCORES IN ORDER OF PLAY	
Alberta (Palinkas)	9-2
Newfoundland (Phillips)	7-4
Nova Scotia (Jones)	6-5
Prince Edward Island (Danks)	9-6
Saskatchewan (Anderson)	10-2
Territories (Aucoin)	6-5
Ontario (Merklinger)	10-1
New Brunswick (Hanlon)	9-4
Manitoba (Laliberte)	5-6
Quebéc (Charette)	6-4
British Columbia (Dalio)	7-6

Team Schmirler had scored 84 points (7.6 per game) and allowed an amazingly low 45 points (4.1 per game) scored against them. They had outscored the opposition by 3.5 points per game. That's understandable at a regional bonspiel if they consistently play their A-game, but to do it at a national championship is truly outstanding.

The team would face their longtime Winnipeg rival in the championship. The Manitoba champions downed Saskatchewan's Sherry Anderson in the semi-final. If Anderson had won, it would have been the first single-province championship ever in national women's competition.

The only way to get a private moment with your teammates after winning a Scott Tournament of Hearts.

The look of success – bringing the Heartware home again, this time from the 1994 Scott in Kitchener-Waterloo

The *Leader-Post's* Ardith Stephanson interviewed 12-time Nova Scotia champion Colleen Jones before the final game. The headline read: "Jones picks Schmirler ahead of everybody." The story went on, "She's a step above everybody else. They're coming by guards by inches, they're playing aggressively, they have much more confidence than last year and it's noticeable. They're clearly ahead of the pack.

"They're several shots ahead of everybody else. I see it as them and us. There's really noticeable separation between their team and the rest."

Looking at their only loss of the week, Jones viewed it this way: "They were fortunate to lose that game when they did. It's too hard to go through the week 12-0. If you lose in the round robin you get it out of your system. We're all human. She didn't lose as much as Connie won. Sandra is definitely the top of the class. Her team is rock solid."

The final scenario was a *déjà vu* of Brandon, 1993. By clinching first place, they received the bye straight to the final. This meant a full day off before the big game. Sandra was determined not to get caught in any unnecessary distractions as in the previous year. Instead of being at the Waterloo Recreation Complex to watch the semi-final, they stayed at their hotel and watched it on TV.

This was the first tournament under curling's new rules, the introduction of the FGZ to Canadian curling, which was expected to create a more aggressive, wide-open style of game.

Sandra recalls her strategic choice to play the new game the old way. "This wasn't a club game, this was the Canadian championship. I felt a conservative approach with us starting the game with hammer was the prudent way to go. Connie leaned this way as well, so the result was a well played, boring game for the fans."

These two curling superpowers had perfected the conservative hit-and-peel game to such a degree that a team with a two-point or greater lead would have little chance of losing. The elite teams were becoming so efficient that the game had to make this fundamental change with the FGZ.

This was akin to the designated hitter in baseball. In reality, baseball's change was like cosmetic surgery; curling's was like major life-saving amputation. A centuries-old part of the game was being altered, and although the purists would say "sacrilege," as with most major changes in life, the FGZ, having been given time, is now an accepted part of the transition. Attendance has increased at most major events; television ratings are setting records; new people are joining local leagues. It is the most significant move in the history of curling. It has helped keep it on the world stage and accelerated the growth of the game.

Team Schmirler was ready to take advantage of the FGZ if it was to their advantage. Sandra says, "We were

At the closing banquet in Kitchener, the team poses with Bob Stewart, president of Scott Paper.

up 2-1 after five ends and Connie could have used the FGZ to create more points. She never did and still got her two points to go up on us 3-2 coming home.

"In the first five ends we had control because we jumped ahead as a result of us having hammer. Connie preferred keeping it clean when she had hammer and was playing for us to miss. She was hoping not so much for wide-open misses but us missing a couple of partial shots. She got her two in the seventh end. Her third, Karen Purdy, made a great split to create the two."

Team Schmirler blanked the eighth and ninth ends to set up the final end. They played the tenth with the FGZ, trying to set up a two-point end. The worst-case scenario would be getting one on last shot and forcing the extra end.

The team threw eight perfect stones in the last end. "Marcia threw her first two rocks dead on," says Joan. "The ice was so keen you barely seemed to let your rocks go. After Marcia made her two shots, I felt so confident when I went to shoot. I had such a strong feeling the way the end was shaping up."

Laliberte's team got a bad break on a peel attempt and rolled to the back of the house early in the end. Joan and Jan were able to muscle a couple of shots on the backing. Joan says, "I threw my last stone, made it, and said out loud, 'I'm done.'"

Jan, who looks so cool on the outside, reveals the inner weather patterns: "Joan said, she's done. I was thinking I wish I was done, I can't wait to get finished."

Laliberte was facing the two potential winning stones of Team Canada on her last shot. She tried a freeze, to either force an extra end or to steal the win. Her rock was a little heavier than she anticipated, nudging the Schmirler stone and rolling the Manitoba rock into the open. All Sandra had to do was make a wide-open hit to win. Even a half-shot, hit correctly, would win the game.

A big part of Team Schmirler's appeal for the fans is their gut-level honesty about their emotional state in these big games. Even though they've achieved the highest honours in the game, they still have those dreaded butterflies that want to evolve into ravens.

Jan was nervously standing at the tee-line holding the broom. "I thought my heart was going to jump out of my chest. All I said to Sandra was, 'Throw it clean.' It was like listening to the ocean while I waited for Sandra to go down the ice and clean her stone.

"I was so relieved I was finished throwing. But my heart was beating so much. There was fear, excitement, and anticipation. You try to maintain an even keel, you have to check the emotions at the door before the game begins. It does get a little easier to keep all these inner emotions in check because of experience, but there's always a degree of tension because of the circumstances."

"I was literally shaking," admits Sandra. "It was a routine open out-turn hit. We'd been throwing out-turn hits all game. My knees were shaking and my hands were, too. My heart was racing a hundred miles an hour. I purposely took a little extra time to calm down. I tried to block out the magnitude of the consequences of this last shot. It's almost like I pretended it was just a routine practice shot. I settled in the hack and got a comfort level and started my delivery. I directed my concentration on the task at hand, not my delivery. Not the fact that we were trying to win our second straight national title."

Sandra threw it clean to help her team win 5-3. She jumped with delight, then dropped to her knees in relief. The other three all met in the far house, hugging and joining arms and heading down the ice to congratulate Sandra. They wept, hugged, and shook with emotion.

Team Schmirler became only the third women's team to win back-to-back Canadian titles. Vera Pezer's Saskatoon dynasty won three in a row from 1971 to 1973, and Heather Houston and her Thunder Bay foursome won back-to-back championships in 1988 and 1989.

The women could now reload and prepare for the world championships in Obertsdorf, Germany. There was a full month to get in gear to defend their title.

Regina wasn't getting tired of celebrating the exploits of one of its favourite ambassadors. Local and provincial media were making them front-page news on a regular basis. There were civic receptions and another Callie sendoff.

They were feeling ready to defend in Obertsdorf. The experience of the previous year in Geneva, as well as the January bonspiel in Berne, helped familiarize them with their international competition. They had faced most of the 10 teams at the 1994 Worlds over the past 12 months.

Going in as obvious favourites, they were feeling positive about their chances. They had a full year of playing the FGZ under their belts, and would feel no fear of the unknown facing the Europeans this time around. They knew they were capable of winning again. It was simply a matter of going out on the ice and playing up to their potential.

Elisabet Gustafson, the Swedish skip, seeking her second world crown, had this observation: "These Canadians have such an air of self confidence about them. As soon as you see them walk into the arena you sense such a great team. Not arrogance, because our team finds them so genuinely friendly.

"In 1993, in our semi-final, the game was so very close, but I felt like the difference between our

Now it's on to Calgary. Departing Kitchener-Waterloo with the trademark white stetson symbolizing the next year's Scott host city.

89

two teams was bigger. You could see the confidence in their faces.

"They are such a strong team. Sandra is so clear in her decision-making. Their approach is so precise. They seek perfect shots every time and think nothing of it. They routinely make their shots or are very close."

Though Gustafson wasn't afraid of Team Schmirler, her respect for their play was immense. Gustafson knew that a foreign team would have to bring their A-plus game to the rink to beat this Canadian juggernaut. This compliment from their Swedish rival was a tribute to the Regina quartet's almost unwavering consistency.

The team left Regina on a Wednesday in order to have a few days to get acclimatized and recover from the jet lag of a trans-Atlantic flight. The first two games would be on Sunday versus the USA and co-favourite Sweden.

The trip to Germany would be a bit of a mara-

thon. Joan kept a diary. "We left Regina on Wednesday and arrived in Toronto. All our fans were on the same flight – Joan and Bill McCusker, Walter and Verna Betker, Ron and Dawn Gudereit, Frank Macera, Shannon England, and Kerry Gudereit. Ardith Stephanson from the Regina *Leader-Post* was also in our group.

"We left Toronto for Frankfurt. At this point our fans had to take a different flight. We departed for Munich and waited another hour for the next flight to arrive with our luggage and our fans. Then it was a three-and-a-half hour bus ride to Obertsdorf.

This turned out to be a 24-hour ordeal to get to the small Bavarian city of 12,000 people. They were relieved to finally arrive and settle into their accommodations. If the team believed in omens, they probably wouldn't have won a game in the upcoming week.

Their first hotel had substantial problems, so

Marcia and Joan, the best sweeping front end in the world, pour it on for a Schmirler shot as they try to repeat as world champions in Obertsdorf.

"Hard!" With a three-second difference in draw time between one direction and the other, the sweepers could never let up.

the next day they changed hotels.

Over the next couple of days the team focussed on preparing their minds and skills on seeking to become the first Canadian and world back-to-back champions.

There was a meeting with the Canadian men's champions from Kelowna – Rick Folk, Pat Ryan, Bert Gretzinger, and Gerry Richard. Sandra enjoyed meeting the Folk team: "Rick was born and raised in Saskatoon. When I was a teenager, he won his first world championship representing Saskatchewan at that time. He was one of my curling heroes as a youth just starting out. Now both of us were trying to win the Worlds for Canada.

"You had to admire Rick. He had just been at his dad's funeral a week before, so that was pretty heavy on his mind. But it's the old story, his dad wanted him to go to the Worlds. It had been 14 years between championships. His dad helped introduce him to the game and they were a tight-knit family."

The team got some much-needed practice time in to get a feel for the ice and the overall venue. Anita Ford and Lindsay Sparkes started the usual book on the stones and the ice. They would seek to match the rocks and make sure that the curl on each individual's two rocks was the same. Some curling

rocks will react a little differently than others because of how they are cut underneath. Folk's team also kept a book, and the two teams often compared the information throughout the week, just to make sure nobody got fooled in the heat of battle.

The team was feeling comfortable with their surroundings and good about their chances. Jet lag was almost over as well. Ardith Stephanson interviewed Joan about this crucial area of preparation. "When the team arrived in Germany it was mid-afternoon, which is eight hours ahead of Regina, but the rink members knew they shouldn't sleep. That's the key to surviving jet lag – get on a German time schedule immediately.

"'That's why they bring us in so much earlier. You don't have any trouble sleeping the first night. It's the second and third night – getting your internal clock to adjust.'"

Sunday finally arrived. Game one was versus Winnipeg-born-and-raised skip Bev Behnke. She was representing the USA. Her Denver, Colorado-based team consisted of three Canadians and two American-born curlers. Behnke had curled with Connie Laliberte and Connie's sister Janet Arnott before Laliberte went on to win the Worlds in 1984. She also skipped her own team in Manitoba, winning a few zones.

The key to their first win may have been the struggles with the ice. The Eislaufzentrum was normally a hockey venue and the floor was not level, so the ice was as much as six inches thicker from one end to the other in an attempt to keep the playing surface level. The ice was generally to the curlers' liking, but draw weight varied by a full three seconds from one end to the other. Marcia said it kept them in the game mentally. "You were thinking constantly about your weight and which direction you were throwing. As sweepers you had to be so aware as well."

The team got rid of any opening game jitters and went on to post an impressive 9-4 victory.

The second game was against the Scandinavian powerhouse Gustafson. This would not be a great week for the Swedish team. They won their share of games but never really got in synch. Team Schmirler beat them, fairly easily, in a 10-5 win. They were 2-0 and on top of the standings after the first day. The first goal was to qualify for one of the four playoff spots, and they were well on their way.

On Monday there would be just the one game against Angela Lutz's team from Switzerland. The Schmirler crew seemed to be adapting much more quickly to the ice surface than some of the other squads, and they beat the Swiss easily, 8-3. They were tied at 3-0 with Scotland at this juncture of the tournament.

On Tuesday the team improved to an impressive 5-0, alone at the top of the round robin. They opened the day against the only winless team. Japan's Ayako Ishigaki, shooting their best game all week, kept with the Canadians most of the way. It turned out to be one of the most difficult games. Team Canada was

only up 5-4 after five ends and maintained a 7-5 lead going into the ninth, when they scored a big two to put the game out of reach.

In the evening draw they faced Norwegian newcomers, skipped by Ingvill Githmark. Although Norway generally plays the Canadians tough, the game was over in six ends as the Schmirler crew took advantage of every opportunity, winning 13-2. The Norwegian skip curled only 25 per cent, her worst effort of the tournament.

The team was beating their opposition by an average of six points per game. They were dominating. "It was the weakest field we had ever faced at the Hearts or the Worlds," Sandra remarked. "Part of that was due to Norway and Switzerland sending good but inexperienced teams. The Americans also struggled. It became only a three-or-four team race. In Canada, every province has a handful or more legitimate contenders. In Europe, the depth isn't that strong. We weren't taking anyone for granted, because upsets can creep up and get you pretty quick. We never took any needless chances."

Ardith Stephanson sent home this article to the *Leader-Post*, at the halfway point of the event:

"Schmirler takes every team seriously here but thinks the curling is more competitive at the Canadian championship.

"'The teams in Canada get more competition throughout the year, and I think that's the big thing. These teams are the best in their home countries, but if they came to Canada, some of them wouldn't fare quite as well.

"'Experience is the best teacher. If you get burned in a couple of situations, you're going to learn not to do that the next time.

"'Some of these teams haven't been burned and they haven't learned that you have to call the right shot and the right strategies and make them. If they came out of Canada I think they would

Feeling great – half-way through the week in Obertsdorf and still undefeated....

But things can change in a hurry. A bad game sees them get clobbered by Denmark.

learn fairly quickly. We've been burned our share over the years.'"

The midpoint of the week is often the toughest mental part of the event for the curlers. The initial games are over, the standings are starting to settle and take shape. The end isn't quite in sight, and mental lapses often occur.

Anita Ford has observed the mid-week blues on many occasions. "It's a long, intense week. Almost all the teams start to suffer mentally at the mid-point. It's awfully hard to maintain high intensity for seven or eight days. The team has to will itself to keep its curling standards up. You have to recognize the tailspin emotionally, and play through it. A bad loss at the midpoint, when you are already struggling emotionally, can hurt a team with loads of momentum. Or it can be a wake-up call to the reality of the situation. The girls go through it like all the other teams, but tend to fight through it all right."

Wednesday was the wake-up call. They met Helena Blach-Lavrsen of Denmark, who beat them 6-3. The Canucks played their worst game of the week and their averages reflected it.

The team took the loss in stride. Besides, they've never gone undefeated at a major competition like the nationals or the Worlds. Past experience taught them to be concerned but not to panic. It had been a long time in playdown competition since they'd lost two or three in a row.

It was the only game of the day for Team Canada, so they did a little shopping and sight-seeing. Joan accepted an invitation to visit a local school. Then it was early to bed to be ready for Thursday's two games.

Finland would be the next victim. Janna Jokela and her Finnish foursome were clearly outplayed in the 8-6 Canadian win, which clinched them a playoff. Scotland's Christine Cannon team was the best of the rest at this stage of the week – Canada was 6-1 and the Scots were 5-2 going into the game. A win for Schmirler and company would wrap up first place; a loss would create the proverbial log-jam.

Sandra curled her best game of the week – an awesome 98 per cent, meaning she missed only a couple of quarter-shots somewhere along the way. It was over in eight, as Canada clinched first overall with a resounding 10-3 score.

The last game of the round robin was a formality for the Canadians, but their German opposition needed the win to avoid a tie-breaker. Josefine Einsle of the host country provided the opposition. Einsle, along with Karin Fischer and Lisa Landle, had faced Schmirler in the 1993 Worlds final in Geneva. Josefine threw third stones for Canadian-born skip, Janet Clews-Strayer, in the previous year's championship. Clews-Strayer now lived in Calgary.

They gave Schmirler her toughest test of the week, the perfect preparation for the next day's

The two Canadian teams, Schmirler and Rick Folk, throw a practice game in the Eislaufzentrum in Obertsdorf.

semi-final. Sandra needed to hit and stick in an extra end to win 6-5.

The team had almost a day and a half to kill before Saturday's semi-final. The CCA took Folk's and Schmirler's teams out for the evening. It was a tension-relief kind of supper. "We had a terrific time," says Joan. "They took us to the Café Baur. We had a little wine, outstanding food, dessert, and some good-natured fun. Pat Ryan was doing his now-famous – in curling circles – Elvis impersonation. Rick Folk was avoiding the karaoke. Sandra was bugging Jan to perform. It was a fun time. We headed back to the hotel to Jim Waite's room for a good-luck Bailey's and then off to bed."

On Saturday the team went for some last-minute shopping and cappuccinos in the outdoor cafés, meeting in time for a mid-afternoon practice. Joan says, "It was kind of counterproductive, as we didn't throw well. Perhaps too much curling?"

Finally the wait was over. They came out strong against the Germans, dominating the first half of the game, but Germany was hanging in there, not letting the game get out of reach. It was 4-2 after five ends and Canada had the hammer. But the

team was more nervous than usual, according to Schmirler. "This is sudden-death, no more second chances. You lose, you're out. I missed my last shot in the sixth and opened the door big time. A steal of two and we're tied 4-4. That probably woke up our nerves. I make that shot or keep the damage down and our butterflies are more in check as well. Thank goodness no one panicked. We still had hammer and at least we're tied with four ends to go."

This was not a typical Team Schmirler kind of game. They got one in the seventh and stole two in the eighth to jump ahead 7-4. It looked like they had finally put Germany away. But the Germans had a tremendous amount of pluck and used the FGZ as best they could to grab two in the ninth. It was only 7-6 for the Canadians coming home.

Sandra needed her last shot to win in the final end, and promptly made a clean hit to score three. The misleading final score was 10-6. They would play Scotland in the final.

The team was noticeably relieved that the semi-final was over. They referred to it as their "character game." Sam Snead (all-time PGA tournament winner) coined the phrase "cool mad." This is a healthy inner anger directed at one's underachieving performance. Team Schmirler was clearly in this mental state in getting ready for Scotland's Christine Cannon and squad. There is a certain pride the team takes in their performance and they knew it needed to be raised to the level they could be satisfied with. "Cool mad" doesn't focus on the potential outside pitfalls in a game. It redirects the team's energy almost entirely on *their* game and the things their team can control.

Sandra has said it many times. "We perform at our best when we dictate the game. When we're concentrating on our strategy and individual performances, we tend to win the vast majority of our games.

"If we're worrying about the opposition, to the point that we allow them to get us off our game plan, that's when we struggle. If we're concerned about the ice conditions and not adapting to it, that's when doubts creep in. We can't let the opposition, the ice, or even the crowd dictate how we play."

The German battle was a definite blessing in disguise.

The final game was played at 11:00 a.m. the following day. Joan comments, "Fortunately, the final was in the morning. Not much time to kill at all."

Both teams played quite conservatively. Because of their first-place finish, Team Canada had the hammer to start the game, and they never lost control.

They were on top of their game and patiently waited for the right opportunity to take control.

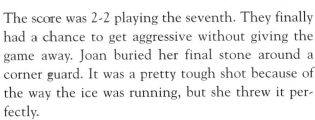

The score was 2-2 playing the seventh. They finally had a chance to get aggressive without giving the game away. Joan buried her final stone around a corner guard. It was a pretty tough shot because of the way the ice was running, but she threw it perfectly.

Scottish third Claire Milne missed her next shot. Jan followed up with a draw to the house for second shot. There was nothing fancy after that, and the Canadians were up 4-2 going into the eighth end, when Scotland caught one of those dreaded hairs and allowed the Canadians to steal a big point and go up 5-2.

The Scots could have blanked the ninth end to have last rock coming home,

"Cool-mad" redirects the team's energy almost entirely on their game and the things their team can control. Cool-mad after a semi-final that was closer than it should have been, Team Schmirler curled with deadly purpose against Scotland in the final.

The result – Team Schmirler, Canada's first back-to-back women's world champions, pose with the spectacular World Curling trophy.

but they elected to take a point, and in the process gave the hammer back to Canada.

The team curled a flawless tenth end and ran the Scots out of rocks. Sandra, for once, never had to throw her final stone in a big game.

They had become Canada's first back-to-back women's world champions. There was the usual celebration, but it was not as emotional as the previous year. Sandra explains, "The main emotion was relief, mixed with satisfaction. It wasn't a flashy win but a game worthy of winning. The team was so steady with no major misses. I like games like this. Just a solid, solid effort. Everyone curled a great game."

It was a devastating loss for Cannon, who left the ice sobbing. She realized her chance to win the Worlds might never come again. In the back of her mind was the shot that caught a hair and turned a one-point game into a near-impossible three-point deficit. The way Team Canada was curling, it probably wouldn't have made a difference anyway.

Team Schmirler put up some impressive statis-tics in the 1993-94 season. They had won over $30,000 to lead all money-winners on the cash cir-cuit. The team was 21-2 at the Scott and Worlds combined.

Their two-year totals on the playdown trail leading to back-to-back world championships will go down in history looking like this:

EVENT(S)	GP	W	L	PCT
92-93 Sask. Playdowns	16	15	1	0.938
92-93 Scott	12	10	2	0.833
92-93 Worlds	11	9	2	0.818
93-94 Scott	12	11	1	0.917
93-94 Worlds	11	10	1	0.907
Total	62	55	7	0.887

Every championship is special, but looking back at the 1993-94 season and its unique set of circum-stances, it may go down as Team Schmirler's best year

A victory parade for both victorious Canadian teams through downtown Obertsdorf, Germany

of curling – the pressure to repeat at two major tournaments and accomplishing the feat; the entry in four major cash bonspiels and winning all of them.

Counting the four cash 'spiels, the Tournament of Hearts, and the Worlds, the team appeared in four quarter-finals, five semi-finals, and six finals. They were an astonishing 15-0 when it really mattered. Going back to the 1993 provincials in Shaunavon, their playoff record when everything was on the line was 19-0. To put this in perspective, they had to beat former provincial, national, and world champions every step of the way. They were constantly beating the best of the best.

These four young women were not just chasing history with this 1993-94 edition of Team Schmirler, they were now carving a whole new standard for teams to pursue. They had pieced together the greatest individual season ever in the history of women's curling, period. This kind of big-game dominance may never be duplicated! ⊙

Good thing they had thought to practise their victory leap on a ski hill before the tournament even started.

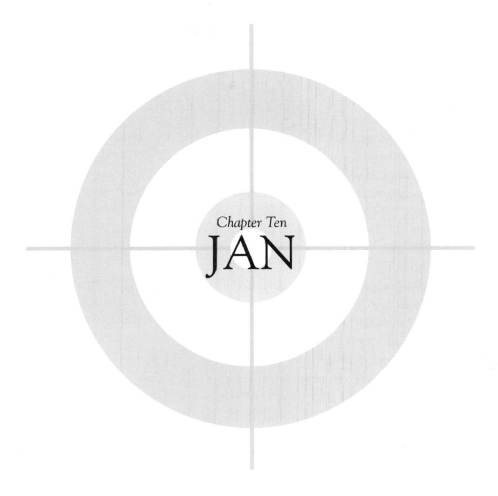

Chapter Ten

JAN

"**S**he never really wanted to go," revealed Jan's parents, Walter and Verna Betker.

"Jan was about 12 years old and we registered her and our two sons in the curling program at the old Regina Wascana Winter Club. Her brothers were slightly older and we figured that we might as well bring all three along, so Jan wouldn't be left alone at home.

"The first couple of times Jan stood there shivering in the cold. She wasn't overly impressed with this family decision. But once she realized she could compete with the other kids, it kind of grew on her."

Quite an inauspicious debut for what many in curling circles consider the best third in the game today. Many think that Jan Betker may be the best individual curler in the world. An equal number of others consider Sandra the best. But you will never hear Sandra and Jan debate the issue. To them it is a non-issue because they are best friends who happen to be on the same team.

Once Jan took to the game, she says, "I was like a duck taking to water. I was small for my age and found a sport where size didn't really matter a whole lot. I was hooked."

Jan comes from an extremely tight-knit family. She is the youngest of four children, all born in Regina. Susan is the oldest, followed by Bill and Warren.

Verna recalls, "Walter and I have always felt very fortunate with our children. They were regular kids but we never really worried about them as parents. I mean they grew up through the late 1960s and 1970s and seemed to avoid the drugs and any other kind of destructive behavior. All four of them had an extremely good circle of friends. They hardly went to any of the dances or parties a lot of their classmates went to.

"Our four kids hung out a lot together as well. Their competitive makeup probably came quite naturally. They were always playing cards or board games or out playing in the back yard. We'd go fishing in the summer

High school curling teammates in 1977 – Jan, Brenda Campbell, Carolyn Nevill, Jayne Duncan. In the rear is their coach, Ruth Lieske.

in a trailer Walter built when the children were still young.

"Jan, being the youngest, had to learn to stand up on her own, and she'd fight back if the situation called for it. We noticed her competitive streak right from the start. She could be very strong-willed, if she believed in something."

According to her teammates, she is flexible in making decisions but will take a strong stand on issues or game strategies she believes in. Once Sandra makes a final decision, Jan will let it go and back Sandra all the way. She'll seldom bring up what the difference in philosophy may have been. If she does bring it up, it's motivation for learning for the next time and not an attempt to prove a point.

Kathy Fahlman and Jan curled together for seven years and Kathy offers this perspective: "She is such a loyal friend, and is one person who doesn't get caught up in gossip or that nit picky stuff. Jan is incredibly intense, but has the ability to let things go once it's over."

Her mom tells the story of a five-year-old Jan who was simply trying to stand up for what she observed to be right. "Her aunt had a really nice winter coat that she took apart and remade for Jan. It wasn't finished; she still had some hemming to do. Jan took one look at it and knew it was too long. We couldn't get through to Jan that it wasn't quite finished. She thought it was the finished product and because it was too long, why go through the hassle of even trying to put it on. She made quite a fuss and actually lost her temper out of pure frustration. We realized the communication breakdown and just let it go.

"The next day, when no one else was around, she consented and tried it on, so I could take some measurements for her aunt. Jan has always been very firm when things are clear to her. She's always had a mind of her own."

Jan grew up with a love for sports and the outdoors. She described her dad as "a sports fanatic. Playing sports, watching it, attending games. He had Roughrider season tickets since 1958. If *Hockey Night in Canada* or CFL football was on TV, we'd all gather around with him to watch.

"With my two brothers we were always playing catch. We'd get our ball gloves on and throw a baseball around. During football season, I'd be out there tossing the football around with them."

Jan's growing-up years were surrounded by the element of sports. Her neighbour across the street was Saskatchewan Roughrider great George Reed and his family. Reed is the holder of more CFL records than any player in the history of the league.

Often her parents would entertain George Reed and other Roughriders in their back yard. This was during an era when the Riders were always competing for the Grey Cup. Now both George and Jan are in the Saskatchewan Sports Hall of Fame.

Maybe some of Jan's never-say-die attitude on the curling ice was adopted from observing Number 34, George Reed. Walter said, "We used to watch George limping around and barely walking up his stairs and then go to the game the next day and watch him steamroll over various defenses for his usual 100-plus yards. He would always play through the pain and battering and give his all. There was never any quit in old George."

Whether Jan adopted this attitude from Mr. Reed

or not, she's got it in volumes. Kathy Fahlman says, "Jan's got no quit in her. She'll fight to the bitter end and never ever give up. She always feels the team has a chance, that it's never too late to mount a comeback until there's not enough rocks to throw."

Jan curled for one year at the Wascana Winter Club. During the summer before the next curling season, the roof collapsed and the club was not rebuilt. Her first instructor was Del Ludvigsen, who was instrumental in getting a lot of young people curling.

Over the next few years Jan sometimes curled out of the town of Kronau, just a 20-minute drive east of Regina. This is a very small community that is similar to Avonlea. Close to a dozen curlers from Kronau have gone on to represent Saskatchewan at various national championships.

During her years in Kronau, Jan would curl lead for her brother Warren. They would bonspiel a bit

over the winter. Walter said, "You could see that both Warren and Jan played to win, even at this early age. I still remember one game where the game was on the line and Warren had to make his shot or give up a big end. Jan very calmly but clearly reminded Warren, as he settled in the hack, that if he missed the shot the other team was going to get five."

Jan curled regularly through high school. She curled both in junior women's and in the Saskatchewan high school provincials. She skipped her teams in those days, even though her preference was to curl at second or third. Verna says, "She took skipping very seriously and always felt that if the team lost it was probably her fault."

Walter and Verna always supported their children and tried to attend their sporting or school extracurricular activities. The most memorable event in Jan's high school curling days was when her team qualified for the southern playdowns in Maple Creek. They travelled there by car, but got caught in a three-day blizzard that stranded the team. Walter said, "The highway was blocked and the only way out seemed to be by train and even it was cancelled. This went on for three days. The girls seemed to be having a good time in spite of the inconvenience."

Jan enjoyed her high school curling years, but says, "We were no real threat. We had fun and did all right. Our junior team made it to provincials once, but we only won one game. Then our high school team made it out of the south on one occasion and we qualified for provincials. We went to Mortlach and got annihilated. We played two games and lost both."

Jan continued her curling after high school. She had always hoped to get a break and join a competitive provincial contender. It took only a year to get noticed. She had joined the Callie Club and got on a team in regular women's play. Before her second year began at the club, Kronau's Kathy Fahlman, a recent provincial junior ladies champion, phoned Jan up to see if they could join forces. Kathy had moved into Regina and had also joined the Callie Club.

Kathy was putting together a very good-looking young team. She would skip, Brenda Campbell curled third, Jan was the second and Sheila Ell threw lead

101

"Jan's got no quit in her. She always feels that the team has a chance, that it's never too late to mount a comeback until there's not enough rocks to throw."

stones. On paper this team was instantly considered one of Saskatchewan's up and comers. They got along well, were about the same age, didn't have family responsibilities, and were able to commit to the competitive cash bonspiel circuit. They were always one of the favourites when the playdown trail would start.

Curling has always been the type of sport where age plus experience has to be a part of a curler's resume. Every now and then a young team will creep through and win a major title. But generally the dominant teams are curlers in their late 20s to mid-40s. Curling is so psychological and demanding from the point of view of mental toughness that curlers need to get toughened up north of the shoulders. That can only occur through the volume of games, experience against top-flight teams, and chronological years.

Kathy and her team were all in their early 20s. From a technical standpoint, they were one of the most solid-looking teams when they stepped out on the ice, but these were to be maturing years. They were favoured to win a city berth to the southern playdowns in their first two seasons together. It was a

reasonable prediction by the press and local fans, because of Team Fahlman's better-than-average success in qualifying in most of their bonspiels throughout western Canada.

Both years were extremely disappointing for Jan, as the team couldn't put it together in the Regina city zone playdowns. But the foundation, which is best built on experience, was growing more solid. Brenda Campbell stepped down from the team in the off-season, so they needed a new player.

When Kathy heard that Sandra Schmirler was moving to Regina, she called her up and had a meeting. Sandra and Kathy hit it off. The team had a new third and Jan was about to meet the lady who would become her new best friend.

The team seemed only a step or two away from winning Saskatchewan. Even though they still hadn't won their zone at the women's level, Team Fahlman was always considered a serious threat. Jan says, "We again went on the cash 'spiel circuit and did very well. We always won our share of 'spiels and money. We were beating teams that had been to the Scott or had won it. But I still wasn't convinced we could

Jan's extended family – "I've been so fortunate that most of my immediate family lives in Regina. I really feel like any success I have is with my whole family."

After the first Worlds in 1993, the nieces, Kirsten, Angela, Kelly and Ashley, were out in force to let Auntie Jan know what they thought of her accomplishment.

play at that level. I was confident in our team and my abilities but wondered if we were really good enough to get over that last hurdle. We could beat the really good teams now and then. But could we beat them when it really mattered?

"With Sandra on board, we seemed a little closer to contending for the province, but our first two years together we again couldn't get out of the cities. Four years in a row of getting close but not getting a zone berth to the south. That creates a few doubts.

"In 1986-87, we finally put it all together. We won our first women's zone, won a berth at the south, and got real hot at provincials. We met Susan Lang in the final up in Nipawin. We curled really well and won our first provincial title.

"I still wasn't convinced, personally, that I was Scott material. Going to Lethbridge and representing Saskatchewan, then curling well, convinced me. We were in every game and curled well against each team. Until you actually make the Scott, you don't really know what to expect."

Jan is a pragmatic person. Even though others may have thought she had an obvious talent for the game, Jan needed to prove it and not just speculate.

Lethbridge was bittersweet for Jan and the team. Kathy struggled. She had her moments, but the consistency she is so capable of wasn't there during the week. Jan, Sandra and Sheila Schneider all made the first all-star team, yet it wasn't enough to secure a playoff spot.

The Calgary Winter Olympics were the following year. Curling would be a demonstration sport. The Canadian Curling Association (CCA) would hold its Olympic trials a couple of months after the

Lethbridge Scott. The CCA wanted eight teams at the Calgary trials. They were choosing individual teams and individual players to form "all-star" teams. Because of Jan, Sandra and Sheila's all-star selection, the team was chosen to curl at the trials.

The team curled well at what organizers were saying was "the toughest field ever for a women's curling event." Team Fahlman got close and lost a tie-breaker to finish fourth.

The seeds of winning a Canadian title were starting to sprout for Jan. She really wanted to experience another Scott, not just to qualify, but to win.

Randy Woytowich thought Jan had arrived at least three years earlier. "Jan curled mixed on my team for a few years. She developed so quickly as a quality curler. We started together in 1981 and won the Canadian mixed in 1984. She was more than capable as our lead."

Walter Betker said that the 1984 team "was one of the most dominant teams on record. As soon as they formed the team, they clicked. They waltzed through the Saskatchewan playdowns and went undefeated at the nationals in Prince Albert. I don't know if they lost two games all year."

Even that Canadian title did not convince Jan she was an elite performer at the women's level. "The mixed has a different emphasis," she explained. "Both the men and women are trying to succeed at the Brier or Scott first. The mixed is a tough event, but you usually only enter when you're eliminated from men's or women's playdowns. I still wanted proof of my abilities by playing in a Scott. I knew I was closer but needed more convincing."

Jan thought the team she was with had finally

Jan ties the knot in 1995, with Regina Ram Canadian football champion Frank Macera.

arrived. Going to the Scott and Olympic trials had settled her thinking that they were ready. Expectations were high and with good reason.

The next two years were years of unfulfilled success. Although the team curled well on the bonspiel circuit, playdowns were absolutely frustrating. Their bid to repeat as provincial champions was cut short by old rival Michelle Schneider.

When Kathy was recruited by Schneider the next year, Sandra and Jan recruited Susan Lang to skip for them. But something wasn't quite right, as another playdown disaster followed.

Jan was in despair. "I was utterly devastated. I knew we were more than good enough to get back to the Scott and have a chance at winning it all.

"In the spring of 1990, I got together with Sandra. I said, I've had enough of this. I need a change. Either I was going to skip or Sandra should skip and that's how our team was born."

Kathy Fahlman wasn't surprised. "They were ready to form their own team. They are so devoted to the game and know it so well, that the two of them needed to launch out on their own."

Jan's years of growing pains built one of the strongest curling foundations on record. The bonspiel circuit, Lethbridge 1987, the Olympic trials, the taste of a national title with the mixed, the many heartbreaking losses in the Saskatchewan playdowns, the hours and hours of bull sessions with Sandra, had all formed a curling philosophy, and passion, rarely seen in the sport. She was on the verge of a breakthrough.

Along the way, family has always been a high priority. Jan says, "I've been so fortunate that my immediate family all lives in Regina, except for my brother Warren and his wife, Vickie, who live in Weyburn.

"They are all supportive. The family comes to all my send-offs and celebrations. My nieces always send pictures, cards, and faxes. I really feel like any success I have is with my whole family.

"My mom and dad were probably my biggest fans. They've enjoyed the whole experience and have taken advantage of all the good spin-offs. They are very social and have got to know all my teammates' families in a pretty close way. They've enjoyed the Scott and Worlds and have gotten to know many of our competition and their families. They've kept in touch with so many of their new friends over the years."

One of Jan's biggest confidants has been her brother Warren, who is a school principal in Weyburn. He took to the game early and has always been a steady curler, representing Saskatchewan twice at the Canadian mixed, winning the sportsmanship award both times.

"He has so many insights into the game and to life in general," Jan observes. "He's always been a great believer in our team's talent and that we could go on to great heights. He used to tell me that we were good enough, and that if we could continued to believe in it, we'd have a chance. As his sister, I knew those words weren't empty phrases. Warren is careful with his praise. He means what he says.

"One of the highlights of my entire career was Brandon '93 and looking in the stands and seeing Warren right behind our sheet. I could see it in his eyes, willing us to win, and a couple of times when we had eye contact, he would nod, like we could do it. That is one image I'll always remember. It was so inspiring and gave me the confidence that we could pull it off."

Jan's husband, Frank Macera, has turned into a huge curling fan. They were married in September of 1995 and have one son – Steven – who was born in July of 1996. Frank is a good athlete, although he has never taken up the game of curling in a serious way.

His passion is football. He played for Canada's

most successful junior team, the Regina Rams, for four years. He was a defensive back who helped the Rams to a couple of National championships.

Frank understands the pressures of high-level competition, Jan says. "He is very competitive and has done well in sports. He teaches at Martin Collegiate and has helped with their football team for most of his teaching career. He understands the commitment it takes to keep your game at a certain level.

"Thank goodness he's not a competitive curler. I don't know how the other three women juggle two curlers in their families.

"He is a big support and totally understanding when I have to drag myself to the rink. Sometimes it must seem like an inconvenience, but he's always been willing to help out and do whatever it takes for our team and for me to be able to play at the most competitive level.

"Frank knew very little about curling when we first met. On one of our first dates he asked me about a draw to the ten foot (there is no such thing in curling). I guess he was trying to understand the game and relate.

"Now he gets upset if he can't watch a game. He follows all the curling on television and wants to be there for all our playdown or cash bonspiel games.

Having Steven has been interesting. When he was only a year old, Frank would bring him down to the rink so he could cheer us on. Then when Steven turned two, it got hard to watch games and babysit. Now he arranges for sitters on his own, for games he really wants to watch."

Steven has become a major part of Jan's life. She has chosen to stay home and spend as much time with him as possible. It's a part of life she really relishes, too.

Until Steven came along, there were the Bichon Frise dogs, Einstein and Boris (named after Boris Becker the famous German tennis player – the close spelling to Betker), who now play second fiddle to the newest member of the family.

Jan is quite candid when she evaluates her sporting makeup. "I'm a perfectionist, ultra-competitive and very, very emotional. The combination of those three can be my own worst enemy. Sandra, Joan, and Marcia have really helped me to be grounded a little bit more.

"I tend to live everything to the max out on the ice. I'm just a range of emotions out there. I can get really, really nervous and can get quite uptight. On the other hand, I've learned a lot about how to relax, have fun, and keep everything in perspective."

Walter and Verna Betker are pleased with the final standings at the 1993 Scott in Brandon.

THE SCOTT TOURNAMENT OF HEARTS		
TEAM	W	L
SASKATCHEWAN	9	2
MANITOBA	8	3
ONTARIO	7	4
TEAM CANADA	6	5
ALBERTA	6	5
BRITISH COLUMBIA	6	5
NOVA SCOTIA	6	5
NEWFOUNDLAND	5	6
PRINCE EDWARD ISLAND	5	6
YUKON / NWT	4	7

This is very revealing, because Jan looks so calm and cool and in control out on the ice. She has that confident look, as if everything is going to work out all right. Jan has obviously learned how to manage her emotions without giving away what's going on deep down in her stomach.

Jan feels fortunate to be on this particular team. She has a very real grasp of Team Schmirler's unique qualities. "Everyone should have an opportunity to play with my teammates, but I'm too selfish. I would never want that to happen," she laughs. Jan goes on, "They really are my three best friends. All of them are such wonderful, gifted people. They conduct themselves with such class.

"Sandra is a people person. Very friendly and outgoing. She is so genuine. What you see is what you get. She's herself, no facade or fakeness to her. As a skip, she is second to none. The best in the game. She really knows the game and, contrary to some observers' opinions, is always in control out on the ice. We tease her about being absent-minded, but she knows what she's doing out there. Sandra is a leader, she somehow has found that fine line of valuing input and taking charge. Believe me – she is the one who calls the shots.

"Joan is our positive, bubbly, upbeat energizer.

One of the strongest people I have ever met from an emotional and mental vantage point. She'll find a silver lining in any situation and it'll make sense. She rubs off on the entire team. Joan can make you feel like you can make any shot. She is instrumental to our success because of her emotional leadership.

"Marcia is the quiet, steady one out on the ice. She goes about her business and is so efficient at her position. Off the ice she loves to have fun and is one

Top left: Frank, Stephen, and Jan, with unidentified curling fan – she stays home with Stephen, when she isn't off winning championships.

Bottom left: Just making the press deadline – Adam Walter was born in August, 1999.

of the leading pranksters. I love her laugh, it is so infectious and can get us all going.

"She complements Joan in the area of positive thinking. Very intense, although she hides it well. Marcia wants to win and takes key losses very hard. Marcia is awfully determined, capable in everything she does, and extremely organized."

Jan has often wondered why their team has had so much success and why they've hung in there so long together. It's not just one dynamic but a mixture of so many things. "It probably starts with the fact that we're all at the same stages of life with young families. We can all relate to each other quite well. We're like a natural new mom's support group.

"All four of us are intensely competitive. We feed off each other. On some teams only one or two may have this intensity. We're all that way, so it naturally inspires us all.

"We're committed to the same curling and family goals. Our families are the priority and curling our main hobby. But we want to excel at our hobby and all do what it takes to succeed.

"We have a great time together. We are the best of friends. We believe in ourselves and each other.

I've got so much confidence that each player will pull her weight and give a maximum effort. If a team is in need of a comeback, I'll take these three any day. We are a team in the true sense of the word and feel we can do anything together on the curling ice."

Jan's intensity is one of the biggest intangibles she brings to the team. She stays 100 per cent focussed on the big picture, allowing nothing to deter the team from the task at hand. The most significant example of this was at their first Worlds in Geneva in 1993, where she pulled the team back on course when dissent could have crept in.

One of Jan's most bittersweet moments in curling happened in Regina at the Scott, immediately following their Olympic triumph. The bitter was not being able to curl at full capacity. The team suffered jet lag throughout the event and never could get the consistency of Nagano into their game. Within 48 hours of arriving back in Regina, they were out on the ice trying to defend their Scott title.

Jan had a conversation with her dad a couple of weeks after the Scott. "I wish the Scott was on now, I finally feel rested and ready to curl."

The sweet was the long standing ovation as they were introduced as Team Canada and the first-ever sanctioned Olympic gold medallists. To be introduced as Olympic champions was one of the highlights of her life.

Jan Betker has come a long way from her first reluctant trip to the defunct Wascana Winter Club. She has traveled a lot of kilometres and curled in scores of club games and bonspiels and has fulfilled her dream of the Scott and Worlds. She has learned to thrive on the pressure and to excel.

Her brother Warren sums up his sister's moxie quite astutely. "Maurice Richard or Gordie Howe would get the big goal in the big game. If there was two on and two out in the bottom of the ninth, you could count on a Mickey Mantle or Pete Rose. Well, my sister is like that in curling. Almost without fail, if the game is on the line and the team needs a crucial shot, she rarely, if ever, misses. Actually, I think she's even more successful than the names I've mentioned." ◉

107

Boris and Einstein filled that gap before Stephen and Adam came along. How do you say "Bichon Frise"?

Chapter Eleven

GETTING BACK
(1994-1996)

Team Schmirler had accomplished what no other Canadian women's team had ever done. As Team Canada they were champions for the second straight season, leading up to their berth at the Scott in Calgary. This meant they could once again bypass the Saskatchewan playdowns, which set them up to pursue the cash bonspiel circuit in earnest. Some observers wondered whether the team's overwhelming success would diminish their competitive instincts.

Sandra says, "I really believe the drive and the commitment were still there. We were all putting off having children for at least one more curling season. We wanted a shot at accomplishing what no other team in the world had ever done. Our team had an unbelievable opportunity to win the world three straight times. No men's or women's curling team had ever done that."

To prepare for Calgary, the women renewed their commitment to getting in as many competitive games as they could. "It was the most cash 'spiels we had ever curled in one season," says Joan. "Of course we were freed up by not having to go through the playdowns at home. But we were driven to make some money. We still didn't have major sponsorship. The team needed to make extra cash to afford the extra bonspiels."

Many cities wanted Team Canada in their major bonspiels. Having a two-time world champion would increase the attendance, the prestige of the event, and the revenue. Most bonspiels covered some of their expenses. Organizers sought to be as generous as they could, but there were extra expenses back home, with the time off work to leave Regina and curl. The team committed to seven bonspiels over an eight-week period. The first one was the Callie Kickoff Bonspiel, more of a warm-up to work the kinks out after a long summer. Team Schmirler advanced to the money round and lost to Milestone's Sharon Garratt in the semi-final. The team earned $280 for its efforts.

The next six 'spiels were major events, drawing the best women's teams from across Canada. Some American and European teams would enter as well.

The first was the Sun Life Grand Prix of Curling in Thunder Bay. Team Schmirler qualified for the final eight, which guaranteed them prize money. They advanced to the semi-final and lost to the Jennifer Jones team from Winnipeg, the reigning junior world champion. This would be Schmirler's lowest paycheck of the major bonspiel circuit – $2,500. Not bad for a weekend's worth of competition.

Sandra reflects back on the autumn of 1994 and the incredible run that was about to happen. "It was some of the best curling we had ever done. We were so steady. After Thunder Bay, all four of us entered that elusive zone, and it never seemed to leave us. The curling was so automatic and effortless. In our minds we were unbeatable."

Jan says, "It was so good, but like a blur. We were so dominant. It's like we just carried on from the 1993-94 season." She wished it could always be like that. "You know in your heart you'll never always be

in that kind of zone. Curling humbles you so quickly. We were aware it wasn't going to last forever, but you do wonder how long can it last."

The Sun Life Ladies' Classic in Saskatoon was the first dividend of being in the extended land of the zone – finishing first by defeating Prince Albert's Sherry Anderson team in the final. The win was worth $9,000.

Nova Scotia was next on the agenda, the Halifax "VG Classic" 'spiel, with the largest purse they had ever played for. Once they advanced to the qualifying round, Schmirler and company simply dominated. The final pitted them against Moncton's Leanne Perron. Team Schmirler jumped into a quick 5-0 lead and cruised to a 7-4 victory. It was worth a cool $10,000.

It was coast to coast for Team Schmirler, as Kelowna, BC, beckoned. It was another $10,000 payday as they won the Canadian Club Double Cashspiel. This pushed their earnings to just under $32,000 in only five 'spiels. To put this in perspective, even the elite teams are happy just to qualify for the

The team gets sent off to the Calgary Scott in 1995, under a banner featuring their rubber-rat mascot.

Women's curling was coming of age in the 1990s; Team Schmirler often beat competitive men's teams in bonspiels.

money. Only one out of four entries will advance to the playoff round that pays.

Team Schmirler was five for five, with three wins and two semi-final losses. There was one more 'spiel before the Christmas break. They would be the only women's entry in a field of 32 teams in Swift Current for the Dynamic Men's Cash Spiel. This event drew most of the Brier-contending teams from the curling hotbeds of Alberta and Saskatchewan – former world champion Eddie Lukowich of Calgary, Brier representatives like Eugene Hritzuk, Brad Heidt, Bob Ellert, Rod Montgomery, and close friend of Team Schmirler, Randy Woytowich of Regina.

Team Schmirler had curled against men's competitive teams in Regina on many occasions. They weren't intimidated, but inwardly wanted to make a statement. Women's curling was coming of age, but the perception for many was that the better men's teams would rarely lose to a competitive women's team. This was an opportunity to prove to the rest of the curling world how far the women's game had come.

The only fear would be if the wheels came off and they came up cold. Every curling team has gone into a bonspiel and lost all their games. It happens! The

team may be off just a bit or the team meets two or three red-hot teams in a row that can't buy a miss.

Maybe the men were a little intimidated by these four young women from Regina, as they won their first two games by scores of 9-2 and 7-2. Both men's teams, Rod Montgomery of Moose Jaw and perennial contender Bob Ellert of Assiniboia, had represented Saskatchewan at the Brier.

Team Schmirler was bringing in the crowds at the local club hosting the event. The building was filled to capacity every time the women were on the ice.

Marcia was pleasantly surprised by the city's support. "We knew we were a novelty to a degree. Whenever we curled, 90 per cent of the crowd would gather behind our sheet or in the stands on the ice by our game."

Joan laughs about it. "It was funny to see. The organizers said the building would start to lean to wherever we were curling. Everybody wanted to watch us against the men. It was a lot of fun, especially as we kept winning."

The team lost their next game to Swift Current's Ron Kloschinsky, which dropped them down to the B Event. It was a minor blip. Two-time provincial

"I was struggling a bit going in to the Scott, feeling tired – we tried to take advantage of as many curling opportunities as we could."

champion Randy Woytowich was up next. They had played Randy's team more than any other men's team over the years.

Sandra tells a story that occurred before this game, about something that could have thrown a serious wrench into their team harmony. "My future husband, Shannon, was curling in Prince Albert in the provincial mixed finals. It was the furthest he had ever advanced in curling. I wanted to be there to support him. Shannon was so supportive of my curling that I felt I owed him as much.

"I thought since we dropped down to the B Event that it would be tough for us to keep winning. Woytowich was so tough that I reasoned our chances were slim in beating them. We'd have to win anywhere from three to five games to qualify for the money. We could only afford one more loss. The odds seemed pretty big.

"I was hoping that the team wouldn't mind if I drove up to Prince Albert to support Shannon if we lost. My reasoning was that if Woytowich beat us, we would drop to the C event and then it gets to be an even longer road to the playoff round.

"The team wasn't overly impressed with my

desire to leave and be with Shannon. They reminded me that the team was in my name, I was the skip, and Swift Current wanted to see all four of us curl. They had paid our full expenses to create interest for the fans. The team felt we made a commitment to the 'spiel and that leaving wasn't a very good idea.

"In hindsight, I should have shared my motivation for wanting to leave. I'd been in some relationships where my partners seldom showed interest in my curling. I know what it's like to not have your partner's support. The other three had terrific husbands who supported them every step of the way. I felt like I was letting Shannon down, although that wasn't the case from his perspective. I thought my loyalties were being challenged between team and my personal life.

"I told the team that if we beat Randy, I'd stay, the implication being that I'd jump in my car and drive to Prince Albert if we lost. The curling gods must have been with us. We beat Woytowich to advance to the B semis. Not that the next game or two would be easier, but Woytowich was one of the pre-bonspiel favourites.

"It's the one time we never really talked through

the issue and came to a consensus. Luckily it was cleared up by our win. Shannon's team kept winning as well. They finished second."

This could have evolved into a volatile situation. It's one of those lessons that reminded the team of the importance of crystal-clear communication. These circumstances have never come up again, yet Sandra knows how she'd respond if they ever did. "The bottom line is to approach it differently, not by the seat of our pants. To be very clear with our team decisions before an event starts. Then to stick with whatever decision we agree on."

The team went on to win their next two games to win a B-qualifier. A statement for women's curling had been made. They went into the eight-team sudden-death money round with an impressive 5-1 record.

They met Calgary's Mickey Pendergast foursome in the championship quarter-final. The Calgary team won 7-6 in an extra end. Team Schmirler finished at 5-2, outscoring their male counterparts 53-34.

The Christmas break was on the horizon. These six bonspiels not only helped pay expenses but put a few extra gifts under their Christmas trees. The final bonspiel before the Calgary Scott was a January trip to Berne, Switzerland, where they went as defending champions of the Berner Cup. The women were looking forward to their Swiss curling holiday. Berne held many sweet memories on and off the ice. It was a perfect preparation for the Scott and the chance to jell even more as a team. It was just the four of them.

Once again, the team advanced to the final. Sandra says it was an ideal time away for the team, but, "We lost the final. I had an opportunity to throw the last rock to win it. I flat out missed my shot and lost. It's very disappointing when the opportunity presents itself and you don't deliver as the skip."

Myriam Ott of Berne won the

"There's no other word to describe what we've been through but fun." Rumours of the team breaking up in 1994-95 were just that – rumours.

final 5-4. Both finalists received gold necklaces and pendants for advancing to the showdown game.

Ardith Stephanson of the *Leader-Post* interviewed Joan on their arrival back from Switzerland, approaching her about rumours that the team might break up and go their separate ways if they won their third straight Canadian title. "I have entertained that thought personally, of quitting at the top," McCusker said. "All of us have felt the struggle of having everybody wanting to knock you off. You do get tired of people cheering against you. If you were to quit, and leave your last competitive game on a winning note, it's an entertaining thought, but to do that we'd have to win Canadians. That's a lot of big wins away.

"It would be very hard, because we have had so much fun. There's no other word to describe what we've been through but fun. It's not something we actually talk about. We entertain the thought more of winning again. Why look at it negatively?"

These rumours were primarily just that – rumours. All four were hoping to have a child in the next year or so. That might entail some time off from curling. They were taking it a year at a time.

Joan was being realistic about the team's future without revealing too much of their individual family plans. They knew a child could extend the time off and a new teammate might fit in a little too well. They respected each other to a fault. No one on the

113

team wanted to slow down the momentum if the others wanted to continue.

Part of Team Schmirler's philosophy off the ice is that family will dictate life's major decisions, and not their favourite recreational pastime. This understanding has always guided the team.

The Saskatchewan women's provincials were held at the Highland Curling Club in Regina. Naturally, the team went down to watch the eight finalists.

"It was very hard to watch for a number of reasons," according to Jan. "The curling was very good and I started to wonder, how can we keep up with this calibre? One of these teams was going to represent Saskatchewan at the Scott. It was pretty bizarre."

Sandra says, "The nervousness and apprehension started to kick in. For me, it was like watching a Scott or world semi-final, with us waiting for the winner. I kept thinking I shouldn't be watching." Sherry

Anderson of Prince Albert defended her title on a last-rock win over Michelle Schneider. For Schneider's team of Atina Ford, Sandi McNabb, and Cindy Ford, it was their first loss in five final-game appearances in a provincial final.

Saskatchewan was going to the Scott with two pre-tournament favourites. After watching the provincials, Team Schmirler was reminded of the enormous depth of Saskatchewan curling. In the week leading up to their third consecutive Scott, the team had their daily practices and meetings.

Joan was not feeling good about her game. "I was struggling a bit going in. I was feeling tired. It had been an outstanding year on the ice. We tried to take advantage of as many curling opportunities as we could. It was catching up to me. I wondered if the others were feeling the same. We have these high standards and expectations and I needed to talk. I felt we could get it back on track. We all did. So we sat down at the Callie."

Sandra was one of the first to speak. "I asked the team, are we ready?"

Joan probed a little further. "I said, let's identify the possible distractions. We talked about the 'three-peat' expectations from the media and even our supporters. I said I hate it when people are cheering hard against us. We attempted to talk through the distracting anxieties each of us was feeling."

In looking back on their pre-Scott preparations, Sandra said, "We tried to prepare as best we could. But we all agreed we didn't properly prepare. We weren't thorough enough. We assumed we were, but we missed a few key elements. I thought we were ready for all the three-peat media attention. I knew they would focus on us being the defending champs, but it was way more than I was used to. I was interviewed every game, win or lose.

"The 70-minute time clock was in play, with two time outs. We never even talked about it and it would haunt us in our very first game.

"We always make an effort to become friends with the venue, to be part of the atmosphere and become familiar with our surroundings. We just gave it a cursory view.

"We prided ourselves at being able to minimize outside distractions...we slipped in that major area in Calgary."

Curling politics – Marcia curled 88 per cent, six points higher than any other lead, but still didn't make the all-star team.

"There aren't any excuses for what was about to transpire, but Calgary 1995 reminded us that we were still learning. You could say it was a character-building Scott with some highlights along the way."

The 1995 Calgary Scott Tournament of Hearts was held in the Max Bell Arena, the same place Schmirler and Betker had played at the 1987 Olympic trial. It was an intimate venue, holding about 2,500 spectators. Being the first team to wear Canada's colours for the second straight time was an exciting honour.

Game number one was against their arch-rivals from Manitoba – Winnipeg's Connie Laliberte. Mark Miller of the Calgary *Sun* reported, "It was billed as a battle of the curling heavyweights – a preview of an expected playoff battle and the rematch of last year's Scott finals. It didn't disappoint."

The Manitoba champion won an old-fashioned, low-scoring match 4-3. Laliberte had hammer coming home, yet Sandra had a perfect opportunity to put a lot of pressure on Connie for her last shot. The time clock came into play. When Sandra came to shoot there was only five seconds left on the clock.

The clock was not Schmirler's friend that night. "I kept thinking, draw, draw, draw, and rushed my last shot," reveals Sandra, looking back. "That game and the circumstances set the tone for the week. I'm still ticked at myself at not preparing for the time clock well enough. I have no one to blame but myself."

"We prided ourselves at being able to minimize the outside distractions and focus on the task at hand," Joan comments. "We slipped in that major area in Calgary. We allowed ourselves to centre our thoughts on the outside circumstances that we couldn't control rather than concentrating on winning games.

"We started to complain about the venue, the Team Canada set-up with all the expectations, the crowd, the media attention, and whatever else. We had faced these things before; the difference was where we chose to focus our attention. Even though we were two-time world champions, we still had to learn or re-learn some lessons."

Jan agreed: "I curled brutal in that first game. We had a lot of chances. We threw a lot of junk up in the first part of the game and never thought through proper clock management. I wasn't ticked at losing, but at how we lost."

The team wasn't in their desired "mental zone," but they had won important games on straight grit and determination in the past. The commitment and desire to three-peat was strong. They had to work through whatever was holding them back. There was no panic, but the seeds of distraction were watered in that first game.

The team rebounded with two wins the following day, beating BC's Marla Geiger 7-5 on Sandra's last-rock draw to the button.

Ardith Stephanson of the *Leader-Post* got some insightful post-game comments from Sandra: "We adjusted after our Manitoba loss. They give you the FGZ and then take away five minutes. You can't play the FGZ when you're trying to bank time. It's boring curling, but that's the way it goes."

There was no joy on Team Schmirler after a loss to Saskatchewan compatriot Sherry Anderson.

Jan had this to say – "It was going to happen sometime this week, that we'd be tight on time. We learned our lesson. We played the first five ends wide open. We had no junk and we tried to have 40 extra minutes left at the half."

Still eating away at Jan was the Manitoba game. "It's not worth the risk. You can't throw a pressure shot with five seconds left. It's ridiculous. But we're not going to win them all. It's just a loss and that's all it is."

Joan was privately hoping that a corner had been turned. "We needed that win over BC. That was a big win, especially the way we won it, with Sandra drawing to the pot. That was a confidence shot. She just put the ice down and said, 'Let's do it.'

"We were back to the old Team Canada that played with a lot of confidence. If we made that shot, we knew things would come together."

Dawn Moses's team from the Territories got caught in the aftershocks of that confidence-builder game as Team Schmirler blasted them 9-2.

The team was getting more consistent, with a pair of wins on Monday over New Brunswick veteran Heidi Hanlon and Québec newcomer Guylaine Crispo,

upping their record to 4-1. They were in second place, one game behind Laliberte. The 1995 Scott adopted for the first time the four-team Page Playoff system, rather than the three teams from previous years. The team was still in control of their destiny.

The roots of the Page system go "down under" to New Zealand and the world softball championships. First and second place teams meet in one game, with the winner advancing to the final and the loser going to the semi-final. Then the third- and fourth-place teams play each other, with the loser eliminated and the winner advancing to the semi-final to play the loser of the first and second place showdown.

The Page system was adopted to allow an extra playoff team, and also to give the top two teams an extra life in case of a loss. It also means two extra games for national television.

Tuesday morning was an all-Saskatchewan confrontation, Sherry Anderson wearing the green and white, and Team Schmirler in Team Canada's red and white.

A conservative, low-scoring affair saw Anderson's Prince Albert team win 4-2. Schmirler's team walked off the ice in a none-too-happy mood.

Theresa Kirkpatrick reported in the Saskatoon *Star-Phoenix* – "Rarely does Sandra lose control...after her loss, she picked up her gym bag and blew through the crowd in the tunnel at Calgary's Max Bell Arena, grim-faced.

"'We were ticked off at ourselves because we played stupid and you can't win this thing when you play stupid. We were one up playing five without hammer and we kind of farted that away and that's not the way to win games,' explained the skip."

"'I was disappointed we didn't play with the confidence we know we have. We played scared and it showed,' said McCusker. 'I wasn't mad, I just thought, what if we lose that momentum-confidence thing, and where can we get it back?'"

They didn't lose because of low averages. Sandra curled 85 per cent in the loss and Marcia was challenging the Scott record for weekly averages among the leads by curling an overall 88 per cent. She would finish the week 6 per cent higher than her nearest competitor. Most amazing was that Marcia wasn't picked as the all-star lead, which proves that even curling has politics.

Nova Scotia had the unenviable task of facing a mad-at-itself team in the evening draw. Team Schmirler generally responds to a shoot-yourself-in-the-foot loss with big wins. This time was no exception, as they beat Virginia Jackson's crew.

Wednesday brought two more games, the first a sound 8-2 thumping of Newfoundland's Laura Phillips. The afternoon game was a battle with second-place Alberta. Returning to the national curling scene was Cathy Borst's Edmonton sharpshooters. Cathy had won two straight Canadian juniors womens titles in the late 1970s. She never totally gave up curling but cut back the bonspieling to begin her family. Team Schmirler pulled off a critical 9-5 win to move in to a second-place tie with the host province.

That night, the team enjoyed a mid-week supper with their families at the new Eau Claire Market near downtown Calgary. It was their opportunity to touch base with their biggest supporters and reload emotionally for the conclusion of the week.

Thursday was the final day of the round robin.

"Calgary 1995 reminded us that we were still learning...it was a character-building Scott, with some highlights along the way."

Tean Schmirler had to win one of their two games to guarantee a playoff spot. First up was rookie Rebecca Jean MacPhee of Prince Edward Island. Being young and from the smallest province, they became the sentimental crowd favourites, curling their best game of the week to defeat Schmirler 7-5.

"We never seem to do it the easy way," commented Marcia. "We had Alison Goring of Ontario for our final game. We were both 7-3 going in. It was simple. We win – we're in and Ontario's out. Ontario wins – they would have made the playoffs and we would have finished out."

Team Canada came out smoking against the former Canadian champion, winning and securing a playoff spot. Manitoba was first with an impressive 10-1 record. Alberta, Prince Edward Island, and Team Canada were all tied for second at 8-3. The three teams went into a special tie-breaker round to determine the second, third, and fourth seeds. Alberta dropped PEI to fourth place, then advanced to play Team Canada.

Schmirler and company beat Borst 6-2 to clinch

117

second place. Next they had to play Manitoba, with the winner advancing to Sunday's final. The loser would play the winner of Alberta and PEI in the semi-final. Team Canada had two chances to get to the final.

Connie Laliberte pulled off a close 6-4 decision to advance to the final. It was a frustratingly close game, right down to the final stone. Manitoba started with last rock and controlled it the whole way. The score was tied on four separate occasions…1-1; 2-2; 3-3; 4-4.

There was one last chance for Team Schmirler to three-peat – their third meeting against Cathy Borst's Alberta champions. At this level it is nearly impossible to beat the same team three times in a row. Borst's team curled well and finished off Team Canada 7-5. It was close until the eighth end. Sandra tried a draw to cut down Borst's chances. Her rock quietly slid through the house and Cathy drew in for four crucial points to go up 7-3.

"What a sick feeling, watching Sandra throw that rock a little too hard," says Joan of the critical eighth end. "It was over and we knew it. We tried to put on a brave face, but we knew a comeback was near impossible. I'm proud of the fact we didn't show any quit. We scored two in the ninth to make it closer. But to steal two coming home against a hot team is pretty tough."

It was over.

Jan had been saying it all week, but especially before the semi-final. "It was like we were the lambs being led to slaughter. The fans were against us, and it affected us a bit. We had really become the target."

"It was a tough crowd," echoes Sandra. "You'd hear people yelling from the stands, 'It's a rat-free zone,' referring to our mascot. You know in your heart it's not with

malice, but the realization is that people want you to lose."

"Maybe it was my emotional state," says Joan. "But it bothered me when a good percentage of fans started singing the 'Na, Na, Na, Na, Good-bye' song. Fans that cheer against you in curling tend to be very polite. It threw me a bit, but I guess it could be seen as a compliment as well."

Marcia was equally affected. "It hurt to know it was over. There was also a sense of relief that someone else would have to wear Team Canada's colours and the demands that go along with it. It was time to start our families as well. Make no mistake, we still wanted to win the red and white back again."

Sandra said the media attention immediately after the game was surprising. "They swarmed me. I wasn't ready for it. Their home province had just beaten us, so I assumed that the attention would be on Alberta.

Sandra was fuming – "We were ticked off at ourselves because we played stupid and you can't win this thing when you play stupid."

118

Team Schmirler gets together with one of their most consistent rivals, the Connie Laliberte rink from Winnipeg, at the 1995 European Masters in Stockholm.

"I felt like a little *peon*. I almost wondered if the media was hoping for a juicy tidbit," she said in frustration.

"There were questions like, 'How do you feel about losing your chance to three-peat? Will your team stick together?'

"My main goal was not to look like an idiot on camera."

The team couldn't wait to hide in the dressing room for some peace and quiet and reflection. Joan says, "We all felt pure relief that our reign was over. We talked for a bit and asked our driver where we could go out for a quiet dinner with our men and parents.

"She found us this great little Italian restaurant. It was just what the doctor ordered."

Carla Scholz, a skilled club curler with a moderate passion for the game, was their driver for the week. She was good for the team because she never tried to offer advice, nor was she star-struck at being with world champions. Her goal was to support the team with her natural humour and to show the expected Calgary hospitality.

Carla says, "After their last loss, I found one of our favourite restaurants. Good thing I was the designated driver. I think they let out three years of pressure. There was only about a dozen of us around the table. We ordered our various pastas.

"They ordered the best wine, which of course was the most expensive. Four or five flasks, to start with. We were there for most of the evening. The waiter kept replacing the wine and the various drinks people were having. Nobody was paying attention.

"Finally it came time for Sandra to pay the bill. It's a good thing they had such a good year on the money trail."

Looking back on that night, Sandra laughs. "It came to over $1,000. For a small-town Saskatchewan girl I almost choked. But we needed a night away like that. We laughed, joked and reminisced. I still get ribbed about the bill. All I remember is signing a whole bunch of traveller's cheques. It seemed like it would never end."

The final continued the following day with Manitoba's Connie Laliberte against Alberta's Cathy Borst. The five playoff games proved to be too much for the Albertans, and Laliberte made a routine take-out in the last end to capture the 1995 Scott Tournament of Hearts Championships – her third Canadian title.

The 1995 Scott was a valuable experience, used many times in the future as a reference point in the lessons learned.

"We had forgotten what a privilege it was to participate," explains Sandra. "We had neglected to maintain our appreciation for what's become the most successful women's sporting event in Canada. We were becoming a little spoiled by our success. We lost our focus on curling and let distractions dictate where we directed our energies. I vowed that it would never happen again."

In 1995, Pam Bryden from Regina was subbing for Joan in Stockholm.

The 1995-96 season would have a different look to the line-up. Joan, planning her second child, was taking the year off, and the team recruited Regina's Pamela Bryden to replace her. In her late 20s at the time, she had been one of the province's better junior players.

In June of 1995, Joan was asked to be a player representative for the upcoming Olympic trials to be held in Brandon in the fall of 1997. Sandra explains, "Joan made a decision to quit for the season. It was an open-ended kind of deal. She went off to the Olympic trials meeting. To say she came back excited would be a huge understatement.

"She said the final format would involve a 10-team round robin with playoffs. There would be four qualifying bonspiels, the 1996 and 1997 Scott winners, a special best-of-three playoff between the 1994 and 1995 Scott winners – that was us against Laliberte – in December in Thunder Bay, two top-money-winner spots, and a final eight-team playoff for a last chance spot.

"Joan thought it was perfect for us. If we claimed a spot in December, we could take the year off and have babies. We wouldn't have to worry about trying to win a bonspiel. We had two years until the trials began.

"Joan would go with us to a 'spiel we were invited to in Sweden and then, a few weeks later, curl in Thunder Bay. Pam Bryden would fill in for our league play, provincial playdowns, and bonspiels. We'd still try to get back to the Scott, but Thunder Bay would become the team's focus."

The team only entered three major cash 'spiels, cutting back more than half from the season before. They went back to Calgary for the Autumn Gold, pocketing $2,200 for a quarter-final loss. Pam Bryden was a capable curler and played as well as, or even better than, expected.

"Pam is a quality person," Jan comments. "She is so nice. We made a real point of allowing her to be herself, and I think she was. She was different from Joan. Quieter personality, with a good sense of humour. We didn't expect her to be the emotional spark plug.

"I tried to be 'the Joan.' Big mistake, because Joan and I are so different in temperament. That didn't last long, thank goodness. We had to find a new way to compensate for missing Joan's emotional leadership.

"It's tough to break in a new curler when you've been together as long as we had been. I don't know if anyone could have stepped in and made an immediate impact in terms of chemistry. Pam did great under the circumstances. She gets full marks.

"But we weren't the same team. We struggled in the first part of the season, yet you could sense that we could click at any time."

The team curled another 'spiel in Regina, the SaskPower Ladies Curling Classic, which drew the top teams from across the country. It was the same result as Calgary. This time the quarter-final cheque was worth $2,500.

Joan rejoined the team for the European Masters in Stockholm, Sweden, alternating with Pam to keep both of them sharp.

Joan remembers the good times in Sweden. "I was the designated driver for the week. I was pregnant. Jan was pregnant as well, but didn't know it yet. We did a lot of tourist stuff and curled fairly well."

Sandra says, "We just had a good time doing things we wouldn't normally do. None of us are horse riders, but we heard about these Icelandic horses that walk a special way. It was loads of fun. We had to wear these funny-looking helmets, and not being too confident around horses just added to the laughs."

The team finished third, losing to the team they were preparing for. Connie Laliberte beat them in a semi-final.

Sandra remembers the turning point as if it were yesterday. "I made an absolutely brutal shot in the sixth end. I threw too hard and hit a straight spot and barely ticked Connie's stone. I left her an open hit for four. Connie made it look routine." But the loss added to their earnings; they pocketed $3,500 for reaching the semi-finals.

The week preceding the Olympic trials playoff berth with Laliberte was not a good one for Sandra. She says it may have been the time she has most doubted her ability to skip. "I felt like a lost puppy, or a lost soul, out on the ice. Our team wasn't where it needed to be to challenge Connie. The consistency wasn't there. I thought I had lost any ice-reading ability I had. I was getting fooled too often and not catching on fast enough.

"Joan had been away. She had that God-given ability to snap me into reality. She could make me feel like I was the best skip in the world. I could be curling the absolute worst and she could keep my head focussed on the game and not my doubts. Thank God she'd be back with us in Thunder Bay.

"We played Joan's sister, Cathy Trowell, in the Tuesday night all-star league. I remember looking around and being consumed with feelings of insecurity. I honestly thought the team could do better without me.

"I would be driving around Regina and just burst into tears. I thought I was losing it. Out of desperation, I called a team meeting on the Wednesday night. We were leaving in a couple of days. I didn't know what to do.

"We had a pretty intense conversation. I shared all my thoughts and doubts. I even told them to go without me. I said, 'I can't play.' The expectations in my head were so overwhelming. This was our shot to qualify and ease up for a full year and to seriously try and start families.

"Good old Joan finally asked the right question to put things in perspective."

Joan zeroed in on the dilemma – What was the worst thing that could happen. The question started

Checking out the unique stride of the Iceland ponies on the Stockholm trip.

121

to snap Sandra back into a healthier mind space.

"We lose! Whatever happens, happens. It's not the end of our lives. Maybe we get a second chance to qualify, maybe we don't, but we've said all along it's our families that are the number-one priority. Curling is our hobby, not our life.

"It took so much pressure off. I knew the team was with me, even if I didn't play up to my potential. I went to Thunder Bay really loose. I wanted to win as much as ever, but I guess I needed to hear that, win or lose, my identity as a person shouldn't be dominated by whether I curl well or not. The people who really care about me are going to love and support me regardless."

The Port Arthur Curling Club hosted the first opportunity for a team to qualify for the Olympic trials to be held two years later in Brandon. Even though Saskatchewan and Manitoba teams were playing off in Ontario, attendance at the games was large. This was another sign that women's curling was coming of age.

The very first end of game one helped Sandra get the old feeling back. "I was facing two stones with last rock. I had to hit and stick against two. It was a big shot I didn't want to face so early in the game. A miss and we give up two. A half-shot and they still get one. I threw it perfect and we were up by one. I remember thinking, 'I can still do it.'"

Team Schmirler controlled game one from that point on, winning in an extra end with a skip's ideal last shot, an open draw to anywhere in the house. Game two was very close until Connie broke it open in the ninth end. The best-of-three would come down to a one-game showdown.

Team Schmirler was curling up to their A-game standards. Even though they lost game two, they felt that, overall, they were outcurling their Manitoba rivals.

The final game was very conservative, with

122

The team stayed in a chalet as guests of Masters organizers Lennart and Lena Olby.

hammer decided in a non-traditional manner – no coin toss but a skip's draw to the house. Marcia remembers this seemingly-insignificant turning point. "Joan and I jumped on it right from the point of Sandra releasing it. We swept it hard the whole way and got it right to the four-foot. We got our last rock."

The team got two points early and never lost the advantage of last rock, meaning they were never losing when they didn't have hammer. Laliberte never took advantage of the FGZ and played very defensively. They were up coming home with hammer and the team gave Sandra her favourite kind of last-rock opportunity – an open hit to win. All she needed was a piece of the opposition's stone. In this scenario a half-shot is a whole shot. Sandra threw it clean and sealed the victory. The Schmirler women won the game 4-2 and were off to the Olympic trials in Brandon.

Sandra says the impact of what they had done never really sank in until a post-game meeting with the Canadian Curling Association (CCA). "Gerry Peckham congratulated us on being the first of ten teams to qualify. He casually reminded us that our spot was secure and that we didn't have to go to a tough qualifying bonspiel to make it.

"It meant we could do some serious family planning without the pressure of trying to qualify for the trials. Joan was pregnant. Jan had recently found out she was pregnant. I knew Marcia and Kerry were making it a priority. Shannon and I really wanted a baby. Not to sound trite, but it's like the curling gods were smiling down on us.

"We left Thunder Bay on quite a high. Our curling was like old times. I felt like my old self. I was so proud of our team. Joan had worked so hard to get ready for Thunder Bay in the preceding weeks and now she could take a curling sabbatical. We were all looking forward to the Christmas break. Then it was playdowns."

The Saskatchewan Scott playdowns were like a tribute to the intestinal fortitude of this team. Walter Betker summed it up best: "Everything went wrong down the playdown trail and they still came within one or two shots of going back to the national championship."

They qualified out of the A side in Regina, with Pam Bryden replacing Joan at second. The south-erns were back in Shaunavon. Marcia got very sick and had to be replaced by Joan's sister, Karen Inglis. To top it off, Jan was pregnant and feeling the energy drain. They struggled, yet qualified out of the C Event to advance to the provincials in Tisdale.

The frozen tundra of Lambeau Field in Green Bay, Wisconsin, would have been a more comfortable location for the eight-team final. Tisdale is a very progressive northern Saskatchewan community, but was in the middle of a -40 degree deep freeze for the entire playdowns.

Team Schmirler played the hand they were dealt. Marcia was still sick, so Karen Daku, a quality curler from Regina, filled in. For a team that thrives on togetherness as an advantage, this would bring their yearly total to seven teammates. Jan was having trouble sleeping because of her growing baby. Karen and Pamela gave it their best effort, with Sandra making big shots and adjusting to her new front end.

They won their first three games to win the A Event, advanced to the B final, and lost to the eventual provincial winner, Sherry Scheirich of Saskatoon. Sandra says, "It was the turning point. We were five up after three ends and blew it." They lost to Scheirich again in the C Event final. Schmirler would have to beat her twice to claim the provincial title, but "Scheirich beat us for the third straight time," says Sandra. "They curled great all week and deserved to represent Saskatchewan.

"They had been knocking on the door for a good handful of years. Jan and I were relieved it was over. We were totally spent emotionally and physically. I felt for Karen and especially Pamela. They were extremely disappointed to be only a game away from going to the Scott.

"It was a rough time between Shaunavon and Tisdale because we were so worried for Marcia. She was in pretty rough shape. We are like sisters, and it hurt not to be in Regina to support her."

The year was over and the team would be reunited for the 1996-97 season. They would crank it up and aim for their third Canadian title. And the pressure to get to the Olympic trials was off. They would let the other contenders worry about that. It was time to relax, have a baby or two, and get that red and white maple leaf back on their backs. ◉

Chapter Twelve
SANDRA

"**I** was nineteen years old and curling in a major cash bonspiel up in Thunder Bay, Ontario. The drawmaster designed the draw for the men and women to be on the ice at the same time, even though the 'spiel was separate. Our junior team was drawn on a sheet beside Sandra Schmirler. They had just won their second straight world championship a few months earlier.

"Our team was in awe. To be on a sheet beside the best women's team in the world. The mystique of this team was unbelievable. As a skip, I watched Sandra come out onto the ice. No fanfare, but for me it was a special moment. It is so fascinating to watch them curl."

These comments are not from a young, upcoming Canadian female skip, but from Mike Peplinski, who skipped two Wisconsin-based men's teams to the world junior curling championship (including a bronze at the 1994 Sofia, Bulgaria, Worlds). He currently lives in Eau Claire, Wisconsin, and curls third for Tim Sommerville's team that finished fourth at the Nagano Olympics.

Sandra and her team have raised the women's side of curling to a level where both young men and women seek to emulate their style and demeanor, bridging not only the gender gap but international boundaries as well.

Sandra has become one of the most recognized athletes in Canada since that first world title in 1993. Her face has been in advertisements. Television promos for curling usually have at least one shot of Sandra's face or of her throwing a rock with her almost flawless delivery. Being the skip usually brings more exposure than other members of the team enjoy, although to Sandra it's always team, because she realizes the important contributions of her three friends and teammates.

The most successful Canadian women's skip in history hails from Biggar, Saskatchewan, an attractive community about an hour west of Saskatoon.

Sandra grows up a sports star and graduates from Biggar High School, here flanked by grad twins, Shelly and Kelly Dielson.

Travellers are greeted at the town limits by a very catchy sign saying, "New York is Big, but This is Biggar." T-shirts and coffee mugs displaying the slogan can be bought in various businesses throughout the town.

Beside that sign is another one proclaiming "Biggar, Saskatchewan – Home of Sandra Schmirler." A subheading explains, "World Curling Champion and Olympic Champion." The years of these four championships are listed below, with space for a few more. Someone in Biggar must have known Sandra wouldn't just settle for one world championship.

Sandra's love for curling began at the local Biggar Curling Club on the corner of Ontario and First Avenue East, next to the Biggar Jubilee Stadium, home to all the town's hockey teams and figure skaters. It looks like most other rural curling clubs in western Canada: reasonable-sized parking lot; giant Quonset-type building; artificial ice plant in the back; and a small entrance into the club. It doesn't say "The Sandra Schmirler Curling Club." It doesn't even say "Biggar Curling Club." Sandra wouldn't want it any other way.

Sandra has firmly held on to her prairie roots. As Lindsay Sparkes has said, "Sandra and her team are just four little girls from Saskatchewan. They have maintained their humility and charm. They all, and especially Sandra, have been thrust into the spotlight.

"She has no cockiness to her. With all of their accomplishments, they have kept such perspective. Sandra knows they are very fortunate. She has that kind of wonder and amazement at their success and just keeps working so hard at staying competitive. Success hasn't changed who she is."

Sandra's mother, Shirley Schmirler, still lives in the same house on the east end of Biggar that Sandra and her two sisters grew up in. Her father, Art, lived there as well, until his death in April of 1999. There is a greenhouse in their backyard, along with a mini fish pond for their goldfish. Shirley says, "We've had people from out of town park in front of our house and take pictures. At first I wondered why, because it's an ordinary house. Then I remember, this is the house Sandra grew up in. Then, I still wonder why."

Sandra's mom goes on to say, "We were a very ordinary family. Even boring, sometimes." But this ordinary upbringing is the stuff Sandra is made of.

In an interview before his passing, Art, along with Shirley, graciously shared their family philosophy. "We emphasized values that were based on honesty, hard work, healthy relationships, getting an education, and trying your best. We always said your best is whatever you can honestly do. If a C was your best and it was an honest effort, we could live with it. But if an A was their best and they underachieved, we'd encourage our girls to pick up the slack. Education was a very high priority.

"In our house all we expected in terms of education was that the girls get a piece of paper. University, tech school, hairdressing, it didn't matter, but get some skill to use or fall back on. Find something they enjoyed and pursue it.

"We were fairly strict and tried to live our values in front of our girls. Sometimes I wonder if it was easier in the 1950s and 1960s than it is for parents today to enforce your values. Not as many conflicting voices as today. We really tried to make our family the priority."

Sandra acknowledges that "the family is real close. I'm the youngest of three girls. My two sisters are married and both live near Calgary. Bev lives in Airdrie and Carol lives on a farm near Acme. They are two of my biggest supporters, along with their husbands and children."

Growing up in Biggar provided a nearly perfect sporting environment for Sandra. "In a smaller town,

the kids have to be versatile when it comes to sports," explained Art. "Most of the children are involved in sports and play as many different kinds as they can. In each sport, the kids play many different positions to fill out a roster. I think it makes for a smarter, more well-rounded athlete, especially if they move on to higher levels."

Biggar is known as an athletic town in an extremely sports-conscious province. It has provincial contenders and champions in hockey, baseball, fastball, figure skating, and, of course, curling. High school sports such as football, volleyball, basketball, track, and badminton produce many athletes who compete at the provincial level.

Sandra wanted to play them all. She excelled at volleyball, fastball, badminton, and even swimming, winning many Saskatchewan summer swim course events and medals at the 1976 Saskatchewan Summer Games in Swift Current. She did track, mostly to get a day or two off from school: "I hated to run, just hated it, any sport but running track. I wanted to play hockey, but that's where my mom put her foot down fairly hard. I was 10 years ahead of my time, for girls to play hockey with the guys."

She feels she got her intense competitive streak from her dad and her grandmother McLeod. Her dad was more of a recreational curler, but played to win and had that never-give-up streak in him. He loved to play pool and often took Sandra down to the pool hall with him, propping her up to watch with a bag of chips. She must have been paying attention, as her now-famous seventh-end Olympics trial shot was as close to billiards as one could get on the curling ice. Actually, many top-level curlers are pretty adept with the pool cue; it reinforces the angles one must play in curling.

Grandmother McLeod, a very good curler in her day, often talked to Sandra about her curling days and the fun her teams would have. She had a reputation as a wily, crafty player who could compete with the best, and she loved to do well and win.

Sandra was a good student, her mom says. "She became a very good student when she chose to apply herself. I remember at the end of Grade 8 how she said it was stupid to make the honour roll when she didn't

Sara is already sceptical of photographers, as Sandra speaks with curling foe turned curling commentator Linda Moore at the 1998 Scott in Regina.

qualify. I wasn't impressed, to say the least, because Sandra was more than able to make the roll. We had a little mother-and-daughter chat. I ended it with, 'All your dad and I expect is your best, just make the effort.'

"Sandra never made reference to it again. A year later she came home with a certificate signifying she had made the honour roll. All she said was, 'That's for you, Mom.'

school provincial title as a third for Anita Silvernagle, then Anita Barber. Sandra loved to play third and would have been content to play that position forever.

She registered at the University of Saskatchewan in the general arts program, hoping to go into computer science. "I gave that up pretty quick, as I'm about totally computer-illiterate. I couldn't really get

The Schmirler Clan – Sandra's dad, Art, passed away in April of 1999. "We were fairly strict," her mom Shirley says.

"Her marks stayed up there through high school. She won three awards at her high school grad, for best overall student, spirit of youth award – Sandra says it was for the childish streak in her – and the sports award. We were proud of her, not just for the awards, but because she tried her best. The rewards aren't always visible, but this time they were. It was the icing on the cake, that's all."

Curling became Sandra's sport of choice as her high school days drew to a close. She won one high

interested, so I went into phys ed, and got my Bachelor's in physical education with a major in recreational administration."

Sandra curled on the U of S team her first two years in Saskatoon. She got a lot of games in, with some limited local successes.

During Sandra's last two years in Saskatoon, Carol Davis invited her to curl on a more competitive team. Heather McMillan and Laurie Secord-Humble made up the front end. In 1983-84 the team advanced all the way to the provincials, but were finally eliminated by Lori McGeary's foursome. In 1984-85, the team curled a lot of games, had a little bonspiel success, but couldn't duplicate their success of the previous year.

After university, Sandra moved to Regina. This was at the time Kathy Fahlman was putting together a competitive team and found out about Sandra, who became her new third. Jan had already been a part of this team and was content to play the second spot. But a new friendship was hatched, as Sandra met a curling soulmate, someone with similar intensity, drive, passion for the game, and even curling philosophy.

Their first season brought bonspiel success but early disappointment on the playdown circuit. Sandra comments, "It was a good year, with high expectations, but I saw a side of myself I didn't like. We had lost a key game in city playdowns. We played stupid and lost. Sometimes you lose and you are outplayed. That's easy to get over. We plain old, flat-out, blew this particular game. I stormed out of the Callie, slammed a door, and showed no class. It was the first time I showed a lot of emotion from a negative perspective. I think it gave me a bit of a reputation as a hothead, for a while. I hope I've grown up some since, because I look back on that with big-time regret."

"Her fire within is so strong," Sandra's mom observes. "She loves to compete and loves to win."

For the most part the "Callie incident" and "the Swallow story" are anomalies along the journey, with Sandra regretting both tremendously. But without the inner fire there would be no Team Schmirler story. Sandra and her team have matured over the years to a deserving reputation of class, sportsmanship, humility, and even self-effacement.

As a former team driver observed, "Her appeal is her humanness and a down-to-earth

way about her. She acknowledges her flaws. Yet she is high on consistently showing sportsmanship in disappointing losses. Having observed her closely for four or five years now, I can say Sandra doesn't blow it often. I'm amazed at how gracious she is, even when she has every right to get upset. If she has taken the low road in the past, I think the weeds have grown over the parts she's walked on. For all the outside pressures and expectations, she's consistently carved a deep path on the high road."

The 1987 season was the highlight of Sandra's blossoming curling career, her first trip to the Scott. The whole family was ecstatic. Shirley says, "I thought Art would self-destruct when he found out Sandra would be wearing the green, he was so proud and excited."

The tournament was a tremendous learning experience, with a lot of individual success but frustration at the team level. This was the year everybody but the skip made the all-star team. Sandra says, "It was a tough situation, because Kathy Fahlman played so well through the playdowns and struggled so much in Lethbridge. It was the first time I've seen a skip lose confidence, up close. I didn't understand it at that point, not like I do now. We tried our best to bring Kathy back into it. It's too bad that hindsight is 20/20, because there's things we could have done differently. We tried to battle through it and lost the tiebreaker to the Quebéc team.

129

Sandra and two of her biggest supporters, sisters Beverly and Carol.

The new, expanded Schmirler-England family photo in the summer of 1999 – Shannon and Sandra hold Jenna and Sara.

"The one positive of the 1987 Scott was that our entire team was selected to go to the Olympic trials two months later in Calgary.

"The team had gone to the first phase of selections in October of 1986 in Edmonton. After this phase, only Kathy Fahlman had formally been invited, because of her reputation and success of previous years. But it was one of the more memorable experiences. We boarded a plane for Edmonton and really had a fun trip. It was Halloween and we decided to dress up as various fruits. Kathy has a real funny sense of humour and can be such a goof. She dressed up as a tomato, Jan was a carrot, and I dressed up as a grape. It seemed like we were the entertainment at the airport. Kathy had all our tickets and went up to the ticket area and pulled them out. Of course everyone is looking and getting a kick out of this 'cute little tomato.' As she pulls the tickets out, they are stuck on something and she can't get them off. They are stuck on a maxi-pad in her purse. So, without missing a beat, she pulls the pad out, with the tickets stuck on it and waves them around. Everyone around, including the ticket person, had a real good laugh. Maybe that's why Kathy was the skip, she can think pretty quick on her feet."

The trials at the Max Bell Arena in Calgary brought together eight of the best teams in Canada, regardless of province. The Fahlman team did a lot of preparation during the two months leading up to it. They threw a ton of rocks, had useful meetings after practice, and consulted one of the most successful women's curlers in Canadian history, Vera Pezer.

Sandra says, "Vera had become a sports psychologist. With that degree, plus being considered one of the greatest curlers of all time, she was a resource we felt we needed to tap into. She was more than happy to sit down with us. Kathy was still feeling a little shaky from her personal disappointment in Lethbridge. Vera helped us to get our team confidence back, and we felt prepared for the trials."

The team curled well, but lost a disappointing tie-breaker to BC's Pat Saunders, who had won the Scott in Lethbridge. So they officially finished fourth in one of the toughest fields ever assembled in Canada. Linda Moore of Vancouver eventually won it all, beating Connie Laliberte in the final.

In the summer of 1987, Sandra married Del Peterson. The relationship did not work out, and when her divorce was finalized in 1992, Sandra said, "My self-esteem probably hit an all-time low. I always thought that by the time I turned 30, I would be happily married with one or two kids. I went through the pain of divorce and started to feel like a loser – single, unattached, and no prospects on the horizon. I threw myself into curling, and in a sense it became my sanctuary. I practiced a lot, studied game tapes of our team, but also of other teams I admired. It was horrible for my personal life, but turned out great for my curling game, although that was never the plan.

"Jan was my main support in Regina. My family could always be counted on, but they were up in Biggar or in the Calgary area. Jan was Miss Reliable. She was my lifeline. She and Frank invited me to go along on their summer vacation to Montana. We camped and played a little golf. It was a lot of what I needed to keep my sanity, Jan's being there for me, galvanizing our friendship even deeper. I cherish our friendship and have probably never thanked her properly for her love and support during that difficult time."

The following season of 1987-88, team Fahlman

set out to defend their provincial crown, but lost to Michelle Schneider's rink in the final game at provincials.

The 1988-89 season would be the last season for Sandra curling third for Kathy Fahlman. At the beginning of the season, longtime lead Sheila Schneider stepped down, as she and her husband were starting a family. Kathy suggested one of the Inglis sisters as a replacement. "I know this lady at the Callie who can slide all the way down the ice. She must be good. Her name is Cathy Trowell."

Cathy was pregnant and could only curl half the season. By the time playdowns arrived, Joan was the full-time lead. The team advanced to the southerns in Maple Creek.

Sandra relates their disasterous performance. "We made it to the A final and lost, then we advanced to the B and C finals and lost them both. Our third and final loss was incredibly tough to get over.

"We're three up playing the eighth and give up two. We're still in control with hammer. In the ninth, things just fall apart and we allow a steal of three. We go from being three up to two down in only two ends.

"I remember Joan's face just turned white. Jan and I thought she'd throw up. She thought this might be her one and only chance and it slipped away so easily. We were all devastated. What made it even worse was that provincials were being held in Regina along with the men's provincials at the Agridome. We had so wanted to be part of this event. It would have been like a Scott, with the attendance and arena atmosphere."

When Kathy stepped down as skip the following season, as has been documented, the search ended with Joan and Marcia.

Sandra had never really skipped at any level. She thinks she may have skipped eight or 10 recreational or fun 'spiel games up to this stage of her career and that was it. "I didn't really know what to do or how to do it. At first it seemed easier than playing third. My shots didn't have to be as precise, for whatever reason, but part of that was that Jan was such a great third.

"This was during the time of my marriage falling

Shirley and Art Schmirler pose with Sandra at the Callie Club in Regina, as they get ready to tackle the Worlds again in 1997.

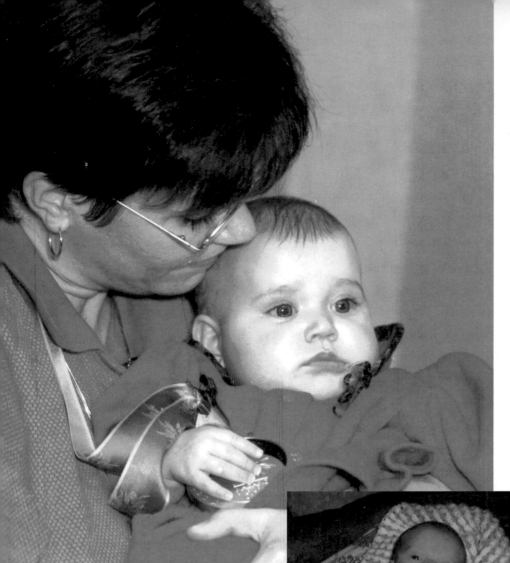

and I looked at each other and thought there was no way we would have seen it.

"It was a skipping lesson that at the time seemed very harsh. But you learn along the way, mostly through those situations that don't go your team's way. You rarely learn something when everything goes right, it's usually when something goes bad."

The team started to curl very well, and won a city berth to the southern playdowns almost without a hitch. The game that stands out for Sandra in southerns was their B semi-final loss to the always-tough Barb Swallow rink from rural Maryfield, Saskatchewan. This became known as the "Swallow Story."

Sandra recalls the game with much remorse but a little humour as well. "It was a struggle, struggle, struggle game. We couldn't put Swallow away. We wound up in an extra end with the hammer. All I had to do was move their shot rock an inch or two and we'd win. It was wide open. I threw it clean. I thought the game was over the moment I released it. At the tee line, it grabbed a hair and literally went sideways into the boards. The rock was only three feet away when it picked. Both teams were absolutely stunned. We lost on a piece of horsehair. We were down to our last life on a stupid pick.

"I was so mad I took a golf swing with my broom and hit the bench between the sheets. Joan hit her broom down on the ice and accidentally chipped a piece of ice. Marcia slammed her broom brush side first, so it made no noise at all. Then she turned her broom around and slammed the ice again with the opposite side of her broom. Jan stood there speechless, just stunned by the miss, but also by our actions.

apart, so I threw myself into it. I studied all those videotapes and practised all the time. I started to study the game with a whole new outlook from a skip's point of view."

Sandra learned a critical lesson during one of the team's first major bonspiels, an autumn event in Kelowna, BC. They were playing one of the better teams from Winnipeg, Sandra recalls. "We were one up coming home with hammer. It was a situation where you had to look at all the possibilities before you threw. It's probably why, even now, I tend to overanalyze too much. I try to look at every single angle and pick the best option. We ended up losing that game because we didn't think things through. I wound up raising them in our very last shot and gave up the two points to lose the game. I was trying to hit the shot rock and blew it. It was a terrible shot, and maybe I just threw it bad, but when it happened, Jan

"The SCA (Saskatchewan Curling Association) officials were Arlene Day and Sandy Rutherford. Arlene said to Sandy, 'I'm going to have to reprimand that team. Could you write out a report on what happened? Everything you witnessed.'

"Sandy looked at Arlene and said very emphatically, 'Everything!'

"So Arlene read us the riot act, and deservedly so. We've shown emotion at other times, but never like that before or since. To say we regretted the incident would be a huge understatement. It was so out of character, especially for Joan and Marcia."

The team recovered and went on to qualify for the provincials, and a few weeks later Team Schmirler won their first provincial championship. At the final banquet was Sylvia Fedoruk, a three-time provincial champion who curled third for Joyce McKee's team in the late 1950s and early 1960s. That team also won two Canadian championships. She was sitting with the provincial organizing committee rep, Mark Lang, who told her the "Swallow story"

from the recent southern playdowns. As Fedoruk got up to leave, she went over to congratulate the team, and added, "Don't you girls worry about the Swallow incident. I like a team with a bit of spunk."

Sylvia was the Lieutenant-Governor of Saskatchewan at the time. When she retired, her farewell dinner was by invitation only, with a very limited guest list. But Sylvia made sure that Team Schmirler was invited. "It was a real honour to be invited, a real elegant affair," Sandra recalls. "To be included on her guest list was such a privilege. She has become one of our biggest boosters over the years. Sylvia constantly encourages our team and says she admires us, but the sentiment is mutual. She is one of our heroes."

The team prepared for the 1991 Scott in Saskatoon. It was Sandra's second appearance, but her first as a skip. She may have accomplished what no other Canadian skip has ever done – going to the nationals in her first year of skipping.

133

Sandra says, "I was so excited to go back. Having it in our home province was a real thrill. But we weren't ready to win and never really went expecting it. In my mind I thought we had a chance, but in my heart I knew it wasn't very realistic. We played below our potential, when you consider how well we were curling in the playdowns and bonspiels."

The biggest lesson of that Scott was in the game versus Heather Houston's Thunder Bay rink. Houston was a two-time Scott champion and the 1989 world champion. "When we played Houston I allowed myself to get totally psyched out by her recent dominance," Sandra explains. "I reasoned that we had no chance to win. How could our team beat their team? It's something I never communicated with the team and I let it affect my play. I threw brutal and they kicked us all over the ice. That was a major learning game for me. If you're going to play at this level, you have to be ready for the challenge and don't worry about the outcome. That game changed my approach to facing the name teams. As a skip, you can't control the future. Just skip the game, put the broom down. You have to try and make as many shots as you can and let the final score take care of itself. Just be concerned with what you and your team can

Sandra has the patience and the respect to spend a great deal of time doing media interviews.

control. If you do that well, the victories will far out-weigh the losses."

Sandra learned another lesson in trying to repeat as Saskatchewan champions during the 1991-92 season. "We came close to repeating but couldn't finish it off. The previous year we went out to seize our wins. When we came to playdowns this season we subtly changed our mindset. We started to play not to lose. We had a taste of playing at the Scott and wanted to get back so badly. So you enter playdowns just hoping not to blow it, instead of playing hard to win and trying to dictate the outcome. You have to remind yourself of past lessons. We knew better but forgot what made us successful in the first place. The lesson would be hard-learned again, after our disappointment at the 1995 Scott in Calgary."

1992-93 would be the breakthrough year for Sandra and her teammates. She says, "We were so driven. I had nothing to hold me back. My marriage was officially over, I was unattached. Other than my

job, all I had for responsibilities was my dog, PJ, and she was easy to make arrangements for.

"I felt my game gaining consistency, and my confidence level as a skip was giving me a reasonable comfort level out on the ice. I really thought our chances at the beginning of the year, and especially through the playdowns, were great. When we finally qualified for the Scott in Brandon, I knew we had a chance to win it all. We all went with the expectation to win."

The team drove to Brandon. It gave them time to settle in and get used to all the venues. Things were running smoothly until they went to get fitted with their green, white, and yellow Saskatchewan curling clothes. "This is usually a highlight," explains Sandra, "because all of us women love to get new clothes. We finally mixed and matched and got all the right sizes. I got back to the hotel and decided to iron my pants. I only had the one pair that could fit."

Jan says, "I was looking at Sandra and thinking,

Saskatchewan's favourite rhyme, but it's only on special occassions that you can get away with using it. Like here, at the sendoff for the Brandon Olympic trials.

'I hope the iron isn't too hot.' She ironed the one side and it was all right. When she turned them over to do the other side, she melted the pants. Well, we all started to roll in laughter, everyone except Sandra!"

"I was just devastated," recalls Sandra. "I ran into the bathroom real upset and started to cry. I can understand the humour in it, but at the time I kept thinking, 'I have no pants.' Then I started to worry that if this was how the week was going to go, I wanted no part of it. Anita let me try on her pants and thank goodness they fit perfectly."

Despite this shaky beginning, Sandra curled up a storm all week, winning her first Canadian title. And the consistency continued at the Worlds in Geneva, Switzerland. Watching in her hometown of Biggar were Art and Shirley. The games were on tape delay back to Canada. Radio would give updates, but her parents tried to avoid them and watch the games in their front living room.

Also watching and listening for scores was Sandra's boarder who lived in her basement suite. Shayne McMillan was a university student from Carnduff, Saskatchewan, who was an avid curler and loved to follow how Team Schmirler was doing. He became a good friend and an informal support-system for Sandra. He was like having a younger brother to talk to and joke with.

When Sandra's team claimed their first world championship, Shayne phoned Art and Shirley to congratulate them. Sandra's parents were hoping to wait for the result by watching the tape-delayed final.

Shayne, all excited, opened the conversation by saying, "I'm living under a world champion!" They forgave Shayne very quickly for breaking the news.

Sandra's mother says, "It's hard to watch them curl in playdowns, especially in finals. We go to all the Scotts but stay home for all the international events. I had a chance during the Olympics to watch my two daughters watch a game. Bev will put a blanket over her head and holler and scream. Carol gets into it and lives and dies with every single shot. During the Olympic final, poor Bev got the flu and had to watch the game all alone in bed. She eventually passed out and watched the game on tape. She just couldn't stay awake – it's as sick as I've ever seen her."

Sandra's first off-season as a world champion brought new demands from the media, the broader curling community, and her home province. She was thrust into a celebrity status that was exciting yet time-consuming. She is known as one of the more accommodating athletes on the Canadian sports scene. Pat Reid, former president of the CCA, has observed, "She takes time for the fans. She'll stand and talk to them and sign autographs. After the Olympics, returning to the Scott in Regina was overwhelming. Yet Sandra would stay after games for a couple of hours doing the PR thing. Sandra has maintained that all that she and the team have accomplished is a real privilege. It's not a hollow exercise of public relations. She's the real deal."

Sandra's pace of life since that first world title has gone into overdrive. She has tried to stay the same on the inside but sometimes she feels like life is going by a little too fast. She confided to her mom shortly after winning in Geneva, "I wish I could find someone to share this dream with and my life. I'd like to think I have a lot to offer someone."

135

Norway's outspoken Dordi Nordby, at the 1993 Worlds. Sandra gets a kick out of her antics.

Life was about to change. The team was renewing a friendship over drinks with Peter Lindholm's Swedish team, which was in Regina for the Callie 'spiel. Marcia got up from the table and bumped into Shannon England, whom she had gone to tech school with in Moose Jaw. He wanted to meet Sandra, one of her world champion friends.

Sandra says, "I wasn't seriously looking to meet anyone. Marcia comes back to our table and says, 'This guy wants to meet you. He's a curler.' So she points him out to me. I said, 'bring him over.' I was thinking it's no big deal, I'll be nice. So we grabbed an extra chair and he hung out with us. He really toughed it out that night and seemed to understand the good time we were having with the Swedes. I needed a ride home and Shannon was kind of like the designated driver. We said our goodnights and Shannon said, 'Give me a call sometime,' and gave me his phone number.

"The next morning I debated about calling him. I'm a Blue Jays fan and the American League playoffs were on. I thought I should invite him over to watch the game. Then my insecurities took over. I thought, why would he want to come over and watch a baseball game with me? So I decided to stay home alone and watch the game.

"About noon, Shannon called. He asked if I wanted to come to his place and watch the Jays game. We had a great time together. It was like I'd known him forever. We became inseparable. He seemed to really understand me and we became fantastic friends.

"He really is the love of my life. He loved the fun world that curling opened up for us. He embraced it and supported it. To me that was the ultimate – someone who understood the game, who realized the cost and sacrifices I was making. He relished it all and loved to watch our games."

Sandra had found her soulmate and more. "He didn't mind me studying videotapes and my amount of practice. He loves to throw rocks and has his own aspirations of getting to the Brier. We spend a lot of time practising together and he's very analytical and wants to know all the nuances of the sport. We would end our practices with these two-end games. The loser would buy cappuccino. Because I'm so competitive I didn't want to lose. He had me so many times and then he'd throw a real stinker and let me back in. I'd win most of the games. In the beginning he'd think, 'I'm beating a world champ, how could I do that?' Those practices got me to what I consider my A-game. I noticed a marked improvement in my consistency, as a result of those two-end battles. At present, Shannon probably works harder on his game than I do. The cappuccinos have evened out a little more as well."

Shannon goes to all the Scotts and was able to go to Germany in 1994 and Nagano in 1998. He understands the behind-the-scenes demands on Sandra, the hundreds of phone calls, the planning, the preparation of Sandra's many speeches and motivational talks, the study of the game, the hours and hours of practice and team meetings.

Sandra says her "number one delivery" was her daughter Sara, who was born on September 15, 1997, nine weeks before the 1997 Olympic trials.

It may have been her best sense of timing as well. Sandra explains, "We really wanted children, but I was having a hard time getting pregnant. I required major surgery in September of 1996 to correct some internal complications. Before we had the green light to try and have a child we needed the medical go-ahead. I knew that the longer I put it off, the more it might affect my chances to curl in Brandon at the trials. The team was so supportive. They kept telling me that family is greater than any Olympic experience could ever be. Yes they'd love to play, but whatever happens, happens.

"I got the doctor's okay right before New Year's. Let me say, Shannon and I ushered in 1997. You could say we had a happy new year. She is truly a miracle baby. My greatest honour in life was to give life. I feel so blessed. For Shannon and me, she really is our pride and joy. I smile at her first thing every morning."

Sandra was nursing Sara at the Olympic trials. Shannon was the key to this juggling act. As Sandra says, "He understands what goes on at these major events. Sometimes I wonder if the curling gods looked down and said, 'This lady is too busy to have a baby that's going to fuss,' because Sara has been minimum maintenance for us rookie parents. She slept through the night right from the beginning.

"The hardest thing was going to Nagano without Sara. My biggest comfort was that she stayed with my two sisters out near Calgary. My sisters are so good, they were really into looking after their new niece. So she wasn't lacking for attention."

Sandra Schmirler has handled herself extremely well in the fast-paced life that fame can bring. Pat Reid has been at every Worlds and the Olympics with Sandra. Pat respects "Sandra's ability to stay humble. She is the same quality person she was before the fame. She's a very gracious, caring champion. A true role model to emulate." ◎

137

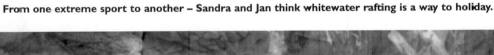

From one extreme sport to another – Sandra and Jan think whitewater rafting is a way to holiday.

Chapter Thirteen

THREE-PEAT
"RELOADING VS. REBUILDING"
(1996-1997)

R eunited, and it felt so good!
January 1997, 14 months after clinching the first Olympic trials berth, Team Schmirler was back to the original four that had started together in the autumn of 1990. It was their longest time apart, and it had been a busy year.

But what a year of ups and downs, highs and lows, to get to the new year. To foresee the next four months and the record-setting pace this team would go on, one would have needed the eyes of a biblical prophet.

Marcia hadn't played a competitive game in almost a year; she had hardly thrown a rock. She had just given birth to her first child, Colin, in December. Joan had had her second child, Christina, in May, and would only miss the upcoming Nipawin 'spiel.

Jan had her first child, Steven, in July. She didn't miss any competitive curling whatsoever.

Sandra married Shannon England in the off-season. And, she was about to get pregnant right near the beginning of the playdown trail.

Three new babies, a new husband, surgery, a pregnant skip, and no games together in the last 14 months – hardly the recipe for curling success. Their first gig together was the city playdowns, phase one of the long trek to get back to the Scott Tournament of Hearts. If Team Schmirler was ever ripe to get eliminated early, this should have been the year. But sabbaticals and starting families often bring fresh perspectives and refill the emotional tank.

Marcia said being away had refuelled her engine. "I would watch them at bonspiels or playdowns and I wanted to get back. I missed the game and my three buddies."

Joan appreciated the time away from the competitive grind. "I was getting burnt out. Family is our priority and I'm glad I could have another baby and spend some quality time with them. I was ready to get back to

Rearrange the trophy shelf – once more they make off with the Heartware, at the 1997 Scott in Vancouver.

the rink. It was fun to be with the girls. The old competitive fire was relit."

The first half of the 1996-97 season was a challenge for this team – Sandra, Jan, sometimes Joan, but mainly various substitutes. Sandra says, "We knew Joan and Marcia would eventually join us again. I knew they'd work hard to get on top of their games. But if we were going to take a serious run at playdowns, Jan and I knew we needed to get games under our belt.

"We were way more prepared for the subs this year, and we curled quite well even with the ongoing changes."

The only glitch in the five major 'spiels they entered was in their home town – the SaskPower Women's Cash Bonspiel. Sandra wishes it could have been different. "I was on the organizing committee. It was busier than I anticipated. I never got any practice in and we got off to a bad start. We didn't qualify for the playoff round. Started out on the wrong foot and never fully recovered. It was a disappointment. After the 'spiel we had to practise our conflict-resolution skills as we were really letting little things irritate each other."

Walter Betker said the rumour mill was busy during this 'spiel. "We heard that the team was fighting and scrapping. Too many subs. All the babies. How could they cope? It's interesting what surfaces when others see a good team struggling.

"Sure they were a little down, but they never entertained any thoughts of a team breakup. Maybe that's what some people wanted."

Sandra tends to wear her emotions on her sleeve and Jan is usually the one in contact with the after-effects. The casual observer could easily misinterpret this the wrong way, though nothing could be further from the truth. Jan is the perfect third for Sandra, in the sense that she gives her skip permission to let off a little steam. And if Sandra does get personal, Jan can stand up for herself. The feeling is mutual, because Jan tends to be the same way.

Often getting out of Regina and away from normal responsibilities can realign the team's consistency in the win column. The inaugural Evergreen Curling Classic in Nipawin was next on their agenda. Sandra and Jan were joined by Cathy Trowell and Laurie Secord-Humble. It was the first time these four had joined ranks and Sandra recalls that, "We jelled just at the right time."

The team dominated the playoff round, winning the quarter-finals 8-5, the semi-finals 7-1, and beating Saskatoon's Kim Hodson 5-3 in the final. It was a healthy first-place cheque of $8,000, and it restored Sandra and Jan's confidence against their primary competition.

There was one more 'spiel without their regular front end, up in Saskatoon. They qualified for playoffs, but were eliminated in the quarter-finals. It did help to pay expenses that they came home with $2,000.

The last major bonspiel was a week before Christmas in Thunder Bay, the first JVC/TSN women's skins game. The men had enjoyed this nationally-televised event for a few years. It was great for the ratings. Only four of Canada's top teams were invited. The teams play 10 ends and are awarded money for ends won, not by how many points are scored. It's really 10 mini-games in one. The team with the most money wins. It's a takeoff on golf's skins game.

This would be the biggest payday ever for women's curling, with $70,000 up for grabs. The skins game has become the most coveted bonspiel on the circuit in only three short years. A team can qualify by winning a Scott, one of two other major selected

bonspiels, or if one is the defending champion.

Joan was back and her sister Cathy moved over to fill in for Marcia. They curled extremely well, winning their semi-final and losing an entertaining final to Thunder Bay's Heather Houston. Houston and her team earned $34,700 for two games of curling. Team Schmirler received $25,600 for finishing second. It was their largest payday ever.

Sandra says, "It was a fun event and the money wasn't bad either. My only regret is that we didn't win it, to guarantee an invitation back for next year.

"The format of a skins game wasn't totally foreign for us. We had about 10 practice games to get the idea in our heads. To win an end, you have to score two or more with hammer or steal just a point without last shot. It's a real aggressive game with lots of rocks in play every end. It was good for my confidence as well. I felt I was struggling somewhat before the 'spiel."

There was one more bonspiel before the full reunion and the beginning of the playdowns – the Regina Highland Men's Cash Spiel. Marcia was back,

141

Taking a moment away from the long thin sheet of ice, in Berne, 1997.

Team Schmirler won their first two games before losing the A Event semi-final. They rebounded with three straight wins to clinch the B Event qualifying spot, and then beat Sherry Linton's youthful Regina team 6-4 in the final. Linton and her team of Nancy Inglis (Joan's sister), Sandi McNabb, and Tanya Kaip were one of Saskatchewan's threats to go on to the Scott.

Provincials were being held in Swift Current at the Centennial Civic Centre. The Saskatchewan Curling Association decided on a new format to decide their representatives to the Scott, an eight-team round robin with the top four teams advancing to a sudden-death playoff. The team loved their chances of reaching the playoff round, but the sudden-death format concerned them. In previous provincials, a team had to lose three games before being eliminated. In this format a team could go undefeated and reach the final, only to lose to a team with three or four losses.

The team jumped out to an impressive 5-0 record, assuring themselves of a playoff spot. At 5-0, they had a shot at advancing straight to the final. All they had to do was win their final two round robin games. Their sixth game was against a winless Myrna Neilson and her struggling team from Yorkton. Schmirler's sense of humour may have been her undoing. In the dressing room before the game, the two teams were teasing each other. When Myrna wasn't looking, Sandra snuck a plastic rat into Myrna's jacket. On the ice during the handshake, Myrna finally put her hand into her pocket, felt the rat, and screamed. It broke both teams up, and put Myrna's team into a very loose mind space for the entire game.

Already eliminated from playoff contention, the Yorkton team squeezed out a 5-4 victory. As so often happens in this slippery game, the team on the bottom of the standings played up to their potential and knocked off the first-place team. Team Schmirler finished the round robin at 6-1 to clinch first place, but

but did not curl every game. The 'spiel was between Christmas and New Year's so family commitments meant "lots of subs," as Sandra remembers. "Maybe it was the Christmas season or whatever, but we were loose and curled well," she says, "even with all the shuffling of personnel. We somehow made the final. Old foe Randy Woytowich was our opponent. Randy was unbelievable." The team won $1,300 for their second-place finish.

The shuffling was finally over. The ups and downs were about to balance out. The team was finally back together and it felt right. "When you step on the ice it all comes back," Marcia said. "The four of us are identical in what we want. We want to do the best we can, make the shots, and win. That part of it you're born with."

The team has acknowledged that there was maybe a little fear that it wouldn't be the same, but after the first few games it really was like old times. Joan says "Having Marcia back really kick-started my game. She joined us for a few club games before playdowns and it was like she never missed a beat. I was struggling, and she was outcurling almost everyone in the building.

"I started thinking if she can do it after a year off and just having a baby, I better keep up with her. I couldn't let her outcurl me, when I'd already been on the ice for a while and at a couple of 'spiels. You know what? I started to get my game back."

The first leg of the Saskatchewan playdowns was the city regionals to qualify for the southern playdowns. Team Schmirler started out the way they left off 14 months earlier. They never lost a game, beating good friend Atina Ford 10-3 in the final.

The SaskPower southern women's playdowns were held at the Tartan Curling Club in Regina.

that rat-infested loss to Neilson meant they had to play a sudden-death semi-final, which they won 7-5 to advance to the final against fellow Reginan and club mate Sherry Linton.

Joan says, "We knew them well. My sister (Nancy Inglis) is the third. We knew if they played like they had all year our hands would be full. Sherry as the skip may have been young. The reality, though, was that she knew all of our team from on and off the ice. This took away any mystique we may have had because of our past successes."

The final was a barn burner. Schmirler was up 4-2 playing the eighth when Linton used the advantage of hammer to tie the game at 4-4. In the ninth, Linton managed to steal a point to lead 5-4 coming home, which set up a very tense last end. Having hammer back meant that the chances of an extra end were good, but Schmirler didn't want an extra end if they could avoid it. They would throw up some cor-

ner guards, get aggressive, and try for the two points. The strategy worked. Linton's second, Sandi Weber, tried to come around a guard to take out a Schmirler stone. She just missed, rubbing on the guard. The experienced Schmirler team had the opportunity they were trying to create. Joan put her rock on the other side of the house to have two shot stones in the house. The teams traded shots from then on. Sherry Linton tried to keep the damage down on her last stone. She didn't quite execute and left her final shot wide open for Sandra. The veteran skip made no mistake, throwing an out-turn hit-and-stick to score three. The team had earned their fifth trip to the Scott.

Sandra says, "The nerves were still there, on that final stone. I was thankful it was a wide-open hit. I've had that similar out-turn hit on three occasions to win either a provincial or Canadian championship. When I threw my final stone it was in the back of my

This is what it's all about at Worlds – the goodies include individual medals and bragging rights on that spectacular world trophy.

mind. Those previous experiences calmed my shaking hands. Experience really is a good teacher, if you remember to apply the lessons.

"We'd been through so many of these nail-biters that you'd think it would get easier. Problem is, the nails keep on growing."

It appeared that Team Schmirler was performing on all cylinders. The fourteen months apart didn't seem to affect their play, but the provincials were only phase one of regaining the world championship.

Brian McCusker didn't question whether the team was back or not. "Our team (Randy Woytowich) had a practice game against them in preparation for the Vancouver Hearts. You could see it in their eyes and in their performance. They were back. The inner drive to win was as strong as I'd ever seen it. Possibly stronger. The time off for Marcia and Joan was good – they were refreshed and refocussed. I thought they should be legitimate favourites to win it all and go back to the Worlds."

The team felt confident about their chances in Vancouver. The chemistry wasn't simply there – it appeared to be even stronger. The passion to prove that they could be the best was once again their prime motivator.

There were a couple of other motivations to win the 1997 Scott. The winner of the Scott would automatically be Team Canada at the following year's championship. It would be a once-in-a-lifetime dream to curl at the Scott in their home city. The Olympics were also coming up in early 1998. If they were to be Canada's team in Nagano, it would be exciting to go as Canadian champions.

The Scott Tournament of Hearts would take place in Vancouver's Pacific National Exhibition Agridome, which seats 3,500 spectators. Small and cozy, the Agridome was a converted livestock showplace, and one unforeseen adjustment the curlers had to make was to the odour of the former tenants. Of course, some of the eastern Canadian teams thought that the 'Chanel Agridome' aroma favoured the prairie teams and their agricultural roots.

This was one of the most experienced Scott fields to date, with only nine of the 48 regular curlers not having any Scott games under their belts. With all the veteran teams in attendance, the general feeling was that a 7-4 record would guarantee one of the final four playoff spots.

Team Schmirler, so meticulous in their pre-tournament preparations, felt as if they were finally able to cope with almost every possible challenge. The team took Sandra's discovery that she was pregnant in stride. She had three teammates who could empathize with her hormonal distractions.

Their opening game was against the current Team Canada, Ontario's Marilyn Bodogh, who was also reigning world champion. Team Schmirler won the opening game 9-2 in eight ends. The tone for

the week seemed to be set, for both rinks.

This was Schmirler's only game on opening day. On day two, Newfoundland's Laura Phillips and her crew pulled off a minor upset, beating Saskatchewan 7-6 in an extra end.

Sandra gave them full marks for their win. "They made a lot of great shots to beat us. I missed a couple at the end of the game I wasn't too pleased with. I was a little down on myself afterward. I thought they were makeable shots and I didn't execute. But we came out strong in our second game of the day against Nova Scotia."

Colleen Jones was back for the twelfth time. Once again Team Schmirler rebounded with a vengeance after a heartbreaking defeat, cruising to an unexpected 12-2 win.

The team was in a logjam at 2-1, tied for second. Cathy Borst of Alberta was the only undefeated team at 3-0.

Day three put them in the first two draws of the

It's a tie game, and they're down to skip rocks against Denmark in the 8th end at the 1997 Worlds in Berne, Switzerland.

day. The first game was against Prince Edward Island and Rebecca Jean MacPhee, who stole her way to a 8-6 win. It was a tough loss, because Sandra wasn't able to make her last shot in the tenth end.

Sandra was a little frustrated. "We were 2-2 and had to put together a string of wins to keep our playoff hopes alive. Both losses were on the last shot. In both defeats I couldn't finish it off and the teams stole points to win. We could have won those two games, because as a team we played reasonably well. We had to keep playing like we were, just a little more consistent, that's all."

The team had a short break between games, but didn't mind, because the sooner they could get on the ice after a loss, the better. Janet Harvey's Manitoba team was next on the agenda. The Saskatchewan women curled a complete game in a 9-6 victory. Sandra was relieved to win, especially after both losses were misses on the final stone. It was a bit of a confidence-booster to gain the win in this way. The victory reset the tone and helped them turn the corner for the rest of the week.

The women had a half-day with no more games, a nice time to rest and visit with friends and family. It's what the team was looking forward to in preparation for day four, when the overall standings start to sift into shape.

Last-rock games were becoming the norm for Saskatchewan. The fourth day brought two more. The team moved to 4-2 in the standings, with an extra-end win over Scott veteran Heidi Hanlon and her New Brunswick team. In the evening draw they played Quebéc, skipped by Chantel Osborne. Osborne had a chance to force an extra-end, but hit and rolled out on her final stone, helping Saskatchewan win it 4-3. This win resulted in a three-way tie for first among Saskatchewan, Alberta, and Ontario.

Joan called day five "destiny day." She knew the schedule. They would play both Alberta and Ontario. Their future in the standings was not dependent upon other team's performances; the possibility of first place and the playoffs was in their own hands. They could determine their own fate. If they could win both, it would assure them of a tie-breaker and most likely a playoff spot. Even a split would improve their chances. Like all champions, they honestly felt they could beat both opponents.

The first game of the day was against former

Canadian champion Alison Goring and her Ontario crew. Team Schmirler disposed of Goring in eight ends with a 7-2 win.

Alberta and Saskatchewan were alone in first when they stepped out on the ice. It was the feature game for TSN's coast-to-coast coverage. Team Schmirler was playing at the top of their game and doled out a 9-2 drubbing, which left them alone in first place at 7-2. Two games remained in the round robin, but all they needed was to split the games to guarantee first place. This meant choice of rocks and hammer throughout the playoff round.

All four curlers were either leading the averages at their individual positions or close to it. Marcia was an unbelievable 87 per cent to top the leads. Joan was the top second at 82 per cent. Jan was an extremely close second among the thirds at 83 per cent, and Sandra was the top skip at 78 per cent. The team was ahead of the pack with an 83 per cent average overall, akin to an NHL team having four of the five top scorers in the whole league.

Experience prevented the possibility of overconfidence. Sandra explains, "We weren't fooled by the scoreboard. We all had to make our shots and Jan made it easier for me with her outstanding play. She wasn't missing anything. We were on a roll and the other teams were curling well, but we took advantage of every opportunity along the way. That can change so quickly. Ice conditions could change. One or two

of us could be off a little. The opposition could get on a similar roll. These were great teams that were capable of knocking us off. How many times in curling has a team beaten another rink in eight ends and lost a rematch the same way? In these five wins in a row, I think each one of us outcurled her opponent in every game. You won't lose too many games when that happens."

The final day of the round robin pitted Saskatchewan against two struggling teams. It would be nice to win both to keep their momentum, though they would be satisfied with only one win, to clinch first place.

In their first game they played the hometown hosts, Kelley Law, one of the pre-tournament favourites, in their fourth trip to the Scott. It was also their worst finish.

The BC team proved to be good hosts as Team Schmirler clinched first place with an extra-end, 6-5 decision. Their first goal was attained, and they were back in the playoffs.

Their final game was a mere formality for both teams. The Territories' Kelly Kaylo was out of the playoff race. Jan pulled a muscle and watched the last game from the stands. Atina Ford replaced her mom, Anita, as the fifth, and played Jan's position, curling a perfect 100 per cent in an 8-4 victory. A 100 per cent game, in curling, is about as common as a no-hitter in baseball. The team finished at 9-2, thanks to

Team Schmirler celebrates after a nerve-wracking semi-final victory over Denmark.

148

their seven-game winning streak.

The Schmirler-Goring confrontation to advance to Sunday's final was a tight affair. Goring outplayed the Regina women in the first five ends, but Schmirler's crew turned it around in the last five. It was 4-4 playing the eighth when Sandra made a difficult straightback double take-out to jump ahead 6-4. Her last stone actually whiskered a guard, but not enough to knock it off line. If Sandra's rock had curled just a millimetre more, Ontario would have been up 5-4 going into the ninth. Ontario got one back in the ninth to close the gap to 6-5, but that's how it ended, as Saskatchewan ran Ontario out of rocks in the final end.

Ontario then played Newfoundland in the semifinal, with the winner advancing against Saskatchewan again for the Canadian title. Goring's crew rebounded for a 9-4 win, to again meet Team Schmirler. It would be Saskatchewan's third game against Ontario in their last six.

The extra day off before the final offered a much-needed rest for the team. Marcia was still breast-feeding her baby and was losing energy as the week wore on. Every window of rest helped her to get her strength back. Sandra, dealing with her first pregnancy, had a lot of empathy from her three teammates, who understood the physical and emotional changes she was experiencing. She valued any extra time off to be on top of her game from the physical standpoint.

The women were quietly confident in their pregame preparations.

They respected Goring and her Ontario team, but beating them twice in the last five games was good for their psyche. In the back of their minds, there was the very real fear of not being able to beat this solid team three straight times.

Joan reflects back, "We were on an eight-game winning streak and playing very consistently. Even after our record was 2-2, I felt we were on the verge. We were getting the kinks out in those early games. Some of the media were surprised when I said we could go on a long winning streak. Sometimes you can sense it; sometimes you can sense a breakdown as well. We were curling well and losing games we controlled and had chances in. I felt if we could correct those correctable things we would start winning in bunches.

"Sandra and Jan, especially, are the type of players who can fix the breakdowns. When they do, they rarely make those kind of misses or errors in the same tournament or bonspiel, again.

"Marcia was so consistent that we all felt we had the upper hand on most teams. She was constantly getting things started for us."

The big game was close. Both teams were fighting consistency. Goring finished the game at 67 per cent. Sandra got into the 60s but was at an uncharacteristically low 50 per cent after five ends.

The game was quite entertaining for the fans because of a lot of half-shots and some complete misses. For the two teams involved, it was a bit frustrating. The Schmirler team jumped out in front with a quick 3-1 lead. Ontario fought back to be deadlocked 4-4 after five ends. The turning point was the seventh end, when Goring missed her final shot. It was a wide-open hit that she flashed cleanly. Sandra, always quick to take advantage of unforced errors, drew in for two. Saskatchewan played it open and clean in the last three ends, finishing off Ontario 8-5, running them out of rocks in the final end.

The team was now in position to become the first three-time women's world champions. There was a full month before they had to fly to Berne, Switzerland. Sandra joked about the curling gods, but going to Berne was about the best comfort zone they could wish for. This was their third trip to Berne. They had twice curled in the Berner Cup, advancing to both finals, and winning over many Swiss fans during their visits.

Beat Jaggi, who had driven for them in 1995,

requested the team again. "Beat was like an over-grown kid who just loved to joke and have fun," Joan says. "Having him as our driver was one of those intangibles that takes off any unnecessary pressure." He had the ability to keep the team loose, yet not meddle when the women had to be serious. He would wear red and white, and even learned how to end his sentences in the traditional Canadian, "eh?" He also opened his home up for Brian McCusker and Kerry Gudereit to stay with his family for the week.

On day one, the Canadians would play two of the tournament prefavourites. Their first game was against another two-time world champion – Norway's Dordi Nordby. The first five ends were played very carefully, wide-open with a lot of hits. Once the team felt more comfortable with the ice at Berne's Allmend Stadium, they started to use the FGZ. Although the match was the first to reach the fifth-end break, by the time it was over they were the last teams off the ice. The Canadians prevailed 5-3, pleased with their effort in the tough first draw. They'd dealt with new ice, a tough opponent,

149

On the victory podium, with second-place Norway on their right, and third place Denmark on their left.

Berne victors – Team Schmirler poses with the men's-side winners, the Peter Lindholme rink from Sweden.

and opening-game jitters.

Nordby teased the Canadians after the game, threatening to order pizza if it took that long again. "Some of the decisions were complicated because of the new ice conditions," explained Sandra. "This is a world championship and we want to be settled in our minds before shooting. But, if Dordi orders pizza, I'll ask for double cheese."

The Canadians' second game would be against the US team, skipped by Midale, Saskatchewan, native Patti Lank, who found her way to the Worlds through the benefit of moving to another country. Schmirler came up with a 9-4 victory, though Jan had to leave the game after the eighth end with a pulled muscle in her right leg. Atina Ford replaced her and would have to curl against their upcoming opponents from Japan. "We brought Atina on board because she is so consistent," Sandra explained. "We could have moved our front end up, but Atina is a regular skip, who is used to holding the broom and calling the line. She seemed to fit our mix quite well."

The Japanese played Schmirler tough right up until the tenth end, though the Candians eventually won 7-4. Ford played well in her first full game at the Worlds.

"Jan told me before the game to play my normal game," she said to the *Leader-Post's* Darrell Davis. "But she also told me that if Sandra makes a decision I don't like, I should stand my ground. So in one end we changed a shot."

Jan still wasn't 100 per cent, but played in the evening game against the host country's Mirjam Ott. The Canadians prevailed 7-5, and their win/loss record went to 4-0. Kevin Martin and his Edmonton team were also 4-0, giving Canada the top teams in both round robins.

Atina curled her last full game against Carolyn Hutchison's Scottish entry. The final score was 8-4 for Canada, bumping their record to 5-0, and all but assuring them of a semi-final spot. Atina went out in a blaze of glory, making a crucial long straight-back double take-out to set up a big two points in the eighth end. The team was back to its original lineup for its two Wednesday games. Though not as crisp as in their previous draws, they earned a split neverthe-

less. Germany, skipped by former world champion Andrea Schopp, beat the Canucks 8-5 in the morning game. Team Schmirler rebounded with a 9-6 victory over Anne Eerikainen's Finnish squad. They were now 6-1 and guaranteed at least a tie-breaker.

Anita Ford, now coaching the team full-time, explained the loss. "The urgency wasn't there. They were undefeated and were four games away from the playoffs. One or two losses wouldn't hurt them at this stage. This was the typical time of the midweek blues for most teams. Physically, they are tired. Some of the teams know they'll probably make the playoffs, and the bottom rinks know they're out of it. The Germans were battling for their playoff lives, so we were ripe for the picking. I thought, thank goodness this day is over and out of their system. They usually recover from the blues and finish up strong."

The last day of the round robin would give them a chance to clinch first overall, which would give the team last rock in each potential playoff game, and a choice of rocks.

After their "so-so" Thursday, Team Canada enjoyed their most dominant day of the round robin, overwhelming Sweden's Cathrine Norberg 12-4, then pasting the Danish team 9-3 in the evening draw. Denmark and Sweden would end up playing a tie-breaker to determine fourth place, the winner of which would play Canada in the semi-finals.

Dordi Nordby and her Norwegians clinched second and would play the Japanese, who finished third. This was Japan's first trip to the playoff round since entering world competition. They were coached by Canadian Elaine Dagg-Jackson of Victoria, BC, and had spent ten weeks training in Canada, which they hoped would give them a higher calibre of competition in preparation for the Worlds.

Helena Blach-Lavrsen of Denmark won the all-

Scandinavian tie-breaker and the right to play Canada.

"Those semi-finals don't get any easier on the nerves," says Sandra, "especially if you're one of the dominant teams in the round robin. It's do or die. The lower seed usually plays with abandon, because they're the underdogs with nothing to lose.

"Being from Canada, everyone expects us to be competing for the championship. Teams get up for us and often save their best for Canadian teams.

"Look what happened to Kevin Martin. They were the first-place team on the men's side and met up with a red-hot skip from Sweden in the semi's. Peter Lindholm never missed a shot in the last five ends. Martin's team curled a great game. If Peter missed any one of his three final shots, the Canadians would have won. These sudden-death playoffs are scary."

Lindsay Sparkes, the Canadian women's team leader and co-coach with Anita, says, "The semi-finals are worse than the finals for a team's preparation. Once the semi-final is out of the way, a team settles down. The sudden-death element magnifies the urgency of winning. Team Schmirler has been through it so many times now at the Hearts and Worlds that they are pretty prepared intellectually for these situations. They are still very nervous, but they have the ability to draw on principles they've learned in the past that have given them a chance to be successful."

The semi-final against Denmark was a low-scoring affair. Canada led 2-1 after five ends and stole a crucial point in the ninth to finally take control. The final score was 5-2.

Norway handled the playoff newcomers from Japan 12-5 to set up a unique final. The winner between Schmirler and Nordby would become the first three-time women's world champions. It was a great lead-in for the CBC and their coverage back to Canada.

Dordi Nordby is well known as a feisty, determined, aggressive, never-say-die skip. She's even known to do a little trash-talking, which is unheard of in most curling circles. Sandra finds Dordi humorous and enjoys the colour she brings to the game.

"She's good for curling. Dordi can be misunderstood, but we don't take her comments in the papers too seriously. She said some things about Marilyn Bodogh in the previous world championships that sounded like sour grapes. It must not have affected Marilyn, because she went out and won the Worlds the next day.

"Before this final, she said that former Canadian champions Julie Sutton and Connie Laliberte were two of the best teams she has ever watched. Stuff like that doesn't affect our team. Our energy is put into concentrating on what we have to do on the ice to win. We won't allow ourselves to get caught up in off-ice comments. We know what we're capable of doing and need to take care of our own game first."

The final game was a typically tight contest until the fifth end. The score was tied at one. When Jan came to shoot her first stone, Canada had one in the back of the four-foot. Jan threw "two absolutely perfect in-turn draws to give us three counters," Sandra recalls. Dordi tried to raise one of her rocks into the four-foot to turn the end around, but her rock curled too much and hit the other side of her target, driving it barely out of the rings.

Sandra then drew her first stone in, to lay four. Dordi tried to freeze on her last shot to at least keep the damage down,

151

First-ever three-time women's world curling champions – six young women from Saskatchewan.

There couldn't be a prouder moment than standing on the victor's podium, while your national anthem is played.

but she came up short, giving Team Canada an opportunity for five points.

"This was the turning point," says Sandra. "Anytime you get five in competitive curling it's a turning point. I was a little nervous. I knew if I drew this one in, we had control in a big way. But I was concerned about Norway's aggressive play and how well they played the four-rock FGZ. I never felt it was over, even if I made my shot. I threw the out-turn draw and made it. We were up 6-1. We made our last five shots and Norway missed all five, by a total of just a few inches."

Norway's never-say-die attitude was now Canada's biggest concern. Norway only got one with hammer in the sixth, but put big pressure on Canada in the seventh. Sandra was facing three on her final shot. A miss and it would be a one- or two-point game with a tremendous momentum shift. Sandra recalls that seventh end: "The turning point was the fifth end, but it was the seventh end that put us back on track. It was straight damage control. We called the double on my last shot. I couldn't miss them both, but I needed to get at least two of their rocks out of there. We made it, and they only stole one. We were still up 6-3, but I felt like we got a little control back with that shot."

Norway stole one more in the eighth to make it 6-4. The ninth end went Canada's way and they got

their deuce to go up 8-4 coming home. Even with the five-ender, it was the first time the women could sense that championship number three was really in their grasp. The tenth end was a mere formality as the Canadians ran Norway out of rocks. It was over, and history would record a new chapter in women's curling. Sandra, Jan, Joan, and Marcia had become the world's first three-time women's world champions.

This one was possibly the sweetest and most memorable. Sandra articulates it well: "To come back after everything we'd been through, three babies in the same year and a fourth on the way; 14 months without the same line-up; winning Saskatchewan all over again; going to the Hearts and winning Canada; going to the Worlds; my pregnancy; Jan's nagging injury; homesickness for all the little ones in Regina. Three-time world champions! Who would have thought it?"

The honours and accolades started to roll in, the theme being "best women's team of all time." Three world championships within a five-year period will be incredibly difficult to duplicate.

The province they were all born and raised in gave them its ultimate sporting honour on June 14, less than two months after Berne – induction into the Saskatchewan Sports Hall of Fame. This honour is usually given to great athletes and teams after their formal retirement from competitive play.

Ironically, Team Schmirler's ultimate goal in 1997 was not the world championship; going to Brandon in November and winning the Olympic trials was still their focus. The 1997 season was off to a fabulous start, but it was only half over.

Lindsay Sparkes gives an insight into the team's primary goal when they began the 1996-97 season. "They are one of the most driven teams I have ever watched or worked with. We met together at a high-performance camp the summer before the 1995-96 curling season. This was after their third-place finish in Calgary. One of the things we talked about was goals. Most teams I work with take it a season at a time. They were talking about Nagano in 1998, the Olympics. They were committed to keeping the team together and improving what they already had. We're talking about a team that had just won two world championships. I had no sense that they thought

they'd arrived. Their humility is one of their assets – constantly looking for ways to improve as individuals and as a team.

"This team doesn't look over their shoulders to past accomplishments. They look ahead, set a target, and seek to meet their goals. They set up a realistic plan over the next few years that kept family first, but gave them the best chance to get to the trials and become Canada's first team to win a sanctioned Olympic medal.

"They leave no stone unturned, to use the curling metaphor. The women plan, prepare to minimize outside distractions, reinforce their family support system, and continually work on their curling game."

As Sandra reveals, "We were thrilled to win our third Worlds, but it didn't slow us down in our preparation for Nagano. It simply reinforced to ourselves that we could get back to the top. Berne created momentum, it was up to us to ride the wave." ◉

Husbands, kids and dogs were all there at the Callie to send the team off to the Olympic trials in 1997.

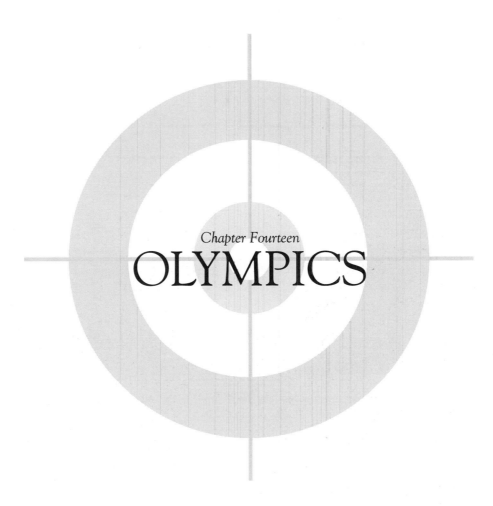

Chapter Fourteen

OLYMPICS

Team Schmirler qualified as Canada's first

sanctioned Olympic female curling team as a result of one of the most memorable pressure shots in the history of the sport.

It was the seventh end of the Olympic trials final between Sandra Schmirler and Shannon Kleibrink's Calgary rink. Kleibrink had wrestled the momentum away from Team Schmirler and was one up playing the seventh end. Because they had hammer, Sandra decided to gamble with the end. It backfired big time. The Calgary team was looking to steal, to go two up, and seize control and a berth in the Olympics.

When Sandra came to throw her first stone, the only shot she had was a run-back off a guard to open things up. The Calgarians had a stone in the four-foot, guarded like Fort Knox. The only consolation was that Schmirler had two healthy second shots, so the end wouldn't get totally out of control.

Sandra's first stone rubbed off a guard and rolled to the side, leaving the Calgary stone still covered. Sandra was disgusted with herself and let a national TV audience know about it with one of her off-the-cuff colourful metaphors.

As Jan and Sandra looked over the mess they were in, they both realized that the miss may have become their only hope, giving them a shot at a long-angle wick (a very fine hit-and-roll off another stone) into Kleibrink's counter in the four foot.

For some reason, Shannon and her team ignored, or never saw, the long-angle wick. Sandra and Jan were whispering to each other at the back of the house when Sandra motioned to Jan that the wick was playable, a low-percentage shot but makeable.

Jan describes the game within the game. "I don't think they even saw the wick. So I said to Sandra, 'Don't even look at it, don't even think it, because they haven't seen it yet.' When I curled with Randy Woytowich

Joan – "When the CCA proposed the playoff (for a position at the Olympic trials)...I started to cry, 'cause I had just quit the team."

he used to always say, 'Don't even think it, because then they'll change their mind. Just be quiet and look disinterested.'

"I was afraid they'd see us talking about it and change their minds and get rid of the shot that gave us the wick. If they played that shot, we literally didn't have a shot and would have to concede a point. They chose to throw another guard to cover part of the four-foot that really didn't matter. Basically they were guarding a very good guard."

Sandra says, "I wholeheartedly agreed with Jan. Not just so Kleibrink's team wouldn't hear, but the crowd as well. Brandon is such a knowledgeable crowd that we've seen them change a skip's mind for the better by cheering certain calls. We had to stay quiet."

It's like Napoleon used to tell his troops – "Don't interrupt the enemy while they're making a mistake." Napoleon must have spent some time in the Scottish highlands observing this new game played on ice in the long winter months.

As soon as Shannon threw her guard stone, Sandra and Jan went straight to the wickable stone, talked about the right weight and where to put the broom. They knew it was their only shot, as incredibly precise as it had to be. If they made it, they could score anywhere from one to three points.

Sandra settled in the hack. "I knew I was going to make it. It was uncanny. I wasn't scared or nervous, because it was such a long shot. It's never happened to me like this before, but everything around me went blurry in my head, and things got all fuzzy except for what was straight down the ice. All I could see was like tunnel vision down to Jan's broom."

Sandra pushed out of the hack and delivered the stone with perfect weight, right on the broom. Halfway down the ice, she let out her now famous shriek. She threw it perfectly, Jan called the sweepers off and on at the right times, Marcia and Joan did the necessary work. The rock wicked off the side stone and rolled into the rings, removing the Kleibrink stone perfectly. They scored a "three-ball," as Sandra refers to it, to go up by two with three ends to go. It was a thing of beauty, the kind of trick shot you'd see in a smoke-filled billiard hall, a sensational shot that captured the essence of curling.

The crowd erupted. Sandra almost lost control. The team hugged and shed a few tears, an unusual mid-game celebration. They took advantage of the three-minute CBC time-out to recompose and get their heads together for the final three ends.

The road to Nagano began as a seed in 1988 and became a passionate dream in the spring of 1995 after the disappointment of the team's third-place finish at the Calgary Scott Tournament of Hearts. At that point, the pressure of trying to three-peat was over. It was time for having children. Joan wanted to take the year off to have her second child. The other three would curl together unless another pregnancy occurred.

In May of 1995, Joan took part in the CCA meetings in Ottawa, to discuss the format for the November 1997 Olympic trials tournament in Brandon. Ten men's and ten women's teams would compete; the two recent Canadian champions would play off for a position in the fall of 1995, and the 1996 and 1997 champions would automatically qualify. The seven other spots would be earned through sanctioned bonspiels across the country. This meant the first spot up for grabs was a best-of-three playoff between Connie Laliberte's rink and Team Schmirler.

Joan had a myriad of emotions going through her as she sat in the meetings. "The CCA really wanted our team to be one of the ten in Brandon, but you had to earn a spot by winning a major 'spiel or the Hearts. When they proposed the playoff of 1994 and 1995 champions as the first route, I started to cry, 'cause I had just quit the team. But I phoned Regina, all excit-ed, and shared the format with my former teammates.

"This was the best opportunity, because it was a one-out-of-two chance. Everything else was a major bonspiel or winning the Hearts.

"They were more than understanding and graciously invited me back for the trials playoff. We had won together and it was our opportunity to go together to the Olympics."

This brought on a natural pressure to qualify in 1995 and not have to worry about winning a bonspiel or Hearts over the next two years.

Sandra explains, "We all wanted to start our families and this for us was the perfect opportunity. If we win the best-of-three against Connie, we don't have to jump through all the hoops of extra curling to qualify. For me, this is when all the negative mental stuff started. One great opportunity, and we are freed up from a lot of extra obligation. We could all have kids and our original team could stay together for our Olympic run. I put a lot of pressure on myself, like never before."

Marcia on trial – "I was confident, yet wondering...these other teams had curled twice as much as us."

157

Realizing that they could use some extra resources in preparing for the trials, the team called up Lindsay Sparkes from Vancouver. Lindsay had been their team leader at each of the Worlds they had won. She was a curling Yoda of the highest order. Lindsay had been a Scott and Worlds winner plus an unsanctioned Olympic gold medallist, curling third for Linda Moore at the 1988 Calgary Winter Olympics, when curling was a demonstration sport. She was a certified coach and a top curling psychologist.

Pat Reid, the CCA rep for Team Schmirler at all three Worlds and the Olympics says, "This team is so coachable. Already a two-time world champion at the time, and they still are looking for ways to improve. Bringing Lindsay in was so wise. I find it amazing that the successful teams like Schmirler are so open to being taught. It's strength drawing from strength."

The team wanted a game plan to get to Nagano. There were issues to be dealt with, issues as basic as how to bring a fifth player in to replace Joan and sort out the transition back to Joan. How to communicate clearly their roles with a shuffling line-up. How to prepare to play Connie Laliberte, whom they were so familiar with. How to make the Olympics their curling focus. Do they make the Scott a serious goal? If they lose, then what?

Calgary 1995 was a fresh wound. How does the team bounce back from that disappointment? This experience revealed a few weak weapons in the arsenal. How do they work on their weaknesses? How do they strengthen what they are competent with?

Lindsay says, "I saw myself more as a facilitator or consultant. I wanted to be a resource. Help them to identify areas of concern, but also to celebrate their triumphs and to build on the positive that was already in place."

Lindsay's focal point in their weekend of meetings was a diagram she drew up labelled MT. OLYMPUS. Sandra still gets excited when talking about this

Team Schmirler at work in Japan – Sandra goes after an opponent's shot stone in Nagano.

Sandra draws a bead on winning it all. "(The Mount Olympus scenario developed by Lindsay Sparkes) was an accurate description of our mind space."

timely illustration. "It was so perfect for our team."

Lindsay drew a range of mountains. A mountain for every year the team had been together. The highest mountains were the back-to-back world championships. After each season the mountain peak would go back to the bottom and they'd have to start the climb all over again. Each new season was a whole new climb. But after their repeat world titles they only went down about half of the mountain because they automatically qualified for the Scott as Team Canada. Lindsay drew a swinging bridge between the mountains for these years. All other Canadian teams had to start at the bottom and work their way back up.

In the diagram there were rocks – teams and distractions – at the bottom of the mountain. Their target was Team Schmirler and these rocks were throwing themselves at the defending champions to try and defeat them. It was a continual battle to stay at the top of the mountain.

Lindsay discerned that the team's success in 1993 and 1994 was that they hardly ever looked down to watch the rocks being fired at them. But a swinging bridge is unstable when opposing forces take aim for sustained periods of time. The bridge needed mechanisms in place to remain stable. They needed to have their focus on moving upward and onward.

So after winning these back-to-back titles, they were losing their grip on the bridge They were more concerned with hanging on than getting across the bridge to resume their summit attempts. In 1995 in Calgary, the team noticed the rocks were getting closer and they started to feel their effect worse than the previous two seasons.

Sandra says, "This was an accurate description for our mind -space. Maybe we would have lost, even with a proper mental approach, but we would have approached 1995 with a healthier outlook, which would have given us a better chance to win."

It also revealed the root of their fall from being number one: focussing on the distractions – other teams, media demands, venue of events, family demands – and not the task at hand.

Lindsay's reasons for putting Mt. Olympus together were becoming clear. She was trying to get

Team Schmirler to look at what made them successful in the first place and to restore the confidence that they felt was slipping away.

Lindsay told the team, "What went wrong was not your talent and ability but what you were looking at. What's needed is to recapture the mental state of when you sustained success." Lindsay referred to this as the ideal performance state.

Recapturing this ideal mental state – they learned ways to cultivate the state – would not guarantee victory, but create a climate that would give them the best possible chance. Without the ideal performance state, winning at the highest level was virtually impossible.

Mt. Olympus was meant to create ways to reinforce their position on the swinging bridge or to minimize the obstacles on the long climb back up the mountain. The mechanisms to strengthen the bridge or to energize the climb would be built through intentional team-building and correct thinking. Lindsay helped the team to cultivate this ideal performance state of mind.

All four team members said that they would go back to their Mt. Olympus summit meeting when times got a little testy and wins were hard to come by. It was the launching of Team Schmirler on their voyage to Thunder Bay, 1995 – Laliberte, best-of-three Olympic trial qualification – Brandon, 1997 and Nagano, 1998.

This Mt. Olympus summit redirected their energy towards the Olympics. There would be ups and downs between that summer of 1995 and the Olympic trials of November, 1997. They accomplished their goal of being the first team to qualify for Brandon. All four women would have babies. They would survive a very disjointed 1995-96 season by finishing second in Saskatchewan, perhaps their gutsiest accomplishment, considering all the outside distractions. Then they would win their third Scott and Worlds in 1996-97. Which brings us to the beginning of the 1997-98 curling season.

Very little thought was going into defending their Canadian championship. They were excited about the Scott because they would be in Regina, but most of their energy was directed at being ready for the Brandon trials.

Sandra had Sara in September, right around the time most curling clubs were putting in the new season's ice. Would she be "game ready," having just had a baby?

The team selected three bonspiels to fine-tune their game against the calibre of teams that would be in Brandon, while most of the other qualifying teams would curl in seven or eight 'spiels. With Sandra's recent delivery, that's all the team felt was feasible under the circumstances.

The team knew that Brandon would be like a Scott Tournament of Hearts with double the pressure and expectations and overall international interest. They wanted to be rested and hungry to win when they arrived.

Sandra's first game was exactly one month after having Sara. They were playing their old foe Kathy Fahlman in the Regina All Star Super-League. Sandra felt comfortable throwing, but she hurt too much to sweep. Sara must have brought her good karma that night because she curled an amazing 99 per cent, missing one half-shot the entire game.

Kathy Fahlman joked afterwards, "Sandra, if you're going to play this well after having your little girl, I'm going to have a baby!"

The team entered their first 'spiel with Sandra about a week later, the Callie Women's Bonspiel, which was a Regina-and-area event. Team Schmirler curled well enough to win it. This was good for the rink's confidence, and Sandra was feeling more and more like her old self back on the ice.

A couple of weeks later, they entered the SaskPower Women's Cash 'Spiel in Regina. This would be a grand test, as most of the Olympic trial teams entered it. The rink got off to a quick start and qualified out of the A Event to go on to the eight-team sudden-death playoff. They won the quarter-final and moved on to play Calgary's Shannon Kleibrink in the semis, a preview of Brandon. Many picked Shannon's team as one of the top two or three to have a chance to win the trials. Team Schmirler

lost a very entertaining game in an extra end.

Sandra says, "We were down in the game and fought back and almost won it with a big three in the tenth. It never quite worked and they beat us in the extra end. Shannon and her team went on to win the 'spiel. They were looking very good."

At this stage, with the trials only a month away, Kleibrink was sending out a strong message that her team was indeed a favourite going in. She had assembled four of Calgary's best shotmakers, and the team clearly defined and accepted their roles and clicked right from the start. They were solid at every position and every aspect of the game both on and off the ice.

Team Schmirler knew they'd have to solve the Kleibrink machine somewhere along the way, and they were hoping they'd get another shot at them in the FlexiCoil Cash 'Spiel in Saskatoon. The women's event was by invitation only, eight teams, most of which would be in Brandon in a couple more weeks. This was a great tune-up opportunity for Schmirler's rink to check for any cracks in their game.

Joan acknowledges that the FlexiCoil "was a perfect preparation for the trials. It was on national television, TSN, it was in an arena, and most of the teams were going to be in Brandon. It was like a dress rehearsal, with some significant cash on the line."

Sandra says, "It was like mini-Brandon, our first out-of-town event of the season. I took Sara along and was able to get a routine for her and me between games. It helped me figure out what I needed to do to be a mom and a curler while living in a hotel. It was a terrific warm-up for trials."

They brought their A-game, beating Kim Hodson in their first game. Then it was Shannon Kleibrink in the A qualifier. If there were any Kleibrink demons to exorcise, they were swept out in a close-fought victory. It was a huge confidence booster.

They played two-time Canadian and world champion Marilyn Bodogh of Ontario in the semis. "We were awesome," Joan recalls. "One of the best games we may have ever played. That's when we finally said, I think we're ready, we've prepared enough. We can play the best and be at our best. The Olympics were in our grasp and we knew we had a legitimate shot."

The team met Kelley Law's Vancouver team in the final. It was close, but Team Schmirler pulled it out to win $13,000 for capturing first. TSN picked Team Schmirler as the pre-trials favourite. And the *Globe and Mail*'s Bob Weeks echoed that prediction. It was amazing, considering that all four women had recently had babies.

As Joan joked, "Marcia and I said our first goal entering the curling season was to fit back into our curling clothes. After that anything was possible. Bring on the trials."

Their curling colleagues were just as impressed with the curling moms and their newborns. Kelley Law may have expressed it the best when she said, "I had a baby about a year ago. When I first went back on the ice, I couldn't even throw it as far as the hog line on fast ice."

Janet Clews-Strayer, 1993 World Silver Medallist, says, "They are my heroes. I'm not ashamed to say that. They've been a model to women athletes all across Canada. You can tell that family is number one, yet they can still pursue their athletic dreams. Having children doesn't slow them down, they just readjust. What they accomplished during their Olympic run is unbelievable, it's unheard of."

Brandon was two short weeks away. The team took the opportunity to rest, to practise a little, and to work on all sorts of things they hadn't had time to do. Then it was off to Brandon.

The lineup was a who's who of Canadian curling. Every team had been to a Scott, and many had had success in winning it.

The Schmirler team exhibited a quiet confidence as they arrived in Brandon. Joan expresses it well. "I never really had a lot of doubt. Our confidence was strong. I really felt we'd find a way to win. I believe in good feelings and bad feelings. And I had a really good feeling going in.

"Brian's Aunt Marion and Uncle Earl Rigby from Ottawa flew in for the trials. They are huge curling fans and Aunt Marion gets these amazing premonitions. So just before opening banquet, I sought out my relatives to see what Aunt Marion was getting. We were getting pretty nervous and needed reassurance. Her words were that they were cancelling their vacation to Florida and getting tickets to Japan to watch us curl."

Marcia was cautiously optimistic. "I was confident, yet still wondered deep down if we had prepared well enough. These other teams had curled twice as much as us. But I knew that we had a realistic chance with the way we'd been curling."

Sandra soon began to realize the magnitude of the trials. "I knew it would be tough, but I didn't realize it would be as mentally draining as it was. It was physically tough for me having to nurse Sara between games. Mentally I never dreamed it would be so intense. Every team was so tough. I felt it was really critical to get off to a good start because it was a long week and there were no breaks in the schedule. We played Connie in our first game and it was close. Had it gone the other way, you never know how your week's going to go. You play Connie and then you have Borst, followed by Law, then Kleibrink, Merklinger. Any of those games can turn, so it was an advantage mentally to get off to a good start. You get behind the eight ball with a field like that and you may not ever get back out."

Jan went into Brandon feeling very positive, but was also taken back by the competitiveness of each draw. "It was hard. Physically it wasn't tougher than any other event. You'd have two games one day and one game the next, so it was different from a Scott,

161

"Adversity builds character." Both Marcia and Joan played despite grieving the loss of grandmothers throughout the Olympics

Grinning victors – The team's motto of "Baby Steps" applied not only to their family life, but to taking their journey to Olympic gold one shot at a time.

where you have two every day. You got a little more time to rest, but there were no easy teams there. Sometimes at a Scott or Worlds you get some teams that are not at the top level. I mean they are good teams, but they aren't contenders. Every single team in Brandon had a shot. Mentally it was very draining. You could never, ever, let your guard down.

"It was like you won one game and said, 'Okay, thank goodness we got them out of the way. So who do we play next?' You find out and go 'Oh, no, they're going to be tough.' It just never got any easier. Every game was a battle and every game affected the standings so much."

Only three of the ten teams would qualify for the playoffs. The first-place team got a bye to the final, while the second- and third-place teams played off in a sudden-death semi-final.

As the week began they had developed a home-grown motivator – "Baby Steps." It was the team motto for their Olympic journey. Joan explains, "It was a reminder not to look ahead. To take it one shot at a time, one end at a time, one game at a time. Being new moms we all naturally could relate to the concept. We knew if we started to look ahead, that's when we'd start to fall apart. We had to concentrate on the moment-by-moment situation. This really

captured our game-by-game approach at the trials and Olympics. Whenever we've had success, be it city playdowns to Worlds, we always tried to take it stone by stone and not look ahead to another opponent or potential playoff victory."

The critical first game that set the tone for the week was against long-time rival Connie Laliberte. It was a typical opening game for a big event, neither brutal nor outstanding. Schmirler had the better of the play and led 4-2 playing the eighth, when the Winnipeg rink stole two, to give Team Schmirler a little wake-up call. They got one back in the ninth to go one up, without hammer, coming home. Then the Laliberte rink made an uncharacteristic sweeping error that cost them a chance at an extra end. Schmirler won 6-4. Connie, one of the favourites, never recovered, and finished tied for second-last at 3-6.

Edmonton's Cathy Borst was next, their second game of the day. Apart from Sandra, the team curled well, although they lost 7-4. "It was a brutal game on my part," recalls the skipper. "What do you do but get over it? Go feed Sara and forget about it. Which for me is next to impossible."

"Sandra was typically worried after losing to Borst," Jan says. "She was bummed out about playing so bad. The rest of us thought, 'Big deal, Sandra!' It never happens for any extended period of time. We know that when she goes back out for the next game, she'll be ticked off at herself and play great, which of course she did."

Kelley Law of Vancouver was in the wrong place at the wrong time, though she managed to get off to a 2-0 start. Sandra came back with a vengeance, winning 7-5 and creating a six-way tie for first.

The team was a little antsy the way things were shaping up in the standings. In most events, they usually won their first three to five games and set themselves up in a playoff driver's seat. Here they weren't leading the pack, and felt as if they were chasing teams.

Jan says, "It was scary. We already had one loss and we're thinking three or four losses will put us out of the playoffs. There were so many great teams still to play. We felt our backs were against the wall and we had to somehow win a few games in a row."

The next day was Monday, with two games on the agenda. The log jam started to separate. Team Schmirler was on a roll, the only team to win both its games. Kleibrink went down 7-5 and Merklinger, from Ottawa, lost 9-6. The Regina team was alone in first at 4-1, with every other team still in contention. Being on top was the place to be, but there was no cushion to allow any comfort.

The key game on Tuesday was against the other Saskatchewan entry – Sherry Scheirich and her rink from Saskatoon. Team Schmirler won the intraprovincial rivalry 8-5, moving them to 5-1 and closer to one of the coveted playoff spots.

Wednesday's games brought on two of the eastern teams. Team Schmirler won their fifth in a row, beating Halifax's Mary Mattatall 6-4. The win guaranteed them at least a tie-breaker. One more win and they'd clinch a playoff spot.

In the evening draw, they met a hungry and hot team. Marilyn Bodogh, fighting for her playoff life, beat the Regina rink 8-5. Bodogh earned full marks for the win, dropping Schmirler's record to 6-2 with one game remaining.

Thursday's game versus Alison Goring of Ontario could clinch first place overall and a bye to the final. A loss could also drop them to fourth place and a tie-breaker or, with all the combinations possible because of the closeness in the standings, they could lose and

still clinch second or third. Regardless of the outcome, they would curl again.

They beat Goring 11-4, clinching first place and a ticket to Sunday's winner-take-all final. They were now one game away from being Team Canada at the Olympics. The only drawback was a 68-hour wait in between games, almost three full days, the longest stretch they'd ever encountered waiting for a final.

Physically, they appreciated the time off leading up to the finals. More time to rest their motherly bodies from early morning feedings and lack of sleep, plus all their preparations for the trials. Mentally, however, the 68 hours felt like 68 days.

THE FINAL STANDINGS AT THE OLYMPIC TRIALS:	
Schmirler	7-2
Kleibrink	6-3
Law	6-3
Bodogh	5-4
Borst	5-4
Merklinger	5-4
Goring	3-6
Laliberte	3-6
Scheirich	3-6
Mattatall	2-7

Kleibrink would play Kelley Law in the semifinals, two of the hottest teams from the autumn 1997 bonspiel circuit. Whomever Schmirler faced, it would be a tension-filled struggle. The Calgary team won the semi-final in a tentative match, with both teams playing quite conservatively. Law was up 3-2 playing the eighth, when Kleibrink blew it open with a huge four-ender, eventually winning 7-4.

Meanwhile, Team Schmirler was trying to fill their time, keep their edge, and not let the butterflies evolve into the dreaded ravens. On Friday, they watched the men's semi-final in their hotel rooms. Kevin Martin's Edmonton rink defeated Toronto's wily veteran Eddie Werenich. After the game, they headed down to the Keystone Centre to practise.

Joan says, "It was so bizarre. A lot of the media was still there and Sandra got bombarded with questions. We finally got on the ice and it was not very good. With the crowd leaving and the lights, the ice conditions really changed drastically. It was worse than we expected."

Team Schmirler keeps a close eye on things as Denmark's Helena Blach-Lavrsen guides a rock to the house.

"It was a waste of time to practise and hope it was like game conditions," Jan explains. "All it did was limber us up a bit. Sandra lost it and complained to the poor ice-makers. We were all feeling the tension."

In the players' lounge after their practise, Anne Merklinger from Ottawa came up to the team and said, "I want to wish your team good luck. You women are the best, go out and win it all, we're really pulling for you."

Sandra burst into tears, with Anne looking at her wondering what she'd said wrong. At this point Jan, Joan, and Marcia started to laugh, realizing the tension leading up to the game was creating an emotional roller coaster that rivaled any Scott or world championship.

It was a release. "It seems to happen before all our big games," Sandra says. "The extremes of laughing and crying somehow help us find that emotional balance to keep our heads. You gotta let it out and then it's gone. We are just so on-edge that any little thing can trigger us off."

On Saturday they shopped and watched the men's final on television, avoiding the emotionally charged atmosphere of the venue and the sometimes invasive attention of fans and the media.

It was time now for Marcia and Joan's cry as they watched the interview with Mike Harris's team after their victory over Kevin Martin. The Toronto skip concluded by saying, "I'm so fortunate to be curling with my best friends."

"I am in the washroom for the interview, when I hear Marcia and Joan sobbing," relates Jan. "I think, 'What now?' So I come out and ask, 'What in the world is going on?' They can hardly talk to me. They are just so moved by Harris's comments. So I'm the only one who hasn't had her cry.

"We go down to the rink to practise and the ice-makers are assuring us that it's close to game conditions. Then the trials committee asks us if it's okay if they practise the special music for the final on Sunday. I thought, no big deal.

"This is my moment. The music is turned way up, and we can't hear each other at either end of the sheet. The ice is really not that good. I lose it at the ice-makers. They are the best, we like them and know them, but it's the tension. I don't cry, but I blow my stack and it's my emotional release. We've all had our

cries and can't wait for Sunday."

"The hours just kept dragging on," Marcia remembers. "Surprisingly, we all slept very well on that Saturday night. We got up and had our breakfast and a pre-game meeting in one of our hotel rooms. We mostly talked about what was the worst that could happen? We got our feelings and fears out in the open. It helped us get a little perspective before the game. It was good for Sandra to deal with the issue of having to leave Sara for almost a month if we won. We could all support her in this because we'd been through it."

Sandra says, "I didn't want to go there with the thoughts of leaving Sara. I mean, it was in the back of my mind, but the time seemed right to bring it to the forefront at this meeting. Once again, I cried, and it helped relieve the pressure. I knew that if we won that my little girl would be in very capable hands, it just helped to verbalize my apprehension with my trusted friends. I knew the support was there, but I'd never gone through leaving my child before."

The final game began and the team maintained control right up to the fifth-end break, leading 3-1 and playing very well.

Then, as Sandra says, "The sixth end was the most innocent three-ball we may have ever surrendered. When I came to shoot they were lying only one shooter. I slid too far on a freeze attempt and they followed it up with a great double. But we were still not in huge trouble. There was a pocket of rocks all in the back twelve-foot that I tried to freeze to on my last shot. A half-shot would keep the damage down, but I rubbed a stone the wrong way and gave her an open shot for three. It's the last scenario we expected. Of course Shannon nailed it for her three."

"It was devastating to go from almost total control to losing by a point," Joan recalls. "Sandra didn't throw it bad on her last stone, it really reacted in an unexpected way. But we know curling can be like that."

The team turned the tide with Sandra's Hollywood shot in the seventh. But as they hugged after that shot, they all reminded each other that three ends still had to be played and they were only two up, without hammer.

Kleibrink's team could have folded their tent and played out the string, but they responded like real champions, taking advantage of the FGZ and hammer to get their two points back and tie the game at six.

The Keystone Centre was electric. Frenzied fans knew they were witnessing an historic game.

One key miss by Shannon Kleibrink in the ninth end opened the door for Sandra on her last shot. It was a wide-open hit for three, Sandra coolly throwing her stone and making a perfect take-out. They could now taste the Olympics – three up coming home and all four women throwing with above-average confidence.

The rest of the game was a mere formality as Team Schmirler ran Kleibrink out of rocks in the tenth end. As Sandra settled into the hack for her final stone, Joan encouraged her by saying, "Just throw it normal."

"Chances of me being normal are not very good," Sandra responded. She threw it up the broom, hitting it perfectly, then buried her face in her hands and started to weep. The expectations of the Olympics, the media attention, a new baby, "wacked-out hormones," all came together. It was the most emotional curling

week they'd ever experienced.

Joan captures much of the team's feelings. "After the game, we were a bit of an emotional mess. We were hugging each other, our husbands, our families. It seemed like everyone we knew was in tears. My mom leaned over the boards, gave me a huge hug and we had a big cry – mostly about the fact that my Dad, who had died that spring, wasn't there to puff out his chest and say, 'That's my daughter!' It seemed like we had been holding that cry in for an awfully long time. Brian said everyone joined us."

The team had a little over two months to prepare for the Olympic Games. During the short flight back to Regina, somewhere over the plains of Saskatchewan, the team made a toast to "Baby Steps," the motivator that captured the essence of their approach to Japan. They had reached phase two of their three-phase process of winning Olympic gold. They knew that having a chance in Nagano would require a step-by-step, stone-by-stone, game-by-game approach. The toast saluted a fine accomplishment and reinforced their team philosophy of what it takes to be successful.

The next couple of months "would be a lesson in frustration in getting ready for the biggest sporting event of our lives," according to Sandra. "The CCA would normally guide us through the hoops of going to a world championship. They were as green as we were, because it was the first time of full-medal status."

"The outside distractions of getting ready for Nagano were like nothing we'd ever experienced,"

165

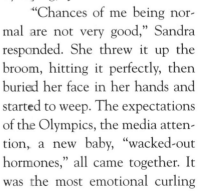

Jan and Joan heat up the ice for an always-crucial free-guard-zone shot by Marcia.

echoes Joan. "We had too much partial information. We heard it would cost $10,000 to get our husbands to Japan. So we almost gave up on that idea until we found ways to bring the costs down. We had to do so much ourselves. We assumed that the COA (Canadian Olympic Association) would take care of most of the logistics. To a degree they did, but in co-operation with our governing body. Since this was the first time of working together, they had to hammer out how to get on the same page."

Everything from team uniforms fitting properly, to the massive media interest, to arranging travel packages for extended family, to team finances from the COA, all became distractions that the team didn't think they'd have to worry about. It was a learning process that was working out the kinks on the go.

"Our practices were often spent in discussing how we would work through the Olympic preparation distractions," Jan reports. "We'd spend half of our time on the ice and cut it short to discuss things that we assumed were taken care of. We needed to spend most of that time on the ice, not working through what we perceived to be minutiae."

Joan says, "It was a genuinely exciting time leading up to the Olympics, but all the outside planning was taking its toll, and our curling did suffer a bit in the process. The CCA will be better prepared for 2002."

Despite all the planning and distractions, the team managed to get in three 'spiels plus a few games in their women's all-star league in Regina. Their first

game after winning the trials was only two days later. The team played Joan's sister, Cathy, in the Regina all-star schedule, losing 5-1. As Joan said, "It is hard to get overconfident in this game. You can get put in your place so quickly."

The team went to Thunder Bay to play in the TSN/JVC skins game just before Christmas. "We curled one game, won some money, but didn't curl very well," Sandra admits. "We had our chances but weren't capitalizing. I remember in one game I had almost an identical shot to that seventh-end wick in Brandon and never even came close."

During the Christmas break they entered the local Highland 'spiel. "We thought it would be a lesson in frustration," says Jan. "Joan went home for the holiday. We'd be using lots of spares because of Christmas dinners and such. We were playing all the top men's teams, and if we didn't do well we'd be uptight about it. But we needed the games. We were the only women's team in it.

"Les Rogers filled in most of the time as a third. We used four or five extra players. Joan got back and phoned to see if we were still alive. We were, and half an hour later she was playing. We stayed hot and won the whole thing.

"For the men, this 'spiel is big because the winner gets a free berth to the city playdowns and doesn't have to go through the process of winning a berth through club play. I remember we broke Randy Bryden's heart in that final. Before the game we teased his team that we could be bought and give him

In preparation for topping the Mount Olympus in Lindsay Sparkes' motivational diagram, Team Schmirler visited the top of the Jung Frau, the highest mountain peak in the Alps.

the game. Our expectations were really low going in and our confidence level was renewed – big time – after we won the whole thing."

The final preparation for Nagano 1998 was in Switzerland for the Berne Ladies International Cup. This was the dress rehearsal for the Olympics. Lindsay Sparkes went along, as she would be the official CCA coach in Nagano.

The team went for three primary reasons. First, most of the eight teams that were going to the Olympics would be in Berne. Jan says, "Winning would be a bonus. We wanted to see the teams we'd be facing. Two of the teams, from Scotland and the US, we had never played. You can watch them on TV or behind the glass and if they are doing real well, your doubts can grow. We never did play these two teams in Berne, but we got to watch them up close and to meet them. It may sound funny, but it helped."

The second reason was to further cement the team concept that is so vital to Team Schmirler's success. Time away together has always strengthened their team and their commitment to each other, which translates into positive vibes on the ice.

Finally, they wanted to consult with Lindsay. The team came with "tons of paper," as Sandra put it. "We spent a few sessions with Lindsay dealing with our emotions and fears of going to the Olympics."

"To be frank, I was scared," says Jan, who always looks so cool on game day. "The Olympics is the biggest sporting stage in the world. We didn't want to come out flat or embarrass ourselves. Lindsay got us

to not just talk about our insecurities but to write them out and to discuss them as a team."

Joan says, "It was great. We all saw that we had the same fears and emotions. We were excited and terrified at the same time. There were so many mixed emotions we were able to work through. It helped us to support each other."

The highlight, Marcia says, was, "going up to the highest peak in the Alps, the Jung Frau. We were literally on top of the world. It was very symbolic for us as a team. The Jung Frau reminded us of the awesome task of climbing to the top. But what a feeling when we got there! We all held hands at the top and jumped together in celebration. Now it was time to climb curling's highest peak, in Japan."

The team made it to the final in Berne, losing 6-5 to friend and rival Elisabet Gustafson of Sweden.

When they arrived back in Regina, Sandra and Jan's broom bag was missing. In it were their brooms, curling shoes, and $150 of Swiss chocolate. The last distraction the team needed was two team members breaking in a new pair of curling shoes before the biggest event of their lives. They ordered new shoes, and finally, about a week later, the broom bag showed up with the brooms and shoes, but no chocolate.

The team was home in Regina for two weeks before heading off to Calgary and then Japan. It was a hectic time of last-minute preparations and parenting. Joan's two children contracted chicken pox right before she left.

Then the team tried a media ban at the sugges-

Joan, Sandra, and Jan, with Team Canada manager Pat Reid, take a break from their Calgary preparations for the trip to Nagano to practise their four-part harmony.

tion of Marnie McBean, a multiple-gold medallist on the Canadian rowing team. "Normally we can deal with all the media requests, but we had no idea how much the Olympics would add to it," Sandra explained. "It was becoming time-consuming. Then Marnie called me just before going to Berne, to encourage our team. We had gotten to know each other through a couple of events for sports. She said that she and Kathleen Heddle had asked the media to stay away three weeks prior to the Olympics so they could work on their training. The Rowing Association worked it out so they would have a big press conference or two before the ban.

"We asked the CCA to send a press release to the Canadian media. There was a bit of a misunderstanding and it came across that all media requests were to be arranged for Team Schmirler through Lindsay Sparkes or the CCA. Just another adjustment on the road to the Olympics!

"We only wanted it for ten days prior. It never really worked, but the local media understood and really respected our training commitments."

The evening before leaving for Calgary, SaskPower sponsored a going-away reception that was first class all the way. "It was a terrific send-off," Marcia said. "About 100 people, and the speeches were short and sweet. Most everyone assured us that even if we didn't win we were still champions and that everyone was pulling for us. SaskPower made a short video of our years together, set to music. It made us all cry. Then Joan spoke on behalf of the team and did a great job and I started to cry again. We were all living on the edge, our emotions were so close to the surface."

The team arrived in Calgary for four days of final preparations and formal Olympic send-offs. Their first task was to pick out Olympic clothing and uniforms. Jan describes the scene: "We were escorted to get our Olympic outfits. Wow! We were taken to a room where they had four piles, and I do mean piles, of clothing in the sizes we indicated on the sizing forms we had completed shortly after winning in Brandon. There were two staff helping us and we got sized for a leather jacket, opening ceremonies jacket,

boots, shoes, a fleece outfit, warm-up suit, pants, blazer, shirt, several tops, luggage, belt, hats, scarf, mitts, curling uniforms – 12 for only nine games maximum. It was so exciting! Unbelievable!"

The formal team was finally all together, the four curlers plus fifth Atina Ford, coach Lindsay Sparkes, team leader and manager Pat Reid, and co-coach Anita Ford. The informal supporters – the husbands and Gary Ford – would meet the team in Japan.

The second day in Calgary Joan picked up the phone at 8 a.m. to hear that her grandmother had just passed away. Joan says, "I read somewhere that to fully appreciate the greatest joys in life, one must experience the greatest sorrows. That's the only way I can explain how horrible I felt at a time of such excitement. This would be a day of many tears and leaning on my teammates, my friends, to help me get through."

On Monday, February 2, the team boarded a plane for Osaka, Japan, and the Olympic experience. Before the plane took off, Jan was philosophizing and joking with Sandra and asked, "Are we really ready? Do we really belong? Have we prepared enough? I wonder if the other atheletes feel this way? All I know is that I am every inch a competitor. I can't wait for it to start."

Jan expresses the question of every Olympic athlete – should they be representing their country? Of course the Schmirler team are worthy representatives for their sport and country. As Lindsay Sparkes has said, "This team is as highly focussed on succeeding at the highest level as any sports team. Their commitment to the sport and seeking to master all of its nuances is second to none. Any athlete or team could learn from the Schmirlers. They easily fulfill the Olympic criteria for competing."

As the team arrived in Japan, they had about five days before their opening round robin game. Their time was filled with team meetings, practice, media interviews, gender testing, Olympic protocol, and rules meetings. They spent a lot of time with the men's curling team of Mike Harris, Richard Hart, Collin Mitchell, George Karrys, and fifth Paul Savage, the savvy veteran with a ton of Brier experience.

When the curlers prepared for opening ceremonies, they enjoyed meeting the other athletes. It was refreshing to discover how many athletes in other sports watched curling, played it, or had family who were members of curling clubs across Canada.

Pat Reid said, "There were a lot of requests by other athletes to get tickets for curling. About a dozen NHL players from Team Canada attended various games. Shae-Lynn Bourne, one of the world's best ice-dancers, wanted the autographs of the whole Schmirler team for her grandfather, who faithfully watches curling on television."

The team stayed at the Curling Olympic Village in Karuizawa, about an hour out of Nagano and the main village. While accommodations in Nagano were first-class, the women felt theirs in Karuizawa were even more impressive.

The opening ceremonies were on February 7, but curling did not begin until February 10. One of the highlights was being marched into the Olympic Stadium in Nagano for the lighting of the torch and all the festivi-

ties of the opening ceremonies.

Jan describes a little of that memorable day. "It was a hurry-up-and-wait kind of day. Everyone was so friendly. We were marching between the figure skaters and women's hockey. The one thing I realized is that people are basically people. You may see them on TV, but they are just as interested in you as you are in them.

"Finally it was time to march in. The chants of 'Go Canada Go' definitely got the heart pumping. As soon as we entered the stadium, we spotted Pat Reid furiously snapping pictures. I must admit the actual entrance and march was a bit disappointing. I was expecting the big roar and it just didn't happen. It was still exciting and we were furiously waving at every Canadian flag we saw in the stands. The Japanese are so polite, they just don't cheer the way North Americans do. The march around the stadium went fairly fast and next thing you know, we were sitting in our seats.

"The highlight was the lighting of the torch. When the fellow entered the stadium, having lost an arm and leg to landmines, surrounded by the little snowlets, I almost started crying – it was so touching and heartwarming. He passed the torch to Midori Ito (gold medal figure skater), who came rising out of the stadium. I will never forget that moment when she lit the flame. It was an incredibly awesome sight – a very powerful moment. Lindsay Sparkes started to cry – and athletes all over just looked awestruck. It was great."

After that, the team headed to Karuizawa for the final preparations for opening game. The next day

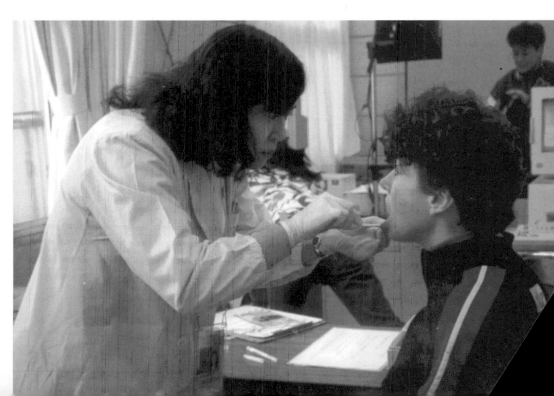

Joan undergoes mandatory gender testing in preparation for competing at the Olympics.

169

the team had one of the longest practice sessions they can remember. They played on every sheet and tried to match all the rocks. Marcia was impressed. "The venue was very pretty and homey. The seating wasn't huge like a hockey arena but could squeeze in over 1,500. But the fans would be close to the ice. The ice was terrific. It had a reasonable curl and ran 25 to 26 seconds from hog to tee."

After practice, the team had a meeting to discuss the importance of playing Atina. Jan explains, "We clarified our understanding that if we medalled and Atina Ford didn't play, all she'd receive was a diploma. All she had to do is throw one rock. She'd done so much for us, it would have been a shame to leave her out. We agreed that when the opportunity came, we'll stick her in, so she could receive a medal."

Finally, the competition began. Game one of the seven-game round robin was against their North American rivals from the US. There were only eight countries that qualified for the Games and the top four teams in the round robin would advance to a single knockout playoff round. The team felt a 5-2 record would guarantee a spot in the playoffs; 4-3 or

less would probably put them in a tie-breaker or totally eliminate them.

Lisa Schoeneberg was skipping the American entry. The Canadians came out strong and caught their southern neighbours flat-footed, building up a 7-2 lead after five ends. And despite a poor showing in the sixth and seventh, they managed a 7-6 win.

The team had a game later that day versus Norwegian Dordi Nordby, but decided to go back to the Olympic village for a quick rest. Mike Harris's team was scheduled to play between the women's two games, and asked Atina Ford to check on their laundry back in the Village. It was the perfect setup for a practical joke.

It was a timely tension-release as they tied all the socks together and strung underwear through them, then tied their masterpiece to the men's doorknobs. The men got a real kick out of it, and the fun between these two Olympic contenders continued throughout the competition.

The women knew their game against Norway would be a battle. Nordby's rink, along with Sweden and Canada, were considered the three favourites

Team Canada marches in for the opening ceremonies of the 1998 Olympic Winter Games in Nagano.

Team Canada hangs out at Athletes' Village.

according to the *Sports Illustrated* pre-Olympic predictions.

Sandra comments on her team's only Olympic loss. "Norway lost a big game to Sweden in the morning draw. We figured they would come out firing. And guess what? Did they ever! Jan and Joan both struggled, and I missed a bad one in the sixth end. We thought there might have been something with the stones, but who knows? We lost in an extra end. Dordi drew three times to count us out of points. Seemed we never could get anything set up with hammer. We knew we'd have to pick up our game as a team pretty quick."

Day two of the round robin brought only one game, against the host nation. The Japanese team gave them a real run for the money until the Canadians broke it open late in the game. Sandra curled a solid 90 per cent and Marcia was steady for her third straight game. Joan and Jan were picking it up, but not yet satisfied with their performances. Atina played for Joan in the first end, so she'd be eligible for a medal.

Jan was struggling with her first-ever middle-of-the-game melt down. It may have helped galvanize the team, because she was usually so even-keeled and steady. She explains the inner turmoil. "I start the game playing poorly and all of a sudden, I'm feeling sorry for myself and wishing I was back in Regina. I think the pressure was getting to me, plus lack of sleep.

"I'm thinking about my son, feeling out of my mind, and I just lose control of my emotions. I can't think of any positive thoughts. I just keep thinking, 'What am I doing here? I can't do this – I want to go home!' Not exactly the thought process you would want in a club game, let alone the Olympics!

"At the fifth end break, everyone can tell I'm teetering on the brink of breaking down. Lindsay is trying to be her positive self and is saying to enjoy the experience, revel in the fact that it's a very challenging game and that we can rise to the occasion. Of course, I know I should be, but just can't. I know I have to be by myself to try and get it together, but when Sandra asks me if I'm okay I literally start bawling. At that moment I am definitely totally out of control. Somehow I manage to hang in there, calm myself down and finish the game, playing much better."

Jan calls this her "mental moment." She got over it, becoming the top-shooting third of the week, and the team dominated the Japanese rink during the last half of the game to win 7-4.

Day three would be a day of lows and highs. Marcia woke up early and sensed she should call home. She got the devastating news that her grandmother had passed away just a few hours earlier. Marcia describes the tragic news in her Olympic diary, "As soon as I got off the phone I went back to my room, because the tears kept coming. Within five minutes Joan was down, followed by Sandra and Jan. I was so grateful I curl with my best friends.

"They asked whether I wanted to curl – I said yes because that's what my grandma would have wanted. Plus, I needed something to keep my mind off things. I was weepy throughout the game against Denmark, but managed to play well."

Both Marcia and Joan were grieving the loss of their grandmothers throughout the Olympics. Not many outside their circle of supporters realized the incredible roller coaster of emotions this whole team was experiencing during what should have been the time of their lives. But the setbacks simply drove this team closer and closer together.

If "adversity builds character" applies to Team Schmirler, it came out with a vengeance in their two

171

games that day. They cruised to a 9-5 win over Denmark's Helena Blach-Lavrsen, and later that evening finished off Great Britain's Kirsty Hay 8-3 in eight ends. Team Schmirler was back to its usual dominant self as all four brought their averages up, and the whole team was clicking. Sandra was feeling very confident in her draw game. Not good news for the upcoming opponents and the playoffs within their sights.

The team looks back on February 11 as their day from hell, and it wasn't just the tragic news of Marcia's grandmother. Jan received an e-mail from Edmonton *Journal* reporter Terry Jones, asking the team about a rumour of being reprimanded for foul language, which turned out to be just that – a rumour – but was upsetting nevertheless.

Joan summed up day three of the round robin with a question and her own answer: "Why is it that a team often plays its best on the worst of all possible days? I think it sometimes takes bad things to make you focus more intently. It's amazing how sadness or controlled anger can make you concentrate so strongly."

The team was now 4-1 and chasing 5-0 Sweden. One more win would clinch a coveted playoff spot. Next up were the Swedish champions. The winner would most likely clinch first overall as well, with only one game remaining after this clash of female champions.

The only game on day four was the showdown for first place. The roll that began during the last half of the game with Japan continued. Jan, despite serious flu symptoms, played possibly her strongest game of the Olympics, and the team clinched a spot in the semi-finals with a solid 7-5 win.

Jan was called for her first-ever hog-line violation. Joan called it "a random violation call, because it didn't appear to be related to sliding over or not." Two days later one of the officials personally apologized, having reviewed the tape and finding no evidence of the violation.

On the fifth and final day of round robin play, each team would play only once. Jan was hit hard with the flu and sat out their final game against Germany's Andrea Schopp. Atina filled in admirably in the team's victory to clinch first overall. The final was 8-5. Canada was awarded first place because of their win over Sweden.

THE FINAL STANDINGS:	
Canada	6-1
Sweden	6-1
Denmark	5-2
Great Britain	4-3
Japan	2-5
Norway	2-5
USA	2-5
Germany	1-6

Canada would play Great Britain's Kirsty Hay in one semi-final, while Sweden would clash with their Scandanavian rivals from Denmark. The losers would play off for the bronze, while the winners would compete for gold and silver. The excitement was building.

The team met their husbands for supper and had a big laugh at the expense of Gary Ford, whose great sense of humour allowed him to laugh along with the ribbing. Jan's husband, Frank, was sharing a room with Gary, and was wakened earlier that morning by Gary talking in his sleep.

Jan records the episode in her Olympic diary. "Frank told me that earlier that day the men had eaten at a traditional Japanese restaurant. They were very polite and ate the dishes set before them. You could tell Gary was having a hard time with some of the food.

"His talking woke the men up at 5 a.m. Frank was laughing so hard he could hardly tell us what he said. 'Great shot. The girls are playing really well. Great sweeping, girls. Raw fish – I ain't eating any friggin' raw fish. Damn raw fish. I just ate horse meat? But I like horses! John Wayne wouldn't eat a horse.'"

The next day was Valentine's Day and the Olympic semi-finals. The team had a tough night of sleeping. With sudden-death semi-finals, there's no second chance.

Kirsty Hay and her Scottish rink were up to the challenge, with Hay playing a scrappy, hang-in-there kind of game. Jan says, "everyone seemed to be calm, cool, and collected. The semi-final is usually the scariest – there's an unbelievable amount of pressure.

"We dodged a bullet in the first end, when Sandra made a nice hit and roll and forced Scotland to take one with hammer. At the fifth-end break, we were one up without last rock. But we were playing a little tentative. Every time we had a chance for two, we'd hit and roll out. The team seemed a little on edge at

172

the break, but I amazed myself with how calm I felt."

The last half of the game was actually fairly poorly played. The ice got quite frosty and straightened out. Both teams were having trouble.

"It was maybe the worst game of my competitive life," Joan says. "I couldn't put any shots together. In the seventh end, I had a meltdown, and Sandra came over, put her arm around me and whispered, 'Hang in there, Joan. Just throw through the tears.'

"I felt like I was letting the team down. I'm usually the positive reinforcer. That's the first time Sandra had ever done that. Her timing was perfect. I finally put it together in the tenth and eleventh ends. But what a horrible feeling to struggle like that."

The team was one up coming home without hammer. Joan redeemed her sub-par performance with a great double, keeping the end clean. When Kirsty went to throw her last rock, all she had was a draw to the full eight-foot, facing two Canadian counters. She had to make it to force the extra end. The way the ice was changing made the shot a little more difficult, but Hay threw it perfectly, and now it all came down to one end to advance to the gold medal game.

Sandra says, "We went to that extra end and I really didn't have a good feeling at all. But the team played a great eleventh end to give me an opportunity on my last shot." She needed a cold draw to the full eight-foot with no backing to win. It was a shot she can't ever remember needing to win a national or international playoff game.

When Sandra released the stone she knew she was close – maybe a little too close. Joan describes the tension that all of Canada felt as the rock made its way down the ice: "It looked good out of her hand. Marcia and I kept the ice clean. Then it wouldn't slow down. We dropped off at the hog line and watched it glide, horrified. In the back of our minds, we knew that Denmark had upset the favoured Swedes, and Sweden would be a tough match for a bronze medal. We watched that rock slide past the tee line and started yelling at it to stop, to sit down! Scotland's third was sweeping it and finally it came to rest. I thought we had lost. Then Jan lifted her broom. It had stopped with about an inch to spare. I have never felt so relieved. We had a group hug at the hogline and put our heads together – we were all feeling the same myriad of emotions, elation, frustration, relief, anticipation. We were guaranteed an Olympic medal – Wow!"

For the record, the final score was 6-5. Jan describes the win as "struggle and emerge, a real character game. After Sandra's last stone, we had our team hug on the ice; the emotions were fairly high. It felt so good to just celebrate by ourselves for a couple of minutes – a real team moment.

"We all went to get hugs from our spouses – even Gary Ford had tears in his eyes.

"I think that was one of the most stressful games we've played – when Sandra went to throw that last draw, I almost couldn't watch. What a great relief to be

After team members themselves, who better to get the first Olympic Gold Medal hug in Canadian curling history than the adoring husbands?

done that semi-final."

The team had less than 24 hours to prepare for an Olympic gold medal clash with Helena Blach-Lavrsen's Danish rink. The Danes were well prepared. Usually a middle-of-the-pack curling nation, Denmark's team was putting in over 20 hours of practice time on the ice each week, an effort that would produce a world championship silver medal later that spring. Helena was one of the best draw skips in the business. If her game was on, Team Canada would need their collective A-game to win.

Marcia described the night before in her Olympic journal. "What a terrible sleep. I tossed and turned all night. I finally got out of bed, packed my things for the trip back to Nagano, and forced myself to eat."

Joan says, "We all had a hard time sleeping. I replayed that semi-final a thousand times in my sleep – willing myself to play better, and that last rock of Sandra's to stop sooner. I tossed and turned all night and just got up early."

After the previous night's pressure cooker win over Great Britain, the team was calm and psychologically ready for Denmark when they finally arrived at the arena. The pressure seemed gone, and normal nervousness and excitement replaced the high anxiety of their semi-final.

The final was a well-played game, without the theatrics of the semi-final, but a good showcase for the sport of curling, which was getting worldwide coverage like never before in its history.

The team had not won a toss for hammer all week, so they elected Marcia to represent the team. She won! The first time all Olympics that they could start the game with hammer.

They made good use of their first last-rock advantage of the Games. Jan describes ends one to five, "First end, we played well and cracked a three-ball. Great way to start. Helena and her team play the freeze game to perfection. Man, they know how to get rocks in play. We were up 5-2 at the break. The first five ends passed really quickly – the last five not so fast."

Sandra describes the last five ends, as the Danes clawed their way back to put a scare into Team Schmirler. "In the sixth we were in trouble. It looked like a sure deuce for Denmark, but I made a good in-turn double across the house and we stole one, to go up four.

"They played a good seventh and got two back with hammer. We were up two playing the eighth end with hammer. We had to make a tap to the four-foot to score. It was a big shot. If I make it, we're three up. If I miss, it's a one-point game, with the four-rock FGZ against one of the best draw teams in the world. I made it, but it went to a measure, it was so close.

"We forced them to take one in nine and we were up 7-5 coming home with hammer. That's about as comfortable as it gets at this level."

But the Danes threw up a couple of perfect guards. The Canadians tried two tough tick shots to move the Danish rocks to the boards. It didn't work. The Danes had two very useable guards covering a rock in the house when Joan came to throw her last stone.

Joan describes her best shot of the Olympics, which set up the winning shot for Sandra. "I had a double peel call for my first shot, but I only got one out of play and the other stone rolled over to the side. On my last shot, Sandra called another double peel. I sat in the hack and thought, 'Throw this good and make sure I get one'. Wouldn't you know it, I got all three rocks and left absolutely nothing in play! I went crazy, jumped in the air, screamed and raised my broom. At that moment, I knew we had clinched it and so did the crowd.

"It was really loud in there as Jan and Marcia made their way down the ice and gave me a high five. We stayed composed as Jan peeled on her two shots. Sandra threw her first stone – a wide open hit for the win. The game ended calmly, no jumping up and down or screaming, for once."

"After Joan made her triple-kill, we all knew it was over," Sandra says. "Jan had two routine open kills. When I went to shoot my first – and thankfully last – stone for the win, I was totally relaxed. After Joan's amazing shot, my nerves went absolutely calm."

After it was over, they shook hands with a very worthy opponent, then had their team hug. "That was a truly great moment," Sandra remembers. "Just the four of us and all we've been through. I didn't want to let go. We had accomplished the greatest conquest in our curling careers. Three world championships were unbelievable, but the Olympics is truly on the entire world stage and we were the first women's gold medallists. Awesome, awesome feeling!"

The team had to wait until the men's final was over before the official medal presentation. They watched most of the men's game between Mike Harris's team and Switzerland's Patrick Hurlimann rink. Harris had dominated play all week, but came out extremely flat to lose in only eight ends. In Harris's defense, he woke up that morning with a bad flu and probably shouldn't have even played. He curled around 25 per cent in the final and felt like he really let his teammates down, but how many chances does a team get at an Olympic gold medal?

The medal presentation was an overwhelming experience. Marcia wrote in her journal, "All of us were emotional on the podium. We received our gold medal plus flowers before the flag-raising and the singing of 'O Canada'. A very humbling yet proud moment.

"The guys' presentation is next. They really have a tough time, especially Collin Mitchell, who breaks down. They were so heavily favoured."

"How do you describe getting a gold medal and watching your flag rise as you sing your national anthem?" wrote Joan. "Unbelievable, emotional, unforgettable. A lot of things race across your mind. Pride – national, provincial, team, and personal – relief, gratification, sacrifice, and a huge longing to

Trays bearing the first-ever official Olympic gold medals awarded to a curling team are carried to the waiting Schmirler rink.

"All of us were emotional on the podium. We received our gold medal plus flowers before the flag-raising and the singing of 'O Canada.' A very humbling yet proud moment."

share this moment with family. My children, brothers and sisters, my mom, and my dad and grandmas who have recently passed away. I know that they would be proud. Silently, I dedicated this moment to them."

"I can hardly wait to get my mitts on my medal," wrote an enthusiastic Jan. "We wait and wait and finally get marched in. There are tons of cameras there, all clicking away.

"We got called up on the podium – it was so exciting. The medal music started and the tray of medals was marched over to us. They looked so awesome.

"As Sandra bowed to get hers, I could see her start to cry. It was a very powerful moment. My turn next – unbelievable. The ceremony was so solemn and dignified, it was incredible. Sandra and I gave each other a big hug. We've really come a long way.

"I was handling my emotions fairly well, and was ready for the anthem – or so I thought. When the flag started rising, I thought of everyone at my house, how proud and excited they must be. The tears came streaming down my face and I couldn't even sing. But it was a moment I will never forget – so proud to be Canadian!"

Sandra recorded her thoughts too. "They marched us out and my heart was just racing. We took our position behind the podium. Then they brought the medals out. And they announced, 'Gold Medallist – CANADA.' We stepped up and I could feel my body shake. They presented the medals; I

started to cry. All our hard work, perseverance, and sacrifice had now paid off. A feeling of being on the top of the world.

"Then they presented to Denmark. It must be very tough being the silver medallist. The gold medallists are happy because they won, the bronze are happy because they won the third-fourth game, but silver just lost and have to face the ceremony with the loss in mind.

"Finally, all the countries have their medals. It's time for the anthem. We know this is going to be emotional. I try to keep myself together. Jan is really feeling the emotion. I put my arm around her to let her know I'm there for her...not sure if she even noticed but it made me feel like a support for her.

"I can hear us all belt out the anthem – what a feeling of pride I feel deep down in my heart. The anthem ends and we bask in the moment. I see Shannon and immediately think of my little Sara back home.

"We finally answer all the media requests, have a formal closing ceremony for curling. By this time we're really tired and hungry, waiting for this to finish. The closing was 'Amazing Grace,' sung and played on the trumpet. It was really quite touching. Dry ice came from their feet...really cool.

"One more function – the mayor, Matsubo, was having a good-bye reception. It was a stand-up affair and lasted until midnight. We never did celebrate with our families that night. When the formal part of the festivities were over, Jan and I went back to our room. I had a long hot bath and off to bed."

The team spent the next few days in Nagano, enjoying various events and meeting many of the athletes. They stayed in the main Olympic village and everyone wanted to see the medal.

"It was so cool, meeting all these big name athletes," Marcia says. "You would see an NHL player in the lounge and go, 'Hi Theo (Fleury), how you doing Patrick (Roy), good to see you Wayne,' – as in *Gretzky*."

Sandra describes the first time they met Gretzky. "Jan and I are headed down to the cafeteria for breakfast. We walk into a lounge; Wayne is sitting by himself on a couch. Jan tries to act cool and goes up to Wayne and says, 'And you're Wayne ...?' She pretends she doesn't know who he is! We're trying not to freak, because these people are so famous. Anyway, he is very gracious. We talk about their upcoming games and he wants to see our medals. He knew who we were, which maybe shouldn't have surprised us. But how do you approach one of the best athletes of all time?"

The team finally flew back to Regina, excited about being with their children and settling back into their routines. But there was a Canadian championship to defend. In less than three days, Regina was hosting the Scott Tournament of Hearts at the Agridome.

Although the team gave it a valiant effort, Ontario's Anne Merklinger beat them in the semifinals. Cathy Borst's Alberta rink would win the championship final. Considering the high-voltage,

emotional Olympic experience, the jet lag, and the anxiety of being away from very young children, a third-place finish at a national championship is an astounding achievement.

There is one moment Team Schmirler will never forget from the 1998 Scott – the opening draw when the teams were introduced. Saving Team Schmirler for the end, the announcer simply said, "Thanks for the gold." The hometown crowd showed their appreciation with a lengthy standing ovation, and all their competitors joined in.

Cathy Borst, who skipped the 1998 Scott champions, remarked afterwards, "It was awesome. We were all happy for them. They deserved it. They have done so much for women's curling. I had tears in my eyes. I felt a warm rush, just being part of it all."

Heather Godberson, Cathy's third, said, "The roar of the crowd was absolutely incredible. For the players on the ice it was an unbelievable experience. Then I hear Sandra say softly, 'I've had enough.' I understood. It was overwhelming, but so deserved."

The 1998 Scott Tournament of Hearts for Team Schmirler was not so much about winning as it was about celebrating Olympic Gold. Joan says it for the whole team, "We would have loved to have won it all again. But that whole week was truly a celebration, and to enjoy it in our home city and home province was such an added thrill."

Is it over? Not according to the skip. "Our sights are set on Salt Lake City." ◉

177

Discovering what just a little Olympic fame can do – the team gets bumped up to first class seats for the flight home.

Acknowledgements

Gold on Ice was a real team effort right from the start.

My wife, Carla Scholz, is the primary reason this book was even conceived. She believed that I could write the story and encouraged me to make "the phone call" to Team Schmirler. A million thanks for her constant encouragement.

I would also like to extend thanks to many others who helped make this book a reality. To Steve Parrish, my personal English teacher and editor in Calgary. He knew I was a hack writer with a story to tell. He is a big reason I stuck with it. His constant vote of confidence and skill at editing provided the light at the end of the tunnel. My only question for Steve is – Are you a curling convert yet?

To my "fifth" players – the typists and computer whizzes in my life. Andy Jones spent hours and hours on the final edit. Your friendship, patience, and attention to detail helped me keep my sanity. Jennifer Wolsey had the toughest deadline of all – getting the rough draft and final manuscript to Coteau on time. Thank you for your extra-mile efforts.

To Anne Jiggins, Karen Jiggins, Ruth Jones, Sue Chedgey (who is now Ireland's only curler), and Janet Clews for all the "bits and pieces" of typing that needed to get done. So much of it was given at the last minute. Thank you for putting your lives on hold for this story.

To the many competitive curlers who sat down for 20-minute interviews that all went into extra ends.

This sport truly does have an air of class to it. Many thanks for your time and interest and pertinent insights that helped shape *Gold on Ice*. The *Gold on Ice* fraternity includes curlers like Cathy Borst, Janet Clews, Karen Cottenie, Kathy Fahlman, Anita Ford, Atina Ford, Gary Ford, Heather Godberson, Elisabet Gustafson, Nancy Inglis, Mike Peplinski, Pat Reid, Michelle Ridgway, Lindsay Sparkes, Cathy Trowell, Ray Turnbull, Sandy Weber, and Randy Woytowich.

Also to Team Schmirler parents – Walter and Verna Betker, Joyce Inglis, Harvey and Mary Schiml, and Art and Shirley Schmirler. These interviews were priceless. The honesty, humour, and healthy pride came through. The husbands deserve a big round of applause for their angle on the team – Kerry Gudereit, Frank Macera, Brian McCusker, and Shannon England.

To Claire Carver-Dias and Doug Dias from our national synchronized swimming program. They supplied insight into the world of competitive sports from a marriage angle, and the demands on women in sports. Good luck in Sydney 2000.

To Dave Poulson and Dave Ridgway, and our *Robokicker* project. The learning experience was unbelievable. Thanks for letting me tag along. You helped water the seed that led to this project.

To Ardith Stephanson, former sports writer of the

Regina *Leader-Post,* who made helpful comments over the years. She has covered Team Schmirler almost from day one of their formation.

To all the following people and their little acts of kindness – Rev. Sid Haugen (the second-best clergy curler in Canada) for picking me up at the airport. Rev. Dan and Wendy Pope for letting me take over your basement during all my Regina interviews. Roger and Anita Ponton for letting me hide away in your Gleichen, Alberta cabin. Jim and Shirley Kane for opening up your basement suite for writing in those summer weeks of relative invasions. Cousin Murray Scholz in Churchbridge, Sask., for stocking up on Scott Tournament of Hearts newsletters, programs, etc. from Regina 1998.

To Gary Pepper and Bernice Merrick of the Calgary Curling Club for help with the Scott rules and for pointing me to certain contacts along the way.

To Gay Fehr of Eau Claire, Wisconsin, for getting us an American perspective on Team Schmirler.

To Ben Fell, my designated driver to Biggar, Saskatoon, Regina, and every town in between – you're a great side-kick and Rookie of the Year lead!

To Jack and Pia Biensch for constant encourage-ment, patience, and all the little things over the whole writing of *Gold on Ice.*

I must mention my parents, Herb and Arni Scholz of Langenburg, Saskatchewan, and in-laws Gunnar and Maisie Samuelson of Hinton, Alberta, for your eagerness to read portions of the manuscript and to cheer me on throughout.

To Chinook Chapel in Calgary, for freeing up my Thursdays, and all of August, 1998, to allow me to con-centrate on writing, and for putting up with the many Biblical parallels from the world of curling on Sundays.

To Sandra, Jan, Joan, and Marcia for being so can-did and transparent. You've let the sporting world into what makes your team tick. You are champions on and off the ice.

To Coteau Books and their entire team for their belief in *Gold on Ice.* Thanks for your commitment. To Geoffrey Ursell and Nora Russell for their fine editing for the publisher. This was not only educational but very enjoyable. And to Nik Burton of Coteau, who believed in *Gold on Ice.*

Finally to my two children, Anah-Jayne and Reed. You both kept everything in perspective. Believe me!

– *Guy Scholz*

Photo Credits:

Photos courtesy of the Canadian Olympic Association; Mike Ridewood, photographer: Page 11;Page 70; Page 72; Page 76; Page 98; Page 154; Page 156; Page 157; Page 159; Page 161; Page 162; Page 164; Page 165; Page 174; Colour Section, Photo #1

Photos courtesy of Scott Paper Ltd.; Mike Burns, Jr., photographer: Front Matter, Page 6, Page 8; Page iv; Page 14; Page 22; Page 44; Page 45; Page 47; Page 49; Page 84; Page 87; Page 88; Page 89; Page 112; Page 114; Page 115; Page 116; Page 138; Page 140; Colour Section, Photo #7, Photo #16

Photos courtesy of Scott Paper Ltd.; Andrew Klaver, photographer: Front Matter, Page 6-7; Page 4; Page 6; Page 12; Page 74; Page 101; Page 127

Photos courtesy of Mike Burns, Jr.: Page 33; Page 73; Page 75; Page 78; Page 141; Page 142; Page 143; Page 144-145; Page 146; Page 147; Page 148-top; Page 149; Page 151; Page 152; Page 153; Colour Section, Photo #6, Photo #12, Photo #15, Photo #17

Photos courtesy of Designer Photographics: Page 102; Colour Section, Photo #18

Photos courtesy of the Leader-Post: Page 3; Page 32; Page 36; Page 60; Page 66; Page 153; Colour Section, Photo #14

Photos courtesy of Peter Hostettler: Page 24; Page 27; Page 69; Page 77; Page 79; Page 80; Page 90; Page 91; Page 92; Page 93; Page 94; Page 95; Page 96; Page 111; Page 113; Page 117; Page 118 ; Page 124.

All other photos courtesy of Team Schmirler.

Rev. Guy Scholz is an avid curler and an experienced curling, sports and inspirational writer. He has a regular Alberta curling report in *Sweep*, and has written feature articles for various curling magazines. Guy was principle researcher for the book *Robokicker: An Odyssey In the CFL*, the story of Saskatchewan Roughrider placekicker Dave Ridgway.

Originally from Langenburg, Saskatchewan, Guy Scholz lives in Calgary, where he also serves as senior pastor at Chinook Chapel, Lutheran Church.